50 Hike

M000209099

APR 0 1 2009

Kachemak Bay clearing after a storm

50 *Hikes*

In Alaska's Kenai Peninsula

Walks, Hikes, and Backpacks through the
Wild Landscapes of Alaska

TAZ TALLY, Ph.D.

First Edition

The Countryman Press
Woodstock, Vermont

With time, access points may change, and trails, signs, and landmarks referred to in this book may be altered. If you find that such changes have occurred on the trails described in this book, please let the author and the publisher know so that corrections may be made in future editions. The author and the publisher also welcome other comments and suggestions. Address all correspondence to:

50 Hikes Editor
The Countryman Press
P.O. Box 748
Woodstock, VT 05091

First Edition

ISBN 978-0-88150-755-3

Text and cover design by Glenn Suokko
Composition by Taz Tally
Location map by Tibor G. Tóth (www.tothgraphix.com)
Hike maps created by Taz Tally with TOPO! © National Geographic Maps
Photographs of the author by Nancy Lasater
Cover and interior photographs by Taz Tally (www.taztallyphotography.com)

Published by The Countryman Press, P.O. Box 748, Woodstock, Vermont 05091

Distributed by W. W. Norton & Company, Inc., 500 Fifth Avenue, New York, NY 10110

Printed in the United States of America

10 9 8 7 6 5 4 3 2 1

I'd rather wake up in the middle of nowhere than in any city on Earth.

— Steve McQueen

DEDICATION

For Dottie, through thick and thin. Thank you!

50 Hikes at a Glance

HIKE	TYPE / DIFFICULTY	REGION
1. Byron Glacier	Streamside / Easy to Moderate	Northern Kenai
2. Gull Rock	Coastal / Moderate	Northern Kenai
3. Hope Point Ridge & Summit	Alpine / Very Difficult	Northern Kenai
4. Resurrection Pass	Alpine / Moderate	Northern Kenai
5. Devils Pass	Alpine / Moderate	Northern Kenai
6. Summit Creek	Alpine / Moderate	Northern Kenai
7. Crescent Creek & Lake	Alpine / Moderate	Northern Kenai
8. Carter Lake	Alpine / Easy to Moderate	Northern Kenai
9. Johnson Pass	Alpine / Moderate	Northern Kenai
10. Lost Lake	Alpine / Easy to Moderate	Northeast Kenai
11. Primrose Creek	Alpine / Moderate	Northeast Kenai
12. Ptarmigan Creek & Lake	Alpine / Easy to Moderate	Northeast Kenai
13. Resurrection River	Streamside / Moderate to Difficult	Northeast Kenai
14. Exit Glacier	Stream & glacier side / Easy	Northeast Kenai
15. Harding Ice Field	Alpine / Moderate to Difficult	Northeast Kenai
16. Mount Marathon	Alpine / Moderate to Very Difficult	Northeast Kenai
17. Caines Head	Coastal / Easy to Moderate	Northeast Kenai
18. Caines Head Alpine	Alpine / Moderate	Northeast Kenai
19. Hideout	Alpine / Moderate	Central Kenai
20. Kenai River	Streamside / Easy	Central Kenai
21. Hidden Creek	Open Forest / Easy	Central Kenai
22. Skilak Lookout & Bear Mountain	Alpine / Moderate	Central Kenai
23. Seven Lakes	Forest & Lakehore / Easy	Central Kenai
24. Skyline Trail & Alpine Traverse	Alpine / Difficult	Central Kenai
25. Fuller Lakes & Alpine Traverse	Forest & Alpine / Moderate to Difficult	Central Kenai

DISTANCE (miles)	CAMPING	GOOD FOR KIDS	WATERFALLS	VIEWS	NOTES
1 to 4 OW	N	★	★	★	Easy access to glacier & challenging primitive extension
10.2 RT	N	★		★	Mostly easy coastal hike with terrific water & mtn. views
5 OW	N			★	Steep challenging climb to spectacular views
39 OW	B		★	★	Long trail through lower forests & high open tundra. Cabins
10.1 OW	B/D		★	★	From forest to alpine tundra through glaciated valley
8.4 OW	B/D		★	★	Forest to tundra through 3 glaciated valleys + high point
6.5 or 18 OW	B/D		★	★	Stream and lakeside & flower-strewn primitive trail
3.3 OW	N/D	★	★	★	Easy to moderate hike to 2 lovely flower-surrounded lakes
23 OW	B/D		★	★	View-rich hike to waterfalls, two scenic lakes and fish
14 rt	B	S	★	★	Beautiful pine lakes, tundra and backcountry access
8.2 OW	D/B	S	★	★	More of a forested hike to Lost Lake (area than Hike 10)
7.5 OW	D/B	S	★	★	Delightful streamside hike to large glacial lake and camp
16 OW	B	S	★	★	Primeval forest hike along a wild river. Easy lower section.
0.25 OW	N	★	★	★	Easy, largely paved access to glacier. Wheelchairs OK
4 OW	B		★	★	Trek to the cathedral of ice, snow and light
2 to 4 OW	B		★	★	Two routes, the race and scenic. Bay and alpine views
11 OW	D	S	★	★	Coastal hike with spectacular views of Resurrection Bay
3+ OW	B		★	★	Coastal hike to alpine tundra. Views of bay and glaciers
1.5 RT	N	★		★	Easy access to sweeping views of Skilak Lake country
6 to 8 RT	N	★		★	Easy hike above and along the Kenai River and Canyon
1.5 OW	N/B	★	★	★	Great first, easy hike to Skilak Lake. Winter hiking
2.5, 0.8 OW	N	S		★	Hike to panoramas of Skilak Lake and surrounding mtns.
4.5 OW	D	S		★	Hike across glacial moraine hills and around lakes
1 to 11 OW	B			★	Rapid access to tundra highcountry and sweeping views
4 to 13.5 OW	B			★	Lovely forest trek to 2 glacial lakes and the alpine tundra

OW = ONE-WAY
RT = ROUND-TRIP

50 Hikes at a Glance

HIKE	TYPE /DIFFICULTY	REGION
26. Russian Lakes	Forest & Alpine / Easy to Moderate	Central Kenai
27. Bishops Beach & Homer Spit	Coastal / Easy	Southeast Kenai–Homer
28. Bishops B. to Diamond Beach	Coastal / Easy to Moderate	Southeast Kenai–Homer
29. Diamond Gulch & Beach	Coastal / Easy to Moderate	Southeast Kenai–Homer
30. Homestead-Demo. Forest	Lowland & Hills / Easy to Moderate	Southeast Kenai–Homer
31. Crossman Ridge	Hills & Ridgeline / Easy to Moderate	Southeast Kenai–Homer
32. Calvin and Coyle	Wetlands / Easy	Southeast Kenai–Homer
33. Anchor Point Beach	Coastal / Easy	Southeast Kenai–Homer
34. Red Mountain	Alpine / Moderate to Difficult	Southeast Kenai–K-Bay
35. Tutka Lake	Lowland Forest / Easy to Moderate	Southeast Kenai–K-Bay
36. Grace Ridge	Alpine/ Moderate to Difficult	Southeast Kenai–K-Bay
37. Sadie Knob	Forest & Alpine / Moderate	Southeast Kenai–K-Bay
38. Wosnesenski River	Streamside / Easy to Moderate	Southeast Kenai–K-Bay
39. China Poot/Leisure Lake	Forest / Moderate	Southeast Kenai–K-Bay
40. Poot Peak Hike & Climb	Alpine / Difficult to Very Difficult	Southeast Kenai–K-Bay
41. Moose Valley	Forest, Meadow & Alpine / Moderate	Southeast Kenai–K-Bay
42. Coalition Loop	Forest / Moderate	Southeast Kenai–K-Bay
43. Goat Rope Spur	Alpine / Very Difficult	Southeast Kenai–K-Bay
44. Alpine Ridge	Alpine / Moderate to Difficult	Southeast Kenai–K-Bay
45. Saddle Trail–Grewingk Glacier Lake	Forest / Moderate	Southeast Kenai–K-Bay
46. Glacier Spit–Grewingk Glacier Lake	Forest / Easy to Moderate	Southeast Kenai–K-Bay
47. Grewingk Glacier	Forest, Alpine / Moderate	Southeast Kenai–K-Bay
48. Humpy Creek South to Glacier Spit	Open forest / Easy + Tram	Southeast Kenai–K-Bay
49. Humpy Creek North to Mallard Bay	Varied Coastal Alpine / Moderate	Southeast Kenai–K-Bay
50. Emerald Lake	Alpine / Moderate	Southeast Kenai–K-Bay

GOOD FOR KIDS
S   for kids with a bit of stamina

CAMPING
B   backcountry camping
D   developed camping available within the park or forest
N   developed camping nearby

DISTANCE (miles)	CAMPING	GOOD FOR KIDS	WATERFALLS	VIEWS	NOTES
22 to 24 OW	D/B	★	★	★	Multiple hikes to lakes, waterfalls, and cabins
5 OW	N	★		★	Easy-access beach hiking, spectacular views across bay
6.5 OW	B	S	★	★	Beach hike along high eroding cliffs, coal layers & tide pools
2+ RT	B	★	★	★	Secluded wild beach, magnificent views & great driftwood
1.5 to 2 OW	N	★		★	Hike the path of Homer's early homesteaders. Great views
4 OW	D/B	★		★	Homestead Trail Extension, unique views of Kachemak Bay
0.5 OW	N	★		★	Flat, short, easy in-town access through moose habitat
1+ OW	D/N	★		★	View five volcanoes across Cook Inlet + rock hounding
8 to 14 OW	B		★	★	Bike & hike trip to views, mining camp, and unique geology
3.5 OW	D	S	★	★	Lowland-forest hike to a lovely waterfall. Good early season
8 OW	B			★	Glorious wildflower-rich ridge hike with magnificent 360° views
4.3 OW	D/B		★	★	Forest hike to flowered alpine tundra + great views of "Woz"
12 OW	D/B		★	★	Glacial river hike through wild country. Many animal tracks
2.8 OW	D	S		★	Forest hike to several lakes. Access to other hikes. Cabins
3.7 to 4 OW	D		★	★	Challenging hike and climb to the top of a landmark peak
6.3 OW	B		★	★	Delightful hike through varied alpine terrain meadows
7 RT	D	S	★	★	Primeval forest hike. Alternate route to Leisure Lake
3 OW	D			★	Steep, flower-strewn scramble to a great view point
2.5 to 5.5 OW	B		★	★	Forest hike to alpine ridges with dramatic glacier overlook
1.1 OW	B	★		★	Easy and fast access to shores of Grewingk Glacier Lake
4.5 OW	B	S		★	Beach and open-forest hike to shores of glacial lake
7 OW	B		★	★	Hike to and touch the glacier. Birding at glacier lake. Tram
6.9 OW	B	S		★	Open-forest hike across alluvial flats to glacier spit. Tram
3 OW	D		★	★	Coastal and alpine hike to a delightful tidal bay.
15 OW	B		★	★	Wonderful alpine hike through tundra and forest with lake

OW = ONE-WAY
RT = ROUND-TRIP

50 HIKES IN ALASKA'S
KENAI PENINSULA

Map by Tibor G. Tóth, Tóth Graphix
www.tothgraphix.com

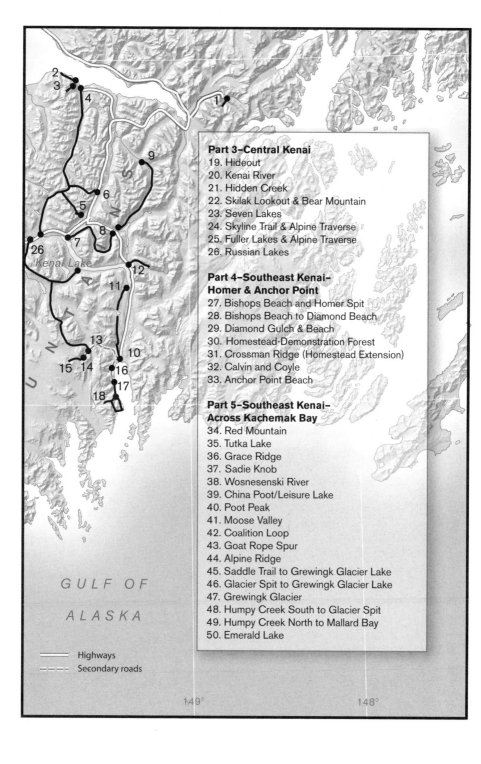

GULF OF

ALASKA

Kenai Lake

MOUNTAINS

Highways
Secondary roads

149°   148°

Contents

Acknowledgments

I would first like to acknowledge and thank cartographer extraordinaire, Tibor G. Tóth, for the wonderful 3D topographic location map he created on pages 10 and 11. Viewing his map allows you to truly visualize the topography of the Kenai Peninsula without actually being here. To see more of his marvelous work, visit him at www.toth-graphix.com.

And for Nancy Lasater, I humbly offer immense praise and gratitude for providing such detailed and inspired editing of this book. Her writing suggestions and editing have made it much clearer, more concise, and interesting for every reader. I marvel at her writing skills. Working through her edits was like taking a writing course . . . just amazing!

To my hiking partners Zip the wonder dog, Katie (Little Tusty), Jaz, Jim Hurd (The Animal), Karen Hurd (Zena the Warrior Love Goddess), Hope (Spicy Chicken), Ellie (Smart Jock), Nancy (Babushka Mama Moose), and Karin, thank you for making my hiking and the creation of this book even more enjoyable!

A special thanks to Candace Ward, Gary Titus and Scott Slavik of the Kenai National Wildlife Refuge for reviewing my book and making fine suggestions.

I also owe a debt of gratitude to my publisher, The Countryman Press, and especially to my Managing Editor Jennifer Thompson, for working with me and showing so much patience.

Finally, thank you to my agent Matt Wagner of FreshBooks for helping me start this project and for his good work at several critical steps along the way!

View of one of the many unnamed mountain peaks in the Kenai Mountains

50 Hikes in Alaska's Kenai Peninsula

Introduction

Like all "The Great Land" that is Alaska, the Kenai Peninsula is like no other place on earth. We often refer to the Kenai as "mini Alaska" because it contains stunning examples of much of what makes Alaska such a compelling landscape to visit, including soaring rugged mountains, crystalline hundred-mile views, wild colorful rivers, grinding glorious glaciers, big land-based wildlife, even bigger marine wildlife, unbelievable fish, grand lakes, huge tides, forests galore, exquisite alpine tundra, and nearly 24 hours of daily sunlight to enjoy it all in summer. This book covers 50 of the most spectacular hikes on the Kenai Peninsula and provides you a guide to visiting these grand Alaskan natural wonders.

This is the first book to comprehensively cover the hikes of the Kenai Peninsula, and so it was written with great love and careful stewardship over several years. The hikes come in all lengths, venues, and levels of difficulty, from easy beach strolls near civilization to hardy multiday treks through remote wilderness, but every hike is meant to provide something marvelous that is uniquely Alaskan. You are invited to lace up your boots and read along with the author, a Ph.D geologist who has chosen every trail, then walked and photographed each one several times in order to give you the most thorough, personally guided, professional tour possible.

Welcome to the Kenai (pronounced Keen-eye) and enjoy! This introduction briefly covers:

- Geography of the Kenai Peninsula
- Geology of the Kenai Peninsula
- Hiking Tips: Gear
- Hiking Techniques and Tips
- Hiking Choices and Ratings
- Information Resources

GEOGRAPHY OF THE KENAI PENINSULA

Located in south-central Alaska, the Kenai (from the Russian word Kenayskaya) extends south from Anchorage and the slicing Turnagain Arm of Cook Inlet for 150 miles. Its maximum width is 80 miles near mid-peninsula.

The Kenai is so large (at 16,013 sq. mi. or 41,473 km²) that it's 50 percent bigger than the entire state of Maryland. It's also larger than New Hampshire, Massachusetts, New Jersey, Hawaii, Connecticut, Delaware, and Rhode Island. It's so big, in fact, that you could combine those last four states and still have enough square miles left to include Delaware again. The Harding Ice Field (Hike 15) alone is larger than the whole state of Rhode Island!

The western portion of the peninsula (see the map on pages 10–11) is primarily flat wetlands dotted with thousands of glacially carved and filled lakes. The northern and eastern parts of the peninsula are dominated by the rugged glacier-carved, and still carving, Kenai Mountains. In between these two extremes are glacially eroded and filled landscapes of lowland lakes and forests, such as the picture-postcard Skilak Lake country.

The peninsula is dominated visually by the Kenai Mountains that extend the entire length of the peninsula, rise from sea level to a maximum of 6,612 feet east of Kachemak Bay, and form the backdrop and backbone for many of these 50 glorious hikes.

BIOMES

The biomes (communities of species) of the Kenai start at sea level with grassy coastal areas, then move to aspen, birch, and hemlock lowland forests higher up. At the mid-elevations, the forest changes to spruce, cottonwood, poplar, aspen, and birch, followed by alder and willow thickets in the subalpine zone. Above them, you will meet treeless dwarf birch, spruce, and low, wind-shaved tundra plants at the highest elevations of the alpine zones. After that, only red algae survives in the snow and ice until it too finally stops trying as the ice field thickens.

Sumptuous wildflowers thrive everywhere starting at the lower elevations in May and at the higher elevations in July and August. It's a short growing season, so Alaskan plants take advantage of every long day to blossom in successive waves of blue lupine, white pushki, mauve roses, purple monkshood, yellow dandelions, and fuchsia fireweed.

The tree line is found at low elevation this far north. Above it, there is first the subalpine zone of willows and alders, followed by the alpine tundra. You will leave the trees behind at around 2,000 feet of elevation and the subalpine bushes above 2,500 feet. Some of the most spectacular cross-country hiking is way up in the alpine zone above 3,000 feet!

One of the many treats of hiking and trekking in Alaska is how relatively easy it is to reach these treeless, view-rich, easy walking regions. In the Lower 48 in contrast, you have to climb to 10,000 feet in the Southern Rockies before reaching the same alpine zone.

THE TIDES

The legendary, fast-moving 20–30 tides of Kachemak Bay and Cook Inlet add excitement and an ever-changing element to the peninsula, but hikers must be wary of them when tackling any coastal trail. For instance, the hikes of Caines Head State Recreation Area (Hikes 17 and 18) can only be accessed on foot at low tide. Be sure to consult a tide-table book before you head out.

WILD AREAS

About 90 percent of the Kenai Peninsula is wild undeveloped land that is home to a striking variety of national and state parks, wilderness areas, wildlife refuges, recreation areas and special management areas.

The following lands provide many of the wonderful hikes in this book:

- Kenai Fjords National Park: 669,000 acres of glacier-covered terrain
- Kenai National Wildlife: 1,970,000 acres of mountains, lowland forests, and thousands of lakes
- Kachemak Bay State Park and Wilderness Area: 368,290 acres of forested peaks
- Caines Head State Recreation Area: 5,961 acres of coastal and alpine hiking near Seward
- Large portions of the Chugach National Forest in the northern part of the peninsula which at 5,900,00 acres is the second-largest national forest in the US (after the Tongas in SE Alaska)
- Anchor River State Recreation Area: 266 acres of beautiful coastal hiking
- Kenai River Special Management Area:

2,170 acres of lowland forest and stream-channel hikes
- Kachemak Bay State Critical Habitat Area: 222,080 acres of protected and managed waterways providing access to the Kachemak Bay State Park and Wilderness Area
- Fox River State Critical Habitat Area: 7,104 acres of accessible and hikeable but wild, untrammeled, and trailless lands located at the north end of Kachemak Bay. (See the Web site www.taztallyphotography.com for more info on this area.)

LAKES AND RIVERS

The Kenai is home to thousands of glacially carved lakes. Among these are two giants: Skilak and Tustemena. At 117 square miles, Tustemena is the 5th largest in the state. Skilak Lake, located midway along the world-famous King Salmon fishing stream that is the Kenai River, serves as a major locale for the hikes in Part 3 of this book. With an area of 38 square miles, a maximum depth of 528 feet, and a mean depth of 240 feet, this glacier-gouged scenic lake is home to many world-trophy-class, and often overlooked, brown and rainbow trout, as well as the much-touted salmon of the Kenai River proper.

Many beautiful, wild streams drain the Kenai Peninsula. The Kenai River is the longest, largest, and most famous. An astonishing aquamarine blue from suspended glacial "rock flour," it forms the backdrop for the Kenai River Hike (Hike 20) in Part 3. Also in Part 3 is the Russian River viewed along the Russian Lakes Trail (Hike 26). Other notable streams include, in Part 4: Deep Creek, the Anchor River (visited on the Anchor Point Beach Hike, which is Hike 33), Stariski Creek, and the Kasilof River.

In Part 2 we visit the Resurrection River (Hike 13).

You will also encounter many smaller, but no less fabulous, streams in the Kenai such as Johnson and Bench creeks along the Johnson Pass Hike (Hike 9) in Part 1. Many of these streams are, like the Kenai, fed by glaciers whose sediments' interaction with the sunlight creates the variety of blue to brown colors characteristic of their waters.

INLETS, SOUNDS, AND BAYS

The Kenai Peninsula is bounded on all three sides by large, fascinating, dynamic bodies of water that are all major northern extensions of the Gulf of Alaska to the south. To the east is Prince William Sound; to the west is Cook Inlet; and to the south is Kachemak Bay. (See the Hike Location Map on pages 10–11.) All three of these ocean arms, with their massive, driving tides, provide breathtaking scenic backdrops for many of the Kenai hikes.

Prince William Sound is rimmed with still actively calving glaciers and dotted with glacially scoured, rocky islands only lately uncovered by the rapidly retreating ice. The sound provides boat access to many active glaciers including those of the Kenai Fjords National Park. The Caines Head hikes in Part 2 (Hikes 17 and 18) are located on the western edge of Prince William Sound. Access to these hikes can be by water or by foot at low tides.

If you have time, be sure to take one of the fabulous Kenai Fjords glacier tours offered out of Seward. Or, you can take plane rides from either Homer or Seward for dramatic aerial views of the amazing rivers of ice flowing off the Harding and Sargent ice fields.

Cook Inlet forms the western shore of the Kenai Peninsula. It is the hugely tidal and often wind-tossed water you look across on the Anchor Point Beach Hike in Part 4 (Hike 33). On the far western shore of Cook Inlet, you can see the wild, rugged, mountainous 200-miles-long Alaska Peninsula with its five active volcanoes. From north to south these are Mt. Spur, Mt. Redoubt, Mt. Iliamna, Augustine, and Mt. Douglas, all of which can be seen on a clear day from the Anchor Point Beach Hike (Hike 33). Don't be surprised to see one of them spewing up an ash and steam spout!

Kachemak Bay (a Yupik term meaning "large cliff by the water") is another extension of the Gulf of Alaska. The bay, at 40 miles long and 1–10 miles wide, is an estuary mixing the freshwater of the Fox River with the salty marine waters of lower Cook Inlet. This is the bay you cross to reach all the amazing hikes discussed in Part 5 of this book. Be prepared for non-stop mouth-dropping views as you navigate around glorious Kachemak Bay.

GLACIERS AND ICE FIELDS

Two major ice sheets blanket the mountainous eastern Kenai Peninsula: the Sargent and Harding ice fields. They are the source of the many glaciers flowing down from the jagged Kenai Mountains. The Sargent Ice Field is located north and east of Seward at the northeast end of the Kenai Peninsula. The Byron Glacier Hike in Part 1 (Hike 1) is part of the Sargent Ice Field system. Other Sargent Ice Field glaciers such as the Prospect, Spoon, and Porcupine glaciers can be seen looking north across Resurrection Bay from the Caines Head and Caines Head Alpine hikes (Hikes 17 and 18).

The Harding Ice Field is massive. It's larger than the state of Rhode Island, covering between 300 square miles and 1,000 square miles, depending on whether you count the more than 40 glaciers that flow

from it. You can visit one of these ice-field offshoots when you take the Exit Glacier Hike in Part 2 (Hike 14). Or, if you are really adventurous, you can actually enter the world of the ice field itself when you venture into the hall of the glacier queen on the Harding Ice Field Hike (Hike 15). If you take this hike—and it's one of my favorites—you will gain a sense of what most of the Kenai Peninsula looked and felt like just 12,000 years ago, when these ice fields and their glaciers covered nearly all of the land that is now the peninsula and its surrounding ocean waters!

CLIMATE, WEATHER

There is one word for the weather in Alaska: changeable. Most high-latitude environments have schizophrenic weather. Summertime temperatures can range from the 30s to the 70s at sea level but can be below freezing in the alpine zone any day of the year. One of the Kenai's blessings is that it's relatively dry, with close to the state average 22 inches of annual rainfall. In fact, the area around Homer (where I live) at the southern tip of the peninsula is known as the banana belt because it's so moderate in temperature and precipitation compared with other parts of the state. For example, the southeastern panhandle area of Alaska (around Juneau and Ketchikan) is a mid-latitude rain forest, with more than 100 inches of rainfall each year.

Keep in mind that rainfall totals rise as you gain elevation. And, it can rain or snow on any day. In fact, we even have our periods of forever-rain, so you should be prepared for any weather, though you may well enjoy the best!

A word of caution about the fickle alpine zone in Alaska. As mentioned earlier, one of the many treats of Alaskan hiking is the relatively easy and quick access to the alpine zone. Though found at much lower elevation than elsewhere, our alpine zone otherwise is like alpine zones everywhere: exposed. The lack of tall vegetation means broad, continuous panoramas and offers you the ability to hike cross-country, but it also means direct, unprotected exposure to wind, rain, and snow. In Alaska, you can encounter a snow storm any day of the year! Always dress in layers and pack extra layers including a hat, gloves, and long pants. (See Gear section.) I don't care how warm and clear it is at the trailhead! In addition always pack water and some food!

DAYLIGHT

In addition to easy hikes into the alpine zone, Alaska offers another truly terrific geographic gift: nearly endless days during the early summer. On June 21st, which is of course the summer solstice and the longest day of the year, you may not want to sleep. The zone of true 24-hour sun above the horizon starts at 66.5° north latitude (this is due to the 23.5° tilt of the Earth's axis to the plane of the ecliptic). In Alaska this line of latitude, known as the Arctic Circle, is found just north of Fairbanks. The Kenai Peninsula sits just a bit south of the Arctic Circle between 59° (Homer) and 61° (Hope), so you will never actually have 24 straight hours of sun above the horizon. But, for a couple of weeks on both sides of June 21st, it won't get dark, just dusk! It's very cool to experience this and especially at high elevation in the alpine zone because you are literally bathed in the never-becomes-night twilight light.

If you are up this way around the summer solstice, think about taking a scramble up into the alpine zone. Hope Point in Part 1 (Hike 3) is one of the fastest ways to get there, or plan a multiday hike on the Resurrection Pass Trail also in Part 1 (Hike 4), or

into the backcountry around Lost Lake in Part 2 (Hike 10), or up another one of my favorites, Grace Ridge in Part 5 (Hike 36). Throughout the months of June, July, and even into August, you will have extended daylight to enjoy your hiking.

GEOLOGY OF THE KENAI PENINSULA

The landscape where you stand is the consequence of a long, complex, and fascinating geology history that continues to evolve even as we hike through it. The mountains, valleys, plateaus, flat wetlands, lakes, streams, cliffs, and beaches comprising today's Kenai Peninsula are the result of many geologic processes, including the creation of the ocean floor, the movement of huge tectonic plates, the work of volcanoes, the building of mountains through folding and faulting, the advance and retreat of glaciers, and finally the inexorable action of water in the form of lakes and streams. In the following section I present the highlights of this history.

A BRIEF GEOLOGIC HISTORY

We could start a couple of billion years ago, but that would take too long, so let's start a mere 200,000,000 (200 million) years ago. Dinosaurs ran rampant on the land, the oceans covered more of the Earth's surface, and palm trees grew in the arctic—talk about global warming!

From our standpoint here in Alaska, one of the key processes was the creation of the ocean floor by volcanic action welling up from the molten mantle beneath the Earth's crust onto and indeed forming the ocean floor. (Note: This same ocean-floor formation by volcanism from the mantle continues today.) So we will start there.

1) Circa 200 million years ago, somewhere near the equator, formation of ocean floor crust, as large crustal

plates, from hot basaltic volcanism originating from the Earth's mantle, erupts and flows out onto the ocean floor about 2 miles beneath the ocean surface! Note: Some of these ancient mantle-source rocks can be seen and touched on the Red Mountain Hike in Part 5 (Hike 34). Remnants of the ocean floor volcanics can be found throughout the Kenai, with some of the best examples available for viewing along the shoreline around Kachemak Bay.

2) ~240 to 200 million years ago, the ocean floor spreads out and collects thousands of feet of ocean sediment. Limestones and radiolarian chert covers the volcanic/basalt ocean crust. Remember, the ocean crust is under water ... lots of water!

3) ~200 to 150 million years ago, the ocean floor spreads out so much it starts to plow into the western edge of what is now the North American continental crust. The collision is not head-on, but rather at an angle, so the continental- ocean-crustal plates slide past as well as into each other.

4) Beginning 150 million years ago and continuing today, these two plates slide into and past each other as other ocean plates slide north and west. Huge slices of rock tens of miles long are shuffled past each other like a deck of cards. All this results in mountain-building due to the folding and faulting of these rocks for several thousand miles from British Columbia up through southern Alaska, forming a long sequence of mountain ranges

The landscape of the Kenai is dominated by peaks and lakes formed by glaciers

including the coast ranges of British Columbia and southeast Alaska, parts of the Wrangle Saint Alias Range, the Alaska Range, and yes, the high peaks of the Kenai Peninsula!

5) Beginning 20 million years ago and continuing today, while all this folding and faulting mountain-building is happening, another section of ancient ocean floor dives under the western end of the Alaska Range and melts from all the heat of that friction, then flows to the surface erupting and forming the five volcanoes you see clearly on the west side of Cook Inlet from the Anchor Point Beach Hike in Part 4 (Hike 33). This same phenomenon also accounts for all the volcanic islands that make up the Aleutian chain.

6) About 1.8 million years ago, North America, and indeed the whole northern hemisphere, starts to catch a cold. The result is huge continental glaciers covering much of North America and large alpine (mountain) glaciers in Alaska. Large parts of Alaska, including nearly all of the current Kenai Peninsula, Cook Inlet, Kachemak Bay, and large portions of Prince William Sound become covered by advancing, carving, grinding glaciers. Sea levels drop and the Bering land bridge is formed. A big land rush of nomadic, ice-age people ensues from Siberia . . . but that's another story! The glaciers advance and retreat four times alternately grinding down the landscape and leaving huge deposits of sediment. We are currently in the fourth withdrawal, anxiously trying to figure out how far this retreat and its resulting rise in sea level will go!

7) About 14,000 years ago and continuing today, the big freeze starts to become the big thaw. The glaciers begin to retreat, leaving a scoured landscape with sharp high peaks (the peaks themselves being the only things the hungry glaciers had not overridden) skirted by newly revealed low, round hills as they melt back. Big dumps of glacial sediment occur all over the place, but especially in low areas, as the glaciers retreat. The foundation of Homer Spit (visited on the Bishops Beach and Homer Spit hikes in Part 4—Hikes 27 and 28) is the result of these dump—and—retreat glacial events, as are the large, lake-dotted terraces of the western Kenai and the Skilak Lake region in Part 3.

8) Today . . . The retreat continues leaving behind a deeply carved fjord coastline that is filled in with rising ocean waters. Glacial-sediment dumping continues, as the surrounding landscape is slowly transformed by stream channels, slope processes such as avalanches, and the constant action of waves and wind. All the big glacial erratics on the Diamond Beach Hike in Part 4 (Hike 29) are there as a result of the interaction of coastal erosion with the glacial deposits.

If you want some actual history to hold in your hand, walk Anchor Point Beach (Hike 33). There, you will find a fabulous variety of igneous, metamorphic, and sedimentary rocks, including basaltic rocks and radiolarian cherts strewn on the sand. These are clear evidence of the underwater volcanic action that happened 200 million years ago. These rocks were formed on the ocean floor by volcanoes and sedimentation under 2,000 feet of water, dragged a few thousand miles north, shuffled in with other oceanic, continental and mantle rocks, folded and faulted into mountain ranges, and finally delivered to the beach by the Kenai glaciers, which have only recently departed. Anchor Point Beach is a rock-hound's paradise!

So as you hike around the Kenai Peninsula on all these marvelous hikes through this spectacular wild terrain, you are walking through an evolving landscape. And, while the results of the recent glaciation are often the most obvious, there is a long and fascinating history contributing to the changing landscape you see today! As you read through my hike descriptions, I will point out some of the key geologic features you see.

HIKING TIPS: GEAR

Controlling body temperature and moisture is key to comfortable and safe hiking. Dress in layers that are lightweight, compress-pack easily, wick moisture, and dry quickly, and be sure to manage those layers as you hike, taking off and adding them as needed. Also important are hiking poles and knee covers. Following is a list of specific recommendations.

CLOTHES

Socks: Perhaps the most important piece of clothing, since your feet experience the greatest wear and tear when hiking. Keeping them dry and comfortable is paramount, for nothing will put a stop to a great hike more quickly than blistered feet. I recommend two layers of socks: a thin inner sock of fast-drying material such as polypropylene (polypro) or silk, and a thicker outer one of wool. Take two pairs of each for each day's hike, and swap them out every hour or so. Hang the just-used ones off your back-

pack to air-dry. Also, stop periodically and take off your boots, to air-dry them as well. As for blisters, see the discussion of mole skins below.

Knee covers: Your knees get cold long before the rest of your legs, partly because blood vessels are closer to the surface there and have no muscles to protect them. I have invented what I call knee covers, which are made locally for me on the Kenai. I use them in all my outdoor sports, and they protect my knees.

Top layer, closest to skin: Either a short-sleeved or long-sleeved underwear top, preferably made of polypro or new wool. If you are a big sweater like me, consider a half-zip front, which is a good way to control moisture.

Top layer, next: Thin, long-sleeved, half-zip jersey, to be removed once you are warmed up. Note: I often wear this for the first half-hour in the morning and then take it off after I am warmed up.

Top layer, last: Thin, lined jacket of water-resistant breathable fabric, preferably a full-zip jacket, that is compressible for easy packing in the top compartment of your backpack. Note: I may wear this at the start of my morning hike on cold mornings but usually shed this once warmed up, often after only 15–20 minutes of hiking. I keep this handy near the top of my pack for rapid access when I stop and/or for bad weather.

Bottom layer, closest to skin: Thin, wicking, short underwear bottom.

Bottom layer, two: Thin, long underwear of polypro or new wool. If the weather is warm, add high socks and knee covers. If cold, add a pair of breathable/waterproof side-zip pants.

Bottom layer three: Breathable/waterproof side-zip pants, sometimes called rain pants or wind pants. Be sure to get full side-zips so they work with boots. I zip down from the top (rather than up from the bottom) while hiking to allow heat and moisture to escape but still provide leg protection.

Zip-off pants option: Another option/ addition to your bottom set is a pair of hiking pants with zip-off lower legs. I use these to control temperature/moisture while providing leg protection when necessary.

Hats: I usually carry two hats. I use a thin, compressible mesh hat with a sun bill for hiking, which I either soak with water or take off and clip to my waist-pack strap once I start sweating. My second hat is a warm cap to wear around camp. (I also use a wide-brim compressible hat for rainy weather.)

Author and Zip with knee covers and layers

photo by Nancy Lasater

Gloves: I always have gloves, even in mid-summer, since early mornings and evenings are often cool. Also, hiking in rainy weather up here causes cold hands. Like your knees, your hands have little protection from heat loss. When hiking, I often wear only thin, polypro under-gloves, which make an enormous difference and facilitate operating my camera and voice-recording equipment.

Rain cover: It can rain any time in Alaska, so be prepared with either a one-piece poncho or a two-piece top and bottom. Your choice. I favor the two-piece option because I always seem to get tangled up in the ponchos. As for your head, the choices are hood or rain hat. I opt for rain hat since I hate trying to turn my head in a hood. Overall, I prefer the less expensive, new-generation coated nylons over the more expensive Goretex® materials, for they seem to work better and pack easier.

Boots: Boots in Alaska must deal with rain and mud. DO NOT bring those light-weight, breathable, mesh hiking boots, but you also don't need a super-heavyweight boot either, unless you plan to pack heavy loads. Just make sure your sole is stiff and thick enough to protect your soles from bruising when hiking on rocks and stable enough to provide you stability when carrying your load. And very important—make sure your boots are not too loose, or too short in the toes, which will kill you coming down-slope.

My purchase recommendations are: 1) never buy boots via the Web or mail order; 2) walk around the store wearing the boots and find an incline, to check whether your foot slides; 3) when trying on boots, wear the same double layers of socks you plan to wear hiking; 4) also lug your backpack to the store and walk around with the pack on your back in the boots; 5) break your boots in by wearing them around the house before heading out on that 25-mile hike!

Gaiters: Seriously, yes, these can be a godsend, especially in the early mornings, to keep the dew from soaking your feet. Gaiters will also keep the tall overgrowth of grasses off your socks and boots when you hike, but be aware that gaiters trap heat and will overheat your feet, so be sure to do the sock swap discussed above under "socks."

Layering Tips: Having all the correct clothing is useless if you don't manage your layers. Layer up in the morning as you set out, but don't keep all that on! You'll start to sweat and pretty soon you aren't just over-heated but wet too . . . not good! Be sure to stop and consciously check your body temperature and moisture often. I do it starting just fifteen minutes into every hike. Then adjust accordingly. As to fleece, I don't carry it because it's bulky. Consider bringing a down coat instead—one that packs in a waterproof sack. Remember, it's easier to add a dry layer and do some squats or pushups to get warm than it is to shiver in thick layers of wet clothing.

Cotton Kills: I am still amazed when I see folks out hiking in blue jeans. First of all, they are tight, heavy and inflexible, the opposite of what you want for hiking. But more important, jeans are made of cotton. They may look great and feel good when you are standing still or riding a horse, but they are not hike-appropriate clothing. Cotton retains moisture—this is bad. Wet cotton clothing is heavy and warmth-sucking. Don't wear cotton, even for your underwear. There are many soft, nice-feeling woven synthetics and even new wools that will feel just fine and won't threaten your life when you get wet, and you will get wet.

Synthetics vs. New Wool: These are the two choices for lightweight, water-wicking clothing. The new wools don't scratch, even next to the skin, and they are warm even when soaking wet. Wool also doesn't smell as much as most synthetics after a couple days' wear. They both work well. It's a matter of personal preference.

PRIMARY GEAR:
I am often baffled by hikers I see with the latest GPS but no water bottle. Before you get fancy, get the basics, as follows:

Hiking poles: I wish I had gotten a set of these decades ago! I used to call them "sissy sticks," but I know now that if you have a raised center of gravity from toting a pack, these poles are a must. They enhance stability, reduce leg strain, and provide greater safety, especially on steep, unstable slopes (like the thrilling Hope Point Trail–Hike 3). As to type, I prefer the clamp rather than twist kind, since I have too many problems with the twist adjusts not working properly.

Mole skin: Carry some of these always for incipient blisters, and remember that hot, wet feet blister faster than cool, dry ones.

Small stuff bags: Organize your things into small, compressible stuff sacks, especially on longer hikes and overnights. These bags will also keep your wet gear away from your dry.

Food: I always keep a few energy bars (often Snickers®) in the lower compartments of my packs. Snack along the way rather than waiting for meal times, as regular intake keeps your blood sugar levels on an even keel. This in turn allows you to hike more comfortably for longer and prevents the low-blood-sugar monster from rearing its ugly head . . . that's the person who snaps and growls at their hiking companions.

Cup: I confess I drink from stream channels and especially snow melt. I'm alive and well. I keep a lightweight plastic cup clipped to my left shoulder strap with a quick release clip. I even have a thin, four-foot string wrapped around the handle that allows me to dip into streams from footbridges.

Water: Especially when hiking at high-elevation along ridgelines in the alpine zone, always bring water. If you use water you find along the trail, it is a good idea to either boil it (time consuming and expensive) or use water treatment tablets.

Camelbacks: I am not a fan of water bottles, which are a pain to carry, but I love water bags. They even make kid-sized ones,

which will keep the tikes entertained. I like to purchase packs with integrated water bags. Note: be sure to dry and air them out between uses.

Sunglasses and sunscreen: Yes to both. Wear polarizing UV-blocking sunglasses, especially around snow, like on the Harding Ice Field (Hike 15), where the reflected sunlight is polarized and intense. Also cover your skin with sunblock of SPF 15 or higher.

Insect repellent: The Alaska state bird is the mosquito, and if you weigh less than 100 lbs. a tag team of two can carry you off at will. OK, so the state bird is actually the willow ptarmigan, and it takes at least three Alaskan mosquitoes to lift a 100 lb. human, but suffice it to say that we do have mammoth, ravenous mosquitoes here. (This is another reason why hiking in the mosquito-free, high,

Hiking in the easy-to-reach, treeless, alpine tundra provides dramatic views and easy trekking

windy alpine zone is so great.) I am no fan of DEET. Just reading the formula makes me uneasy. My recommendation is lemon eucalyptus oil. It's non-toxic, smells nice, and works. You will have to apply it a bit more frequently than DEET-based compounds, but you won't grow a second head!

Knife: I carry a Leatherman® and a small fixed-blade knife. The Leatherman® is especially good when repairs are necessary. The fixed blade is for shaving wood to make fires and cutting food.

Hand cloth: On overnight and multiday trips, a small, quick-dry hand cloth is a lightweight luxury worth having. It's a terrific multipurpose tool for stream-dipping and cooling off, hand-drying, pot-holding, face-wiping, and even dish washing with sand. I am always glad when I have one and sorry when I don't.

First aid kit: I don't carry a big first aid kit but only these essentials: mole skin for blisters, tweezers, band aids or gauze and tape (which work better than band aids for me), small scissors, Tylenol® for altitude-related headaches, triple-antibiotic cream, lip balm, and aloe (which I use to treat everything from sunburn to puski burns to itchy beards.)

Maps: You only need to buy three maps to cover all 50 hikes in this book. They are all part of the National Geographic Trails Illustrated Maps series: Kachemak Bay State Park, Kenai Fjords National Park, and the Kenai National Wildlife Refuge. See the Resource section at the end of this introduction for ordering information.

Compass: A compass is a useful tool to have. If you brought your own and have traveled to Alaska from afar, remember to test your magnetic variation (the deviation from true north of your magnetic needle), as it is likely to be quite different from the declination you are used to. The magnetic variation on the Kenai was approximately 22° west in 1997 with an annual change of 12' west.

Fire starter: In a small Ziplock® bag, I carry brown paper bag material, which has a higher BTU content than toilet paper or newspaper, along with wood matches, a lighter, some small, dry kindling, and a small fixed-blade knife for shaving wood. Being able quickly and easily to build a fire on a rainy day while stopping for lunch, waiting for your water-taxi pickup, or making dinner at your campsite is welcome indeed. Be sure to replenish your dry kindling, which I do as soon as my fire is built so I don't forget!

Toilet kit: Carry a Ziplock® bag with a lighter and some biodegradable toilet paper, and be sure to burn the used toilet paper and cover your waste when done.

Tent and sleeping bag: If you are camping overnight, you'll want a tent and a sleeping bag. A self-standing, three-season tent is usually fine for Alaska from May through September. As to material, you have your choice of many new lightweight fabrics.

Sleeping pad/chair: Hard-core tough-guys/gals may snicker derisively at this—I don't care. I use a three-quarters-length, self-expanding sleeping pad that doubles as a chair when organized in its form. New-generation pads/chair combos are so light and easily packed it's hard not to bring one along—and I can snicker back while I sit comfortably.

OTHER GEAR YOU MIGHT BE GLAD YOU REMEMBERED TO BRING

Cameras: One of the great benefits of digital photography is the availability of small, high-quality cameras with amazing zooms. They are also light and pack well. Put your camera in a small Ziplock®-bag along with an extra memory card. There are even video cameras that are small enough to pack these days. (Don't count on the video function in your cell phone, since you won't bother carrying your cell phone on all the hikes. Cell phone service on the Kenai is spotty.)

Binoculars: Carry a small, lightweight pair for bear-viewing, distance-seeing, and all-around entertainment throughout the day and night (terrific also for planet- and star-gazing away from the lights).

GPS: Not necessary, as most of the trails in this book do not require a GPS for location and navigation. They can be useful, though,

Katie crossing stream with twin poles upstream

for cross-country hiking and for charting points for later return.

Tide book: A must-have if you are beach hiking, like at Caines Head in Part 2 (Hikes 17 and 18) and Diamond Beach in Part 4 (Hike 29), where tides can restrict beach access and/or returns.

Head lamp: Good for overnight stays. The new LED head lamps are light and efficient with batteries lasting many nights.

Cooking gear: I use a simple, high-powered stove that fits in my single cook-pot to minimize weight and volume. I plan mostly simple but tasty single-pot meals to keep cooking, eating, and cleanup fast and easy.

HIKING TECHNIQUES AND TIPS

Here are some hiking tips I think will make your hiking more enjoyable:

- *Use your hiking poles:* Poles make hiking easier, safer, and less tiring. You can hike with either one or two poles. Shorten your poles when hiking uphill and lengthen them for hiking down. When hiking down steep, unstable slopes, reach first with your pole(s) and then step toward the pole(s). This allows you to descend more safely and with less wear and tear on your knees. When navigating downfalls, use your poles to stabilize yourself over and off the down-fall. Make sure to recheck the tightness of your poles prior to committing your weight to them.
- *Stream crossing:* If you are hiking alone and need to cross stream channels, your hiking pole is your best friend. Hiking poles provide third and fourth points of balance and support. Typically you will want to place your pole upstream, but there are times due to rock placement

and footing where you will place them downstream. If you pole downstream, be sure to lengthen them and check the tightness of the lock. Unhook your waist and sternum straps and loosen the shoulder straps of your pack so you can easily slide out of your pack if you do fall in the water. If you do fall in, slide out of your pack. You can retrieve it after you retrieve yourself. If the water is deep enough that you are floating downstream, place your feet downstream and then try to maneuver away from the main current. I discourage you from crossing streams barefoot. Cold water will quickly numb your feet, reducing your balance and ability to feel purchase. Plus, being barefoot is an easy way to injure your feet in an unstable stream channel. I carry either dive booties or my current favorite solution–Crocs®–and thick wool socks. The Crocs are lightweight, don't soak up water, dry quickly, and are good around camp as well. If you are hiking with companions, you can lock arm-in-arm, making a circle with three people, and cross together stepping in unison. Avoid water more than thigh deep, as deeper water is likely to sweep you downstream. Sometimes the best solution is to wait for later in the day or the next morning for stream flow to subside prior to crossing. Many glacially-fed streams are at their highest and most dangerous flows in mid-afternoon. Waiting for an early-morning or evening crossing may be the best decision.

- *Sock-swapping:* Do get into the habit of sock-swapping during your hike. You will have fewer foot problems and hike more comfortably and happier.
- *Stretching:* Hiking tends to tighten up your legs, back, and neck. Stretching during sock-swapping breaks and in the evening will help work out the kinks and ward off injury.
- *Toenail trimming and shoe fit:* Before you leave for any hike, but particularly long and/or steep hikes, trim your toenails. Long toenails will get jammed into the toes of your boots, even in the best fitting ones, as well as on long and/or steep downhills, causing pain, bruising, and even torn toenails.
- *Get to camp early:* On multiday hikes, plan to get to camp early. Allow yourself plenty of time to unwind, stretch, set up your tent and sleep space, gather fire wood, dry out your clothes, make dinner, eat and cleanup, explore the area around your campsite, do some photography and/or binoc-scaping, and just plan chill. When you are camping in the alpine zone there is always much viewing to do!

DEALING WITH BEARS AND MOOSE

One of the most commonly asked questions is "What about bears?" My first response is usually, "Oh, they are no problem. I always make sure I hike with someone I can outrun." This response typically elicits nervous laughter, as my conversation partners gauge whether they can outrun ME. Short of sacrificing your hiking companions, here are a few common recommendations for managing your interaction with large, and sometimes hungry, wildlife.

- *First and foremost, understand these are wild animals, not pets, and should be respected and treated as such.* No matter how cute or docile a moose looks, make no mistake–they are dangerous and unpredictable. Don't be a moron and try to sidle up close to one so your buddy can take a picture. This is why we have telephoto lenses. Avoidance is the best policy. The truth is most wildlife would rather not interact with us. They think we look and smell funny.

- *Make some noise* as you hike through tight areas with limited visibility such as tall grass and willow thickets. Hike slowly through these areas to give wildlife the chance to vacate. I am not a fan of bear bells but some folks use them.
- *Another important avoidance behavior* is not to leave and not to store food in your tent. Bears have an excellent sense of smell and will seek out your food. Seal up your unused food and store it well away from your tent/campsite.
- *Hang food well off the ground in trees.* Many of the trails in this book have bear-proof food boxes located near established camping sites. Use them!
- *Be aware of wind direction.* If the wind is blowing in your face as you hike, you will be downwind from any bears or moose and they will not be able to smell you. Make more noise in these circumstances and be extra alert.
- *If you encounter wildlife, do not make quick movements.* Stand tall to look big, speak in a normal tone of voice to let the bear know you are human, and back away slowly. DO NOT RUN or you become game!
- *Never get between a mother and her young.* If you see a young moose or bear, you can assume the mom is around. Clear out quickly. Don't wait for the mama viewing. You may experience a more intimate encounter than you like.
- *Stand your ground.* This is a tough one. If a moose or bear charges you, stand your ground, since most charges are bluffs. After the first charge, back away slowly, since that's what they want.
- *If the charge is no bluff* (which is very rare), ball up into the fetal position to protect your head and vital organs.

- *A weapon is no substitute for safe, sensible behavior.*

Note: I have been hiking in bear and wolf country for decades, have had numerous encounters, and never been attacked. Bear attacks, while sensationalized, are rare. With the use of bear avoidance behavior you can enjoy worry-free backcountry experiences.

LEAVE NO TRACE

As vast and wild as Alaska still is, it is still in need of respectful care. The 50 hikes covered in this book are along established trails or well-used cross-country routes. A lot of people use these trails, so please engage in some simple, easy, largely common-sense behavior that will ensure we all enjoy these hikes for a long time to come. Here are some simple, no-trace suggestions:

- *Pack out whatever you pack in.* There is no need to leave anything behind.
- *Camp in previously established campsites.* This minimizes the impact of your camping. If you do camp away from an established campsite, camp far from any established trail—usually more than 100 feet off-trail. You will have more privacy.
- *Do not cut live vegetation for any use.* And remember, during the winter living vegetation is often dormant and may look dead. Moreover, even if a large tree is in fact dead, many old snags serve as habitat for birds and other wildlife. If it is upright, assume it is alive and/or useful.
- *If you make a fire, keep it modest.* You do not need to create a bonfire to enjoy it. Once you are through with your fire, douse it completely and spread the pieces to remove as much evidence as possible.
- *When camping in established campsites,* set your tent up in areas designated for tents or on previous tent sites.

This minimizes the impact of multiple tent setups.

- *If outhouses are not available,* pick a site at least 200 feet away from any water source, stream, or lake. Burn your toilet paper and cover your waste in a shallow hole. Deep holes are necessary or in fact required. Consuming bacterial activity is highest in the top layers of soils.
- *When hiking on established trails,* remain on them as much as possible to reduce the wear and tear on the near-trail environment.
- *When hiking off-trail and cross-country,* avoid stepping on vegetation when you can. If you have a choice walk on exposed rocks. Especially avoid the cryptozoic soil (the dark, patterned soil you find in the alpine zone), for this solid takes many years to establish and grow.
- *Many trails traverse private property.* Please respect any and all private property signs and resist taking any souvenirs no matter how abandoned a site appears.
- *Minimize or don't use soap.* I wash all my cooking gear with fine sand and dirt. We are so accustomed to using soap we may feel that nothing can get clean without it. In fact, I have been cleaning my cooking gear for decades with sand and dirt with no ill effects, and a lot less hassle! If you do use soap, use biodegradable soap and rinse away (200+ feet) from water sources.

HIKING CHOICES AND RATINGS

HIKING CHOICES
I have divided this book into five parts based on the geographic location of the hikes running roughly north to south on the Kenai Peninsula.

Part 1. Northern Kenai
This area includes nine hikes on the northern third of the Kenai Peninsula. They are closest to Anchorage, which makes them easy to sample if you are staying there. They offer a full range of length and difficulty from the casual couple-hour Byron Glacier Hike (Hike 1) to the multiday trek over Resurrection Pass (Hike 4).

Part 2. Northeast Kenai
This area offers nine hikes in the northeast corner of the Kenai near the town of Seward. These varied hiking environments include coastal trails (Caines Head–Hikes 17 and 18), glacier hikes (Exit and Harding Ice Field–Hikes 14 and 15), and the famous Mount Marathon race hike (Hike 16).

Part 3. Central Kenai
This area takes you into the heart of the Kenai National Wildlife Refuge near the towns of Kenai and Soldotna. Here you will find eight hikes traversing a variety of forested lowlands (Seven Lakes–Hike 23), forested uplands (Hideout–Hike 19), long mountain hikes (Russian Lakes–Hike 26), and highcountry traverses (Skyline–Hike 24).

Part 4. Southeast Kenai–Homer & Anchor Point
This area offers seven trails around my town of Homer (Cosmic Hamlet by the Sea). These include several spectacular beach hikes (Anchor Point and Diamond Beach–Hikes 33 and 29), as well as some open-slope hikes (Homestead and Crossman Ridge–Hikes 30 and 31).

Part 5. Southeast Kenai–Across Kachemak Bay
This area includes 17 hikes accessible only across the bay in the Kachemak Bay State Park and Wilderness Area. There, you have

access to high-ridge hikes (Grace and Alpine ridges–Hikes 36 and 44), lowland forest (Moose Valley–Hike 41), and full-on mountain-climbing (Poot Peak–Hike 40).

Whatever your skill level or level of adventure, you are sure to find a hike to suit your fancy.

RATINGS

At the beginning of each hike and in the Hikes at a Glance chart at the front of this book, I rate each hike and provide some basic information. Following is an explanation of the major descriptive topics:

Total distance: Unless otherwise indicated, this is the total length of the trail. Some trails are circle trails. Some are one-way, and some are out-and-back. On the out-and-back trails, I indicate whether the distance given is one-way or roundtrip. For instance, the Summit Creek Hike (Hike 6) is listed as 8.4 miles one way. This would indicate the total hiking distance is 16.8 miles for the roundtrip.

Elevation Change: This figure is determined by subtracting the starting elevation from the highest elevation point on the trail.

Rating: I rank each hike by difficulty as easy, moderate, difficult, or very difficult. In deciding this designation for each hike, I take into account the following: length of hike, steepness, cumulative elevation change, and trail conditions. For instance, a trail that is short and not too steep might still garner a rating of moderate if the footing on the trail is challenging. Note: I am very fit, so what I rate as "moderate" may be "difficult" for those who are less fit or unused to hiking.

Best Season: While many of these hikes can be hiked in spring, summer and fall, here I indicate the best seasons. For example, some trails are choked with tall grasses and are best hiked either early or late in summer. Other trails might be particularly good autumn-color treks.

HIKES AT A GLANCE

In the chart labeled Hikes at a Glance, check out the hikes in the geographic region of your choice and then turn in the book to the hikes that caught your fancy to read more!

Map and Profile Statistics: The maps I created for this book using the National Geographic Topo map software are shaded relief maps that better show the contours of the topography. In addition, you will see each map has an accompanying longitudinal profile, which shows you visually the ups and downs as well as the relative steepness of the hiking route. Located in the lower right corner of each profile are three Gain statistic numbers, which show you, in order from left to right, the total positive elevation increase, the total negative elevation loss, and the net loss or gain of elevation. For instance, the profile statistics for Hike 7 (Crescent Creek) show Gain: +1167' − 264' = +903'. This indicates that along the Crescent Creek Trail a hiker will gain 1167 feet, lose 264 feet and achieve a net elevation change of +903 feet. And, by adding the two gain and loss numbers together, you can calculate the cumulative elevation change, which for the Crescent Creek Hike = 1167' + 264' = 1428 feet.

INFORMATION RESOURCES

Here are some sources of hiking and camping information on the Kenai Peninsula. I have listed Area/Part–specific resources as well as general resources.

BOOK WEB SITES

- Book and author Web site: Taz Tally, www.taztallyphotography.com

- Book publisher: Countryman Press, www.countrymanpress.com

MAP RESOURCES

- The fabulous 3D hike location map of the Kenai: Tóth Graphix Cartographic Studios, www.tothgraphix.com
- National Geographic Maps, Trails Illustrated Series: Kachemak Bay State Park, Kenai Fjords National Park, and Kenai National Wildlife Refuge. These three maps cover all 50 Hikes. www.trailsillustrated.com, www.nationalgeographic.com/maps, 800-962-1643
- Digital Mapping Software: TOPO! www.nationalgeographic.com/topo, topo@ngs.org, 800-962-1643
- Exit Glacier: Exit Glacier Map (large-scale detail map), Alaska Natural History Association, www.alaskaanha.org
- Alaska Atlas and Gazetteer: Includes small-scale/large-area maps of the Kenai as well as GPS tools. www.delorme.com, (http://shop.delorme.com/OA_HTML/DELibeCCtdItemDetail.jsp?beginIndex=0&item=52&section=10096)

PART 1: NORTHERN KENAI

- Chugach National Forest, www.fs.fed.us/r10/chugach
- Hiking Map: Kenai National Wildlife Refuge. National Geographic Maps, Trails Illustrated Series: www.trailsillustrated.com, www.nationalgeographic.com/maps, 800-962-1643
- Cabin Reservations–Federal: (http://www.recreation.gov/marketing.do?goto=/welcomeToNewRecreationGov.html or http://www.mid nightsun.com/usfsch.htm)
- Hiking Map: Kenai Fjords National Park. National Geographic Maps, Trails Illustrated Series: www.trailsillustrated.com, www.nationalgeographic.com/maps, 800-962-1643

PART 2: NORTHEAST KENAI

- Kenai Fjord National Park (Part 2: Seward Area), www.nps.gov/kefi
- Cabin Reservations–Alaska State Park Cabins: (http://www.dnr.state.ak.us/parks/cabins/kenai.htm)
- Cabin Reservation–Federal: (http://www.recreation.gov/marketing.do?goto=/welcomeToNewRecreationGov.html) or (http://www.midnightsun.com/usfsch.htm)
- Water-Taxi Service/Kayak Rental–Miller's Landing, Seward, www.millerslandingak.com, 866-541-5739
- Hiking + Kayak Trip–Kayak Adventures, www.KayakAK.com, 907.224.3960

PART 3: CENTRAL KENAI

- Kenai National Wildlife Refuge. (http://kenai.fws.gov/), E-mail: kenai@fws.go, 907-262-7021
- Hiking Map: Kenai National Wildlife Refuge. National Geographic Maps, Trails Illustrated Series: www.trailsillustrated.com, www.nationalgeographic.com/maps, 800-962-1643
- Cabin Reservations–Federal: (http://www.recreation.gov/marketing.do?goto=/welcomeToNewRecreationGov.html) or (http://www.midnightsun.com/usfsch.htm)
- Skilak Lake: www.skilaklake.com

PARTS 4 AND 5: SOUTHEAST KENAI

- Hiking Map: Kachemak Bay State Park. National Geographic Maps, Trails Illustrated Series: www.trailsillustrated.com, www.nationalgeographic.com/maps, 800-962-1643
- Kachemak Bay Trail Conditions: (http://www.dnr.state.ak.us/parks/asp/trailcondition.htm)
- Cabin Reservations–Alaska State Park Cabins: (http://www.dnr.state.ak.us/parks/cabins/kenai.htm)
- Alaska Natural History Association:

Kachemak Bay Research Reserve
- Kachemak Bay State Park Detail Map: (http://www.dnr.state.ak.us/parks/units/kbay/kbaymap.htm)
- Bike and gear rental and sales: Homer Saw and Cycle located at the base of the spit, www.homersaw.com, 800-478-8405 or 907-235-8406
- Outdoor clothing, high quality and custom: Nomar, 104 East Pioneer Ave., Homer, AK 99603, 907-235-8363, www.nomaralaska.com
- Outdoor gear sales: Ulmer's Hardware, 3858 Lake St., Homer, AK 99603, 907-235-8594, 800-478-8634

WATER TAXI SERVICE
- Mako's, www.makoswatertaxi.com
- Smoke Wagon, www.homerwatertaxi.com
- Bay Excursions, (www.xyz.net/~bay/)
- Homer Ocean, www.homerocean.com
- True North, www.truenorthkayak.com
- Jakolof Ferry, www.jakolofferryservice.com
- Tutka Bay Taxi, tutkabaytaxi.com

HIKING AND OUTDOOR CLUBS
- Happy Hikers–Anchorage, (http://donnagene53.tripod.com/happyhikers/)
- Kenai Peninsula Outdoor Club (KPOC), Contact: Todd Stone (Todd.Stone@bakerpetrolite.com 907-283-8426), Steve Ford (Lforward@ptialaska.net), or Tony Oliver (slowdotnawildbrand@yahoo.com)

GENERAL RESOURCES
- Alaska Public Lands Information Centers, (http://www.nps.gov/aplc)
- Alaska Division of Parks and Recreation, (http://www.dnr.state.ak.us/parks/)
- Alaska State Park Cabins, (http://www.dnr.state.ak.us/parks/cabins/kenai.htm)
- Alaska Natural History Association, www.alaskanha.org

- Alaska Marine Highway, http://www.dot.state.ak.us/amhs/index.html
- Alaska Department of Natural Resources, DNR State of AK, (http://www.dnr.state.ak.us/parks)
- Alaska Department of Fish & Game State of AK, (http://www.adfg.state.ak.us)
- Discover Alaska's Kenai Peninsula, www.kenaipeninsula.org/7_Natural_Wonders
- Cabin Reservations–Federal, (http://www.recreation.gov/marketing.do?goto=/welcomeToNewRecreationGov.html) or (http://www.midnightsun.com/usfsch.htm)
- Alaskan Custom Photo Adventure Trips–Taz Tally Photography, www.taztallyphotography.com
- Wildlife Photography–Wild North Photography, http://www.wildnorthphoto.com/
- Yoga Info–For good stretches to limber up before, during and after a hike, www.yogatoday.com

GEAR
- Pack rafts, Alpacka Rafts, www.alpackaraft.com
- Knee covers, www.taztallyphotography.com

FIELD GUIDES
- Tide Charts: Tide charts are everywhere. Ask at all outdoor stores, water taxis, even banks!
- Alaska Trees & Wildflowers: Waterproof folding pocket guide–A Pocket Naturalist Guide (one of several available) by Waterford Press, www.waterfordpress.com, 800-434-2555
- Alaska's Kenai Peninsula Wildlife Viewing Trail Map: www.AQPpublishing.com
- Alaska's Wild Plants–A Guide to Alaska's Edible Harvest, by Janice J. Schofield; Alaska Pocket Guide, AlaskaNorthwest Books–Graphic Art Center Publishing, www.gacpc.com

- *Alaska's Kenai Peninsula–A Traveler's Guide*, by Greg Daniels and Bill Sherwonit, *An Alaska Pocket Guide,*–AlaskaNorthwest Books–Graphic Art Center Publishing, www.gacpc.com
- *Roadside Geology of Alaska*, by Cathy Conner and Daniel O'Haire, Mountain Press Publishing, http://mountain-press.com
- *A Recreational Guide to Kachemak Bay State Park and Wilderness Park*, by Joshua Duffus, Wizard Works, P.O. Box 1125, Homer, AK 99603

Spring hiking view of natural sculpture of snow, ice, water, mountains and clouds around Lake Kenai

I. Northern Kenai

1

Byron Glacier

Total distance: 1 to 4 miles

Hiking time: 2 to 4 hours

Elevation change: 100 to 1000 feet

Rating: Easy to moderate

Best season: Year-round

Maps: Kenai National Wildlife Refuge by National Geographic Trails Illustrated; Alaska Road and Recreation Map; USGS Seward D-8

Special features: For even the most casual hiker, this hike provides easy access to excellent views of a glacier. For more adventurous folks, you can hike up along the sides of the glacier and get up-close and personal with the glacier, its stream channel, avalanche snow cones and snow caves and massive and varied morainal (glacial) and landslide deposits. The Portage Valley you drive through on your way to the Byron Glacier is the transition zone between the north Kenai Mountains to the south and the Chugach Mountains to the north. So as you climb you are treated to ever more expansive views of the spectacular glaciated peaks of both the northern Kenai and Chugach mountains.

The Byron Glacier trail is a good warm-up introduction to hiking on the Kenai Peninsula and the first trail in this guide you come to on the Kenai Peninsula as you drive south from Anchorage. This is an often overlooked trail by serious hikers, but it should not be because beyond the wide gravel trail there is serious adventure and fun.

GETTING THERE

The Byron Glacier Trail is only a one-hour drive east from Anchorage on the Seward Highway along the Turnagain Arm of Cook Inlet all on paved roads. From the intersection of the Seward Highway and Portage Glacier Valley Road, drive 5 miles east up the Portage Valley toward the visitor center. There are several worthwhile viewpoint stops along the way, including a nice lakefront view of Explorer Glacier at about mile 2.5 on the right or south side of the road. At mile 5 turn left and follow the signs to Byron Glacier and the Portage Cruises. The trailhead is about 1 mile down on the right-hand side. There is ample paved parking at the trailhead for small and big rigs. There is additional parking at a large gravel lot 200 meters past the trailhead parking on the right.

THE TRAIL

The trail leading from the parking lot is wide, about 2 meters, well packed and level gravel that is easily negotiated with a wheel chair with minimal push assist. The initial portion of the trail is through an open

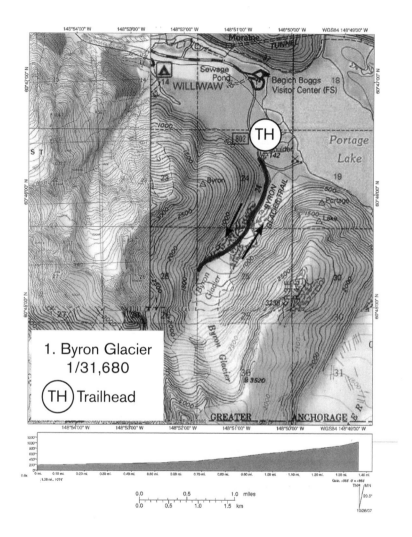

1. Byron Glacier
1/31,680

(TH) Trailhead

Map created with TOPO! © National Geographic Maps

canopy of alder trees along with grasses, fireweed, and large cottonwood and poplar trees. About 100 meters along the trail, it meets the stream channel flowing off the front of Byron Glacier. You will note the milky appearance of the water, created by the fine rock flour glacial sediment carried by the stream. There are numerous opportunities to step off the trail and out into the bed of the stream channel. Do this to enjoy watching and listening to the stream and to enjoy some good views upstream toward the glacier. During high spring runoff this channel will fill side-to-side with rushing sediment-filled water. Viewing the cobblestone-sized sediments that blanket the exposed gravel bars in the stream channel gives you some idea of how powerful this stream can be. Alder bushes, which have large, dark green leaves with serrated edges, and bushes of willows with their smaller, lighter green smooth-edged leaves are found all along the trail. In addition to regular fuschia-colored fireweed, look for dwarf fireweed with its smaller leaves that rarely grow over a foot tall. You will also find some large-leafed plants called devil's club along the trail. Carefully turn these large leaves over to see and feel from where this plant received its name!

One of the dandy features of this valley is the massive snow avalanche fans that form in the winter. Time and again unstable snow accumulates on high slopes and ridges, and then thunders down spreading out in a fan when it reaches the valley floor. So much snow accumulates that these snow avalanche cones will last well into and often through the summer. You will notice that both the Byron Glacier stream and the stream channels flowing down the now snow-free avalanche chutes run under the massive snow cones creating sculpted snow caves. These caves should

be viewed but not entered, because unlike ice caves they are highly unstable.

The trail follows the stream channel up to the end of the maintained gravel path at a viewing bench about 1 mile from the trailhead. From this viewing area you have excellent views of the Byron Glacier as well the multiple massive avalanche-formed snow cones. As you look up at the glacier, keep in mind that the current glacier is a tiny remnant of the glacier ice and snow that filled this valley just a few thousand years ago. Step back in time, and you would be sitting under about 1,000 feet of ice at the viewing bench.

The most fun hiking however starts at the end of the maintained trail, where you begin hiking across glacial ground moraine and avalanche debris. The footing is uneven and usually unstable, and completely fun but NOT recommended for young children. Good sturdy footwear with good ankle support is a must, and having dual hiking poles is a big advantage. One of your first destinations might be the edge of the nearest avalanche snow cone. The interaction of the stream channel with the snow cones with their snow caves and sculptures is fascinating. But do not hike on the snow cones themselves. They are unstable and often have thin roofs over the underlying stream channels.

About a quarter mile from the end of the maintained trail, there is a large ridge composed of larger angular boulders. This is an avalanche debris pile that caromed down from high on the west slope and exploded across the valley. If you look high up on the west slope, you can see the fresh face of the scar from where most of this debris fell. The Byron Glacier stream channel as been rerouted around the eastern end of this avalanche debris pile. The easiest way to navigate this debris ridge is to hike around the east end near the stream channel . . . besides it's fun over there. Once you leave the avalanche debris behind, near the stream channel you will be crossing the outwash plain of the glacier, formed by the deposition of sediment from the Byron Glacier stream channel. Notice how little vegetation there is here, due to the recent exposure of this area by the rapidly retreating glacier. Venture up toward the front of the glacier near where the stream channel exits the bottom of the glacier to admire the small ice caves that have formed at the front of the glacier. But do not enter these caves.

As you move up and out from the outwash plain you will be hiking across a variety of glacial and avalanche debris deposits. Look for striations on the rock faces, evidence of these rocks having been dragged along by the glacier. Most of this debris is highly unstable. As you hike and especially up and down the steeper sections be sure to test your footing, for failure to do so may result in turned and sprained ankles. Hike as far up the debris piles as you like. When you are near the glacier you may be surprised to find you are actually walking on the glacier, even though you thought you were on the rocks. It is common for the surface of a retreating glacier to be covered with sediment and other debris. When you find you are on the ice, simply move off toward the valley walls until you are sure you are on safer ground. While the glacial ice is more stable than the snow avalanche cones, they can still hide unseen dangers such as thin roofs and crevasses.

Once you have gained about 500 feet of elevation, turn around and start looking back north up the valley you have just tra-versed. As you climb you will see increasingly revealing views of the Byron Glacier valley and its stream channel, Portage Lake and the high Chugach Mountains. From high on the debris you will also have a good perspective of the debris avalanche deposit and be better able to visualize how it came crashing down the western slope and flowed out across the valley. Look carefully and you will see the tongue of the debris flow where it came to rest. Hike as far over the debris deposits and along the sides of the glacier as you like.

SPECIAL NOTES

Both the Byron Glacier and Exit Glacier (Hike 46) hikes provide easy and rapid access to a close-up view of a glacier. The Exit Glacier does indeed take you within throwing distance of the glacier itself on the maintained trail. The Byron Glacier, while providing excellent views, does not take you right up to the glacier on the maintained trail. Exit Glacier is also larger, more towering, and overall more impressive than the Byron, especially up close. But the big advantage of the Byron Glacier is that it does not fill its valley from side-to-side as the Exit Glacier does, which means that the Byron Glacier provides more access to the glacier's sides and its associated ice, snow, and glacial debris.

Once you leave the maintained trail and continue up the valley toward the glacier, even more adventure awaits you. You can investigate the interaction of the snow avalanche cones with the Byron Glacier creek, or you can hike up the margin of the glacier and explore the glacial and avalanche debris along the glacial margins. There is easily a full day of exploration and you could still return for more.

Northern Kenai and Chugach Mountains meet near Byron Glacier

50 Hikes in Alaska's Kenai Peninsula

2

Gull Rock

Total distance: 10.2 miles round trip

Hiking time: 4 to 5 hours

Elevation change: 550 feet

Rating: Moderate

Best season: Year-round

Maps: Kenai National Wildlife Refuge by National Geographic Trails Illustrated; Alaska Road and Recreation Map; USGS Seward D-8

Special features: Gull Rock's and trail views of Northern Cook Inlet, Turnagain Arm and surrounding Chugach Mountains, plus myriad hidden corners and little meadows filled with grasses, trees, lichens, and mosses.

The Gull Rock Trail offers a delightful forested coastal hike with great views of Turnagain Arm, Cook Inlet, and the Chugach Range beyond. By the way, mountain bikers may also be enjoying this lovely trail so be on the lookout for them.

GETTING THERE

From the intersection of the Seward and Hope highways, drive 17 delightful miles northwest through alternating spruce and aspen-dominated forests, with stands of large cottonwood near the stream channel, to the town of Hope. The road follows the shoreline of Sixmile Creek. Go another 1.1 miles west on the other side of town on the continuation of the Hope Highway to the end of the road at Porcupine Creek Campground with sites to accommodate small to medium-sized rigs. The trailhead is at the west end of the campground.

THE TRAIL

Gull Rock Trail is a well-maintained remnant of an old wagon road from the 1920s that wrapped around the north end of the Kenai Peninsula. It was initially used as a wagon road that was part of the trail to Johnson Creek, where a saw mill was located. Then this path was used as a route by trappers.

From the trailhead, at an elevation of 100 feet, you follow the coastline that forms the southern rim of Turnagain Arm as you hike through a spruce, aspen, birch, and hemlock forest all the way to Gull Rock. The trail sometimes snuggles right up against the shoreline and sometimes runs a short distance away. At the beginning of the trail you hike through a canopied forest of large stately birch trees with an understory of lush, bright, spring green ferns, including 6-foot-tall fiddleheads. Look for stands of wild roses and dwarf dogwoods. As you peer back into the dense surrounding forest you will see many dead snags, which are pointy deceased trees piercing the sky. These are dead spruces, the result of the spruce beetle infestation that rolled through the Kenai between 2001 and 2002 killing over 90 percent of the mature spruce. But also notice how the forest, especially the young

spruces, is already recuperating, growing up nicely all around the snags.

The trail rises gradually to the high point of 650 feet at about mile 3, passing well-known Halfway Island a short distance offshore at about the 2-mile mark. From mile 3, the trail trends gradually down to Gull Rock at mile 5, about 150 feet above sea level. Where the trail is close to the water, you can stop and enjoy the frequent peak-a-boo views through the trees across Turnagain Arm to the high Chugach Mountains beyond.

You will surely see bear and moose sign along the trail. Look for the frequent scratch

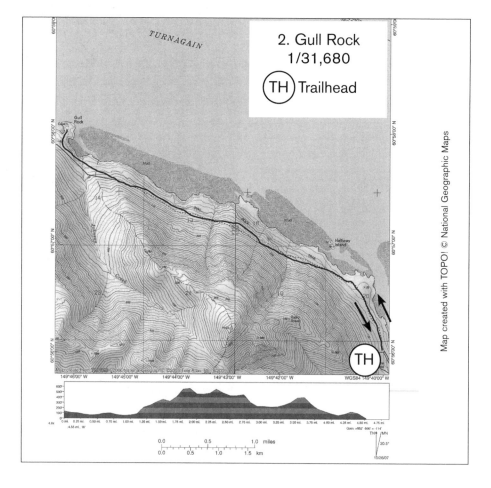

View across Turnagain Arm of Cook Inlet to the high Chugach Mountains

marks in the dirt and dug plants created by scavenging bears. Bears here are generally black, and not brown, but even black bears should be taken very seriously.

Also keep a sharp coastal eye out for beluga whales, which have a habit of hanging out in this section of Cook Inlet.

The trail continues down to Gull Rock, which is a large outcropping that juts out into the western end of Turnagain Arm, near where it meets the more open waters of Cook Inlet. From various perches on the rocky promontory, you can enjoy views east and west. To the east are wide-open vistas of Turnagain Arm, Cook Inlet, and the high Chugach Mountains. To the west are panoramic views of the north end of Cook Inlet and the northern end of the Alaska Peninsula, which is dotted with volcanoes that may be active.

Plan to spend some time nosing around the Gull Rock area at the end of the trail, as it contains many fascinating ecosystems with various mixtures of mosses, grasses, berries, and trees. And Gull Rock itself is just plain fun just to scramble on. It also provides the only real campsite opportunity along the entire trail. If you don't want to stay overnight, this is a great lunch and relaxation stop while you watch the ebb and flow of the world's second-largest tidal range in Turnagain Arm.

You can continue past Gull Rock, but the unmaintained trail is overgrown and covered with downfalls. Those who have tried haven't had much fun—and then there is the nasty-tempered Gull Rock troglodyte who lives about a mile past the rock . . .

SPECIAL NOTES

As you hike along the trail you might notice that the soil profiles are very thin—with many of the trees growing in soil—only a few inches deep, and some right out of the rocks, the result of the area only recently being vacated by a scouring glacier.

3

Hope Point Ridge & Summit

Total distance: 5 miles one way

Hiking time: 4 to 6 hours or more, depending upon how far up the ridgeline you go

Elevation change: 3,608 feet

Rating: Very difficult

Best season: Late May through September

Maps: Kenai National Wildlife Refuge by National Geographic Trails Illustrated; Alaska Road and Recreation Map; USGS Seward D-8

Special features: The first third of a mile through the forest along Porcupine Creek can be hiked and enjoyed by the whole family. Above the creek, spectacular views with my favorite view and perspective of Turnagain Arm and the Chugach Mountains. The name Turnagain comes from the description of Captain Cook when he sailed into these waters, noting he had to keep turning again and again to avoid grounding his ship. NOTE: Take your own water. There is none on the trail but for snow early in the season, which will be long gone for any summer hikers. Also wear sturdy footwear with good ankle support (sneakers not recommended), and hiking poles (two if you have them) will be a welcome aid, particularly during your descent.

This steep hike takes you rapidly above tree line close to the coastline of Turnagain Arm. Above tree line, which you will arrive at in short order, you will be walking first through low bush alders and willows you can see over with wide-open views, and then across even more wide-open tundra.

GETTING THERE

From the intersection of the Seward and Hope highways, drive 17 delightful miles through alternating spruce and aspen-dominated forests, with stands of large cottonwood near the stream channel to the town of Hope. The road follows the shoreline of Sixmile Creek. Go another 1.1 miles west on the continuation of the Hope Highway to the end of the road at Porcupine Creek Campground with sites to accommodate small to medium-sized rigs. The trailhead is at the west end of the campground.

The trailhead is at the east entrance to the campground, the opposite end from the Gull Rock trailhead (Hike 2). There is no trailhead sign on the map, and in fact the trail is not at all obvious. Drive into the campground and park at the first parking area on the right side, which is marked as a day-use area. Walk back out ~200 meters the way you drove in until you reach the spot where the road crosses Porcupine Creek (the only obvious stream channel.) The trailhead is on the south side of the road (away from Turnagain Arm). Walk in 25 meters and you will see a trailhead sign reading HOPE POINT TRAIL EXTREME GRADE NOT

MAINTAINED. This is your warning that there is a steep trail ahead. Interestingly, I found this trail to be one of the easiest to follow with the fewest obstructions. Other trails have encroaching grasses, pushki or down falls, this has none . . . it's too steep for any of that nonsense! So slather on your mosquito repellent and prepare for a delicious challenge!

THE TRAIL

This little-used trail is a treasure. The first third of a mile is a lovely low-gradient hike under a forest canopy of large cottonwoods, birch and spruce trees with understory ferns, moss and big leaf devil's club, none of which encroach, along the west side of Porcupine Creek. Porcupine Creek will sing to you as you hike along its edge. The old-growth forest swallows all outside noise, while shafts of sunlight and sounds of burbling water create a quiet, relaxing ambiance.

After this lazy section, you begin to

climb steeply, and I mean steeply, out of the stream channel directly up the fall line of the slope toward the ridgeline that leads to Hope Point Summit. It is a good idea to attack this step section early in the morning while the air temperature is still cool . . . besides the views you seek from the ridge above are best in the morning light. The lower section of the trail is one of the steepest and gnarliest sections with loose footing and nasty roots. If you survive the first quarter mile, you are probably good to go for the remainder of the trail. As you continue directly up the fall line along the ridge the trees eventually thin out. You are still hiking through spruce and aspen forest, though they too are clinging for dear life to the steep-sided slope. If you are in good shape and love to climb, you will revel in this hike! And to add to your delight, you are greeted with a variety of wildflowers including the lovely red columbine and white four-petaled dwarf dogwood. As you rapidly gain elevation the trees begin to thin, the slope

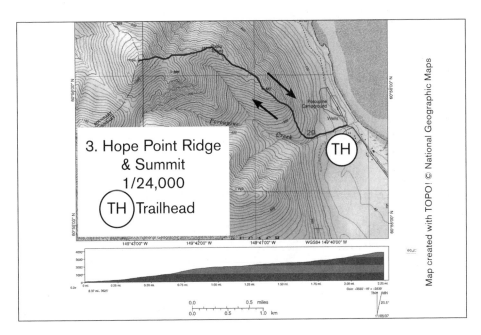

Turnagain Arm of Cook Inlet from high on the Hope Point Trail

50 Hikes in Alaska's Kenai Peninsula

opens up and the grasses and wildflowers become more common. The thick copses of tall spruce and aspen retreat to more diminutive widely spaced stands.

After about three-quarters of a mile and at about 700 to 800 feet of elevation, you reach tree line—the real reason you took this trail. This is where the great views start. You are greeted with spectacular views of the Hope Valley through which you drove, as well as my favorite views of Turnagain Arm and the high Chugach Mountains beyond. Between the tree line and the Hope Point Ridge line you hike through fields of ferns and wildflowers packed with violet blue lupine, red Indian paintbrush, pink wild roses, yellow yarrow, white Queen Anne's lace, wild purple geraniums low to the ground, and the fuschia spires of fireweed along with the aforementioned red columbines that look like shooting comets.

The slope varies between moderate, to steep, to really steep. Hiking poles are a bonus through these steep sections. And as you gain more elevation, hemlocks with their flat leaves join the spruce.

The trail continues steeply until about the 2-mile mark where you reach the first cairn and gain the ridgeline. After that, things gradually level off to a more moderately sloped path as you head up toward the 3,708-foot summit. Stop at the first cairn to change socks, have a bite to eat, and enjoy the view.

From the first cairn, the trail continues up and down along the ridgeline through alternating low-profile spruce/hemlock-dominated sections and grasslands with wildflowers. As you gain more elevation the trees and grasses fall away and the alpine tundra takes hold. Hiking west along the ridge, the western view opens up to outstanding views of the northwestern Kenai Mountains, The Kenai Wildlife refuge flats, Cook Inlet and the Kink Arm, and beyond to the Alaska Peninsula.

As you approach Hope Point, you are hiking mostly across alpine tundra, and the trail slowly disappears. A trail isn't really necessary on the tundra, and once you gain the open ridgeline the summit is obvious. The real joy is exploring around the tundra well above sea level and enjoying the views across Turnagain Arm and the rest of upper Cook Inlet. On clear days you have stunning views of the Chugach Mountains, as well as the volcanoes and other alpine peaks of the Alaska Peninsula across the inlet. And on a very clear day you can see northeast all the way to Denali. You need not stop at the summit, either. You can continue southwest along the ridgeline that separates the Porcupine Creek and Johnson Creek drainages, and even beyond. Your only limitation is water, as none is available on the trail except as snow early in the season.

One note for your climb down. I think hiking down the steep lower slopes is actually much more treacherous than hiking up, and much tougher on the knees. Having double hiking poles is an enormous advantage. Extend both poles so you can reach forward to keep your weight forward on your toes. This posture will help minimize the slip potential. Plus, you can use the poles to help soften the wear and tear on your knees.

SPECIAL NOTES

The farther south you hike up and down the ridgeline from Hope Point the more expansive will be your views, and the more isolated you will feel. Just pay attention to the weather, as it can quickly turn windy and stormy up here. And as always dress in layers and carry extra clothing as well as food and water.

4

Resurrection Pass

Total distance: 39 miles one way

*Hiking time: 3 to 6 days but shorter seg-
ments can also be done*

Elevation change: 2,600 feet

Rating: Moderate

*Best season: Mid-June through Septem-
ber (fall is my favorite)*

*Maps: Kenai National Wildlife Refuge by
National Geographic Trails Illustrated;
Alaska Road and Recreation Map; USGS
Seward B-8, C-8, and D-8*

*Special features: The Resurrection Pass
Trail is considered one of the great
must-do classic signature trails in the
Kenai Peninsula. From its heights, you
have outstanding panoramic views of the
northern Kenai Mountains and Cook Inlet
from along the high alpine trail sections,
and you can see northeast all the way to
Denali on clear days. Well-spaced public-use cabins and campsites make this
an excellent choice for a multiday trek.
There are lots of opportunities for side
hikes, and especially across alpine tundra
terrain. There is also good winter skiing
along the trail with use of the hut system.
Take this hike in the fall when you can
enjoy the fall colors of the vast expanses
of tundra as well as the trees.*

This is a multiday traverse over Resurrection Pass across lower-elevation forested
slopes and higher-elevation tundra-covered
ridgelines of the southern Kenai Mountains
from Cooper Landing to Hope, with excellent views of the northern Kenai from the
alpine zone.

GETTING THERE

From the Hope turnoff on the Seward
Highway 70 miles south of Anchorage,
drive about 16 miles north to Palmer Creek
Road. Turn left and drive south 0.5 mile
and take the right fork onto Resurrection
Creek Road. Continue 4 miles to the Hope
trailhead, which is one of two trailheads
for this long hike. The other is at Cooper
Landing, which can be reached by driving
to mile 53 on the Sterling Highway, where
there is another marked Resurrection Pass
trailhead at the other end. To reach the
Cooper Landing access, park on the north
side of the Sterling Highway at mile 53 at
the marked trailhead for the Resurrection
Pass Trail.

THE TRAIL

The Resurrection Pass Trail can be hiked
from either the Hope or Cooper Landing trailheads, but we'll start from Hope
because the overall slope of the trail is
lower from this side, as you can see from
the long profile for this hike. From the
Hope trailhead, you begin through spruce,
aspen, and alder forests, with interspersed
wildflower meadows, mostly along the
west side of Resurrection Creek. The trail

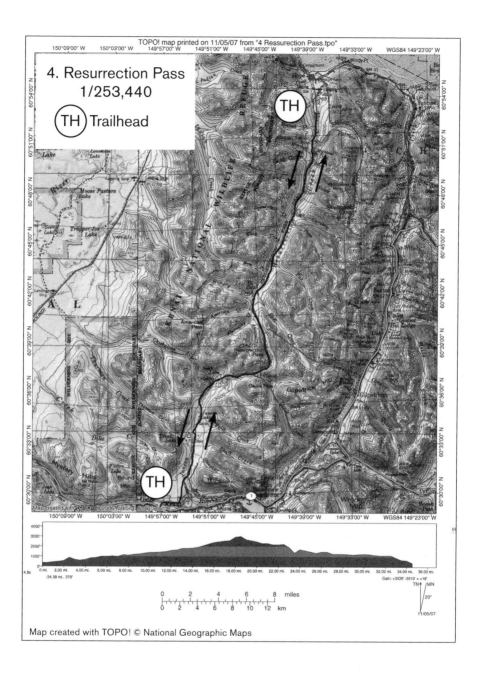

4. Resurrection Pass
1/253,440

(TH) Trailhead

Map created with TOPO! © National Geographic Maps

generally follows the stream, occasionally diverting up the side slopes. Look for networks of beaver dams along the lower stretches of Resurrection Creek. If you're planning to stay in the public-use cabins on this hike, the Caribou Creek Cabin 7 miles in is a good destination for the first night, as the next cabin is not until 12 and one-half miles at Fox Creek. There is also a campsite at Caribou Creek. If you prefer not to hike this far on day one, the Wolf Creek campsite is at about 5 and one-half miles. Cross Resurrection Creek at Caribou Creek. You are hiking mostly under forest canopy and away from the stream channel now. The East Creek Cabin and campsite just past mile 14 at 2,000 feet is a good place to stay for your second night after another 7-mile day.

This next section of the traverse up and over Resurrection Pass to the Devils Pass Cabin at about mile 21 is my favorite. Much of it is above tree line and across wide, low slopes of alpine tundra that from mid to late summer are covered with wildflowers. And of course there are spectacular views. Keep an eye open for wildlife too, including the ubiquitous marmots (aka bear burritos), Dall sheep, grizzly bears, and even caribou.

Take some time to linger near the top of Resurrection Pass at mile 19 (2,600 feet of elevation) to enjoy the expansive vistas and alpine tundra. On clear days you are treated to views toward Cook Inlet and the Alaska Range to the west, the Chugach Mountains to the north across Turnagain Arm, and all the mountains on the northern half of the Kenai Peninsula. I usually take at least a full hour, weather permitting, to do a thorough binocular survey of the Kenai kingdom below. If you have more time and can stay overnight, and especially at the Devils Pass Cabin or Campground, plan to enjoy some off-trail hiking along and across several of the many highcountry tundra-covered alpine ridges and/or explore the upper reaches of the Summit Creek and Devils Pass trails.

As you travel through the tundra take note of the many glacial features. Most of the lower slopes and ridges are rounded because they were overridden and smoothed off by glaciers that flowed over them not long ago. You will also see ridges and small terraces of sediment all along the trail. These are deposits of glacial sediments. You will hike directly through one of these large glacial deposits about a quarter of a mile north of the Devils Pass Cabin. Here, the trail passes through the middle of a ridge that runs perpendicular to the trail and the valley. This is a glacial deposit known as a recessional moraine, formed when the front of a glacier stalled here during its retreat. While stalled, it dumped tons of sediment at its terminus like a conveyor belt. Flat-topped terraces, often visible along the margins of the high valleys, were formed where sediments collected along the edges of the glaciers.

And don't forget the berry picking! In late summer and fall you will find troves of berries—blueberries are my favorites—throughout the tundra. Gathering bunches of fresh berries can add some nice zest to your granola!

Another wonderful pastime in the high tundra is to simply lay down and feel the often-blowing breeze wash over you as you listen for the sounds of the alpine birds flitting about. The Summit Creek Trail (Hike 6) intersects the Resurrection Pass Trail here near the summit. Two miles farther at about mile 21.4, you reach the junction with the Devils Pass Trail (Hike 5) and cabin. If you have time and can stay overnight, and especially at the Devils Pass Cabin or

Campground, plan to enjoy some off-trail hiking along and across several of the many highcountry tundra-covered alpine ridges and/or explore the upper reaches of the Summit Creek and Devils Pass trails. The Devils Pass campsite is just down the trail on the south side. From Devils Pass, you move from the wide-open alpine tundra back down into the forests.

The trail to the Swan Lake Cabin at mile 26 is the steepest on the traverse, with the last mile or so dropping down fairly steep switchbacks. So be sure to have your hiking poles ready. The Swan Lake Cabin is about 0.3 mile off the main trail to the west. This secluded cabin sits on the eastern end of beautiful Swan Lake. If you have an extra day, you might consider bushwhacking along the shoreline to spend an extra night at the West Swan Lake Cabin at the other end of the lake.

Day five is from Swan Lake down to the Trout Lake Cabin at mile 32. This is an easy 6- to 7-mile hike down the Juneau Creek drainage past Juneau Lake. The relatively low gradient makes for a pleasant cruise through the forested uplands. The sixth and final day takes you on an easy 7-mile downhill trek along a mostly forested section of trail to the Cooper Landing trailhead. If you are pressed for time, you could easily combine days five and six and hike all the way from Swan Lake down to the Cooper Landing trailhead. This would be a 13-mile day, but it's a relatively easy downhill journey.

SPECIAL NOTES

I love the high-altitude section of this trail between Devils Pass and Resurrection Pass with its wide-open cross-tundra views and many obvious glacially formed features

The Resurrection Pass highcountry offers many stunning views of glacier-carved peaks and ridges

such as paternoster lakes (strings of lakes connected by small streams formed by sediment deposition of the retreating glacier), moraines and kame terraces. Be sure to take time to hike up onto and explore the recessional moraine located just north of the Devils Pass Cabin where the trail bisects a large gravel ridge. Stand on top of the ridge and look south for some nice views across the tundra. And imagine that only a few thousand years ago the valley where you are standing was completely covered with flowing ice.

I often hike into the Resurrection Pass area via the Devils Pass Trail (Hike 5) or, one of my favorite trails, the Summit Creek Trail (Hike 6), rather than from the Resurrection Pass trailheads. Both of these trails provide more rapid access to the high alpine country, bypassing many miles of hiking though forest cover. Once you are in the vicinity of the Resurrection Pass you have so many choices of places to hike and explore along the Resurrection Pass, Devils Pass and Summit Creek trails, and their surrounding country.

If you intend to secure cabin reservations for your multiday Resurrection Pass trek, do so early in the season (January or February is not too early!). This is one of the favorite trails, and cabin reservations fill up quickly and early in the year. But if you do not have cabin reservations, don't let this deter you from this grand hike. The many camping spots are well located and offer fine respite. In either case plan to arrive at your camp or cabin early so you can enjoy the areas surrounding each location. The 5- to 7-mile distance between camping/cabin locations allows for leisurely travel as well as early arrival.

The Resurrection Pass Trail is designated a National Recreation Trail, and it's popular with mountain bikers. The southern section up to the Juneau and Swan Lake Cabins is used in winter by Nordic skiers who ski in for overnight stays. I actually enjoy this piece of trail more on skis than as a hiking section. If you are interested in a multiweek trip, you can link three locally connected trails—the Resurrection River Trail (Hike 47), the Russian Lakes Trail (Hike 34), and this Resurrection Pass Trail—to form a splendid 72-mile trek from the Seward area, where Exit Glacier tumbles down from the Harding Ice Field, to Hope on the southern shore of the Turnagain Arm of Cook Inlet. Whether you are just hiking the Resurrection Pass Trail or doing a longer combination trail, be sure to make your cabin reservations early to minimize the nights you'll have to spend camping—unless, of course, you could care less about staying in the cabins.

If you are planning a bike return, this route from north to south is the route to take. The bike ride from the southern Sterling Highway trailhead to the Hope trailhead while lengthy, is largely DOWNHILL!

5

Devils Pass

Total distance: 10.1 miles one way

Hiking time: 2 days round trip or access to longer multiday hikes along the Resurrection Pass Trail (27 miles to Cooper Landing trailhead, 31 miles to the Hope trailhead)

Elevation change: 1,500 feet

Rating: Moderate

Best season: Mid-June through September

Maps: Kenai National Wildlife Refuge by National Geographic Trails Illustrated; Alaska Road and Recreation Map; USGS Seward C-7 and C-8

Special features: Easy to moderate climb on shallow-sloped trail through a glaciated valley to the gorgeous high-alpine areas and lakes, and great views of the north-central Kenai Mountains and valleys below.

This is a moderately difficult climb from the Seward Highway up through forested lowlands to the tundra ridgelines of the Resurrection Pass Trail at Devils Pass. It provides rapid access to the alpine country and sweeping views.

GETTING THERE

From the intersection with the Sterling and Seaward highways, drive 2 miles north on the Seward Highway. Trailhead parking is at mile 39.5 on the west side of the highway. There are restrooms and ample parking for more than a dozen vehicles. There is also a secondary staging area on the west end of the parking lot used for horses. Devils Pass Trail is a favorite with riders. BTW: Do you know how to tell horse poop from bear poop? . . . The bear poop has bear bells in it . . . as well as lots of berries.

THE TRAIL

In the first 2 miles, the trail crosses a lowland with an open-canopy forest of spruce, aspen, birch, hemlock, and cottonwood trees with little elevation gain. In the autumn this part of the trail is covered with a golden carpet of aspen and cottonwood leaves and often lined with gray-green lichen and moss. At about one-half mile, you reach a wooden bridge over the south fork of Quartz Creek. At about 1 mile, you cross under power lines and thankfully leave civilization behind. Then you hike up and over a lower hill section dominated more by spruce trees at the lower elevations. They are the spiky ones that pierce the sky. You will hike through a

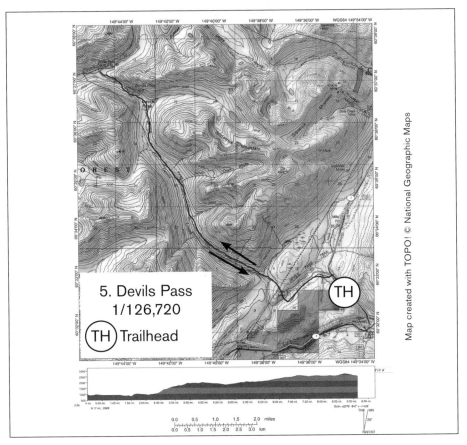

Map created with TOPO! © National Geographic Maps

5. Devils Pass
1/126,720

(TH) Trailhead

short quarter-mile of subalpine alders at the top of the up-and-over, after which the trees drop away and your views open up with great views into the highcountry.

The trail then heads back down into the spruces again as it approaches the north fork of Quartz Creek. At 2 miles you reach the north fork of Quartz Creek and a small side trail. Take this side trail 0.1 mile north (right) to a backcountry campsite known as the Beaver Pond Site. This campground is a nice and easy day hike for families with young children.

Spruce and hemlock trees surround Quartz Creek. Mile 2 to mile 3 is the steepest section of the trail. You cross Quartz Creek and gain about 500 feet of elevation through a long switchback to 1,500 feet at tree line, where the payback is the start of excellent views of the Devils Creek Canyon. From mile 3 to mile 8, the trail parallels Devils Creek as it climbs gradually into the upper-alpine country, offering progressively more spectacular views. In the fall, the vista offers an autumn-meets-winter landscape with the lower slopes painted lavishly in reds and golds and the high charcoal peaks already carpeted with snow. If you're not in a hurry, you can make cross-country forays in many directions. (Please, never feel constrained by this guidebook.)

50 Hikes in Alaska's Kenai Peninsula

Around mile 6, you reach perennial Henry Creek, which means it is always flowing . . . temperature permitting. It is the largest stream channel you'll cross on this trail, draining the western slopes of massive Gilpatrick Mountain, which itself boasts nice ridgeline hikes on all sides.

About 200 meters past Henry Creek, you will come to a small side trail leading northeast, which ends at a small campsite offering protection from the wind, a fire ring, and a bear box. This would be a dandy base camp, near as it is to the refreshing, icy waters of Henry Creek, if you want to befriend the slopes of Gilpatrick Mountain. Even if you don't, you might want to take a moment to visit the campsite anyway, as there is a nice view of the valley opposite the campground.

Giant Gilpatrick Mountain dominates this part of the valley. Its peak is a classic triangular-faceted glacier horn, like the famous Matterhorn, carved by eroding glaciers that resided in "cirques" (ice-filled basins that are the sources glaciers) on three sides of it.

The entire middle portion of the trail treats you to the rushing sounds of Devils Creek. The upper chink of the valley broadens into a classic U-shaped glacially carved half-pipe. Stop and look at it. You may never see the likes of it again, this grand and perfectly formed, outside Alaska.

While alders populate the subalpine ground around you, they rarely tower and therefore do not usually restrict your views. As you hike farther up the valley, you will cross several large-slab scree slopes formed by winter avalanches dragging rocks downslope along with the snow. As you pass through these avalanche deposits, give thanks to the forest service trail construction crews who have oriented these slabs to make passage less limb-threatening.

Glorious views of the wide-open highcountry tundra and lush lowland forests

You reach Devils Pass and its drainage divide after 8 miles. The trail levels out at about 2,500 feet. Here you cross over Devils Creek on a wooden bridge, a great place to dawdle for awhile, dip your toes, and enjoy the stream. Soon thereafter you work around the southwest side of Devils Pass Lake,

Once you reach Devils Lake, you are well into the drainage of Juneau Creek. You will notice that Devils Creek, which flows east, does not drain into Devils Pass Lake, and that the lake in fact drains west into the Juneau Creek drainage.

If you have time, take a hike across the tundra east of the lake for more serene views of the quiet, highcountry water and a terrific lunch stop. Step lightly as you cross the tundra, for the vegetation is delicate and you may be one of the rare humans to cross it this year. Please always leave Alaska as you found it. There is a reason we Alaskans reverently call it The Great Land.

Hiking another mile past Devils Lake, you will hike along a sequence of stream-channel-linked lakes, known as Paternoster lakes, which drain one into the other. This connected sequence of little lakes was formed by the scouring and subsequent retreat of the glacier that carved this pass and valley. You might also notice the industrious work of a local population of busy beavers, an interesting interaction of physical and biological processes. As the Paternoster lakes end, the character of the valley changes to a more open plain filled with stream channels and dotted with small ponds. This new flatness is also the result of glacial action, and it is called a glacial outwash plain. It was formed by the deposit of sediments at the front of the glacier as it retreated up through what is now Devils Pass. It's hard to imagine given how

huge and unmoving they appear to be. As they inch back, they build up sediment and rock and all kinds of debris at the front in a sort of glacial shoreline. They also leave flat earth, denuded of vegetation from thousands of years under ice. From high promontories, you will see on your hikes in Alaska the progression of ice, then sediment, then muddy flats, then small green close to the ground, then ever larger and larger trees as the distance from the fleeing glacier increases. This is especially evident from the Harding Ice Field Hike, (Hike 15) as you look down the riverbed left by Exit Glacier, although you will see many smaller examples left behind here.

You again see how beavers have enhanced these many smaller ponds and their interconnecting stream channels.

The end of the trail brings you to the intersection with the Resurrection Pass Trail, still at about 2,500 feet, and the Devils Pass public-use cabin. The previous A-frame cabin has been replaced with a nifty new, more spacious cabin situated along Juneau Creek and complete with a dandy Adriatic diesel stove and a sun deck. This new cabin faces south and looks out along the gorgeous length of the glacially carved alpine tundra terrain along Resurrection Trail. If you do not have a reservation, which you need to make many months in advance, and are camping instead, the Devils Pass Campground is about a half mile south (left) from the cabin.

You can hike north or south along the Resurrection Pass Trail from Devils Pass. Even if you don't intend to hike to either of the Resurrection Pass trailheads, I recommend at least hiking the 1.5 miles north to the top of Resurrection Pass at 2,600 feet. The views are spectacular! Plus, there are opportunities for cross-country hikes across the alpine tundra. As always when hiking on tundra, step on rocks instead of the fragile vegetation when you can.

SUMMIT CREEK TRAIL LOOPS

The Summit Creek Trail (Hike 6), whose unmarked trailhead is between miles 43 and 44 on the Seward Highway about 3 miles north of the Devils Pass trailhead, is similar in nature to the Devils Pass Trail, but steeper and only 8.4 miles long versus 10.1 miles. The Summit Creek Trail intersects the Resurrection Pass Trail at Resurrection Pass. Although it's not an actual loop unless you walk back along the highway, a hike up the Devils Pass Trail, along the Resurrection Pass Trail to the north, and then down the Summit Creek Trail makes a nice 20-mile trek. You can also do a shorter, though less well-defined, combination hike with the Summit Creek Trail via Devils Pass Lake. Refer to the Summit Creek Trail (Hike 6) description for more details.

SPECIAL NOTES

You can hike this trail in a very long day, for a total of about 20 miles round trip, but this would leave you little time to enjoy the highcountry, so plan to spend at least two days here. Hike up on day one, spend half a day on top of Resurrection Pass, and then descend the 10 easy miles back in the second half of day two. Or better yet, take a whole day to explore the alpine tundra around Resurrection Pass and return on day three. Though you should always be respectful of the temperatures and challenges of hiking here in Alaska, we do enjoy much longer sunlight hours in the summers, so you can give yourself more time to hike in the evenings than you otherwise would in the Lower 48.

The upper alpine zone around the Devils Pass Trail reveals the carving and smoothing action of retreating glaciers a mere few thousand years ago. You will notice that Devils Creek, which concentrates its erosive power right along the stream channel, is reshaping the U-shaped valley commonly carved by glaciers into a "V." Look for this same notching in the lower portions of many of the stream channels flowing through the canyons of the Kenai.

6

Summit Creek

Total distance: 8.4 miles one way

Hiking time: 1 to 2 days up and back or as part of a longer multiday hike along the Resurrection Pass Trail

Elevation change: 2,100 feet

Rating: Moderate

Best season: Mid-June through September

Maps: Kenai National Wildlife Refuge by National Geographic Trails Illustrated; Alaska Road and Recreation Map; USGS Seward C-7 and C-8

Special features: One of my favorites! A varied and rapid ascent to the alpine tundra highcountry above Resurrection Pass. The top of this trail, at 3,400 feet, is one of the highest points of any maintained trail on the Kenai. On your way to the top, you traverse three separate glaciated valleys, each more spectacular than the last. In the autumn . . . there is none better!

Summit Creek is my favorite hike in the northern Kenai. The trail has a similar location and destination to the Devils Pass Trail (Hike 5), but it is shorter by almost 2 miles and offers even more spectacular scenery on its glorious trek through the alpine zone. In fact, it takes you to a perch *above* and then directly *down* into the Resurrection Pass summit. Moreover, along the way you'll traverse three different valleys that offer a splendid variety of Alaskan geological and biological treats.

GETTING THERE

You will locate the trailhead nestled between mile markers 43 and 44 on the Seward Highway about 0.5 mile south of Summit Lake and Pass. (On the Kenai, we locate things often by the marker signs along the highways, as the roads and towns are few.) This trailhead is little used and there is no formal trailhead sign, and no facilities. Heading south along the highway as you approach, look on the right side of the road for a banana-shaped parking area tucked in behind some trees. *There is no trailhead sign along Seward Highway so this pullout is easy to miss.* This trail is not as highly publicized or frequented as its neighbor Devils Pass (Hike 5) and horses are not permitted . . . all of which are good things! To be honest, I was tempted to not even include this hike in my book in order to keep it more of a secret . . . but it's just too good not to share. Please treat it kindly if you use it. I'll be checking!

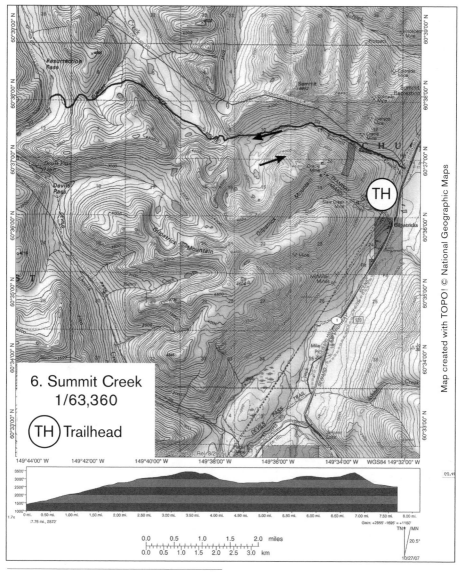

6. Summit Creek
1/63,360

(TH) Trailhead

THE TRAIL

This is a little-known trail, and for the life of me I can't figure out why. The Devils Pass Trail is much more heavily used, but I find Summit Creek far more interesting. The hiking is more varied as you move over two saddles and through three separate valleys and drainages. In addition, you have close-up access to some really stunning glacial features. Well, you get the point—this is a way-cool trail.

The trail begins already at about 1,300 feet on the Seward Highway with a sign-in kiosk and moves immediately up and out of the stream channel bottom of Quartz Creek. At the start, you are very near the

Open tundra surrounding streams and lakes in three drainages await you on the Summit Creek Hike.

headwaters of Quartz Creek and close to the drainage divide with Canyon Creek that flows north down into Upper Summit Lake just 0.5 mile up the highway. You move immediately up onto a bench—a sort of rounded ridge with a flat top—populated with spruce and aspen trees. In the autumn the breeze plays a quaking symphony as it rustles through the aspen branches and the falling leaves create a golden sunlit carpet.

At one-half mile you will pass under the power lines and leave human signs behind. You then hike though a section of open fields filled with willows, fireweed, aspens, and a few spruce as well as low bearberry and elderberry bushes. You begin your brief climb up to the alpine zone. If you are hiking this section in the early morning, rain pants or gators are appropriate to fend off the wet of the grasses. In August, these fields are ablaze with the fuschia of the fireweed, which grows in spires so fast you can almost see it move. Later in August, when almost all the tourists have gone home, these spikes turn into clouds of cottony billows that then break free and snow the air in pollination. We say in Alaska that when the fireweed cottons, summer is soon forgotten, as this early snow is a harbinger of the real thing.

My favorite time to hike this trail is around the third week of September at the peak of the autumn colors. That is when you can revel in the wonderful contrast between the golden yellow of the willow and aspen trees and the deep dark saturated greens of the spruce trees, both of which in turn contrast so spectacularly with the bright white of the termination dust at the higher elevations. ("Termination dust" is what we Alaskans call the early snow that falls in September on the peaks, which "terminates" the tourist season and leaves the state for us "crazies" who love dark nights and subfreezing temperatures.)

The first 3 miles take you along a gradual climb up the north side of the Summit Creek drainage, the first of three valleys you'll traverse. (The Summit Creek Trail seems misnamed to me; it could more accurately be called The Triple Creek Trail or Three Valley Trail.) The lower portion of the hike is brushy, but you move quickly up to some alpine areas with great views. In fact of all the hikes in the Kenai, Summit Creek takes you into the alpine zones faster than any other . . . more quickly than even the Skyline Trail (Hike 24)!

As you hike the lower sections of this trail, turn around to see the resplendent alpine panorama across the east side of the valley. In the fall, the kaleidoscope of color and texture is stunning, including a classic view of a glacially carved U-shaped valley that is in the process of being modified by a stream channel cutting a "V" in its bottom.

The trail follows a long lazy switchback as it climbs into the alpine zone within the first mile. You will cross several sidestream channels. In the valley bottom, look for reluctant remnant snows from the previous year with snow caves formed by Summit Creek as it flows through. Also look up onto the southern slope to see a zigzag pattern on the high slope that leads up to an abandoned mining claim. Note how the alders have used this mining road to work their way further up the slope than they normally would. While you are looking up, note the contrast between the craggy upper slopes that were never covered by the glacier and the lower slopes smoothed by the heavy, slow passage of the ice. Along this trail, look for flattened paths through the grass where the local bears have crushed their way through the fields.

At 1.5 miles, the scrubby willows give way to the open alpine tundra. Stop here for your first glorious 360-degree view. Feel free to put this guidebook down and explore the tundra, taking care to step on rocks wherever you can to protect the delicate vegetation. I always like to venture down to the nearby stream channel of Summit Creek to explore the snow caves that are often present. DO NOT go into any snow caves on any of these hikes, as they are unstable, being formed by moving waters and ice you cannot see.

As you hike higher once more, you will head across large-slab scree slopes where large sandstone slabs have been deposited during winter snow avalanches.

I think the most stunning view in this section is just past mile 3 as you approach the headwaters of Summit Creek at about 2,500 feet. When the trail begins to level out as you approach the saddle above the East Creek valley, look to the south into a huge amphitheater that soars up to 4,800-foot Gilpatrick Mountain. This cirque was once the zone of accumulation for the glacier that filled and carved out the Summit Creek valley. One terrific side hike, with many treasures to discover, is up into this massive cirque bowl basin of Gilpatrick Mountain. In fact, such a hike into this cirque bowl basin with its tundra tussocks, rivulets, streams, and ponds makes a terrific one-day hiking adventure.

From the drainage divide saddle between Summit and East creeks, head downhill into the southern end of the East Creek drainage. The second section of the hike follows the southwest edge of this drainage along the lower slopes of massive Gilpatrick Mountain across beautiful alpine tundra. The head of this valley is rugged, with lots of wonderful waterfalls. Where the trail crosses upper East Creek, you might find the channel crossing a bit easier about 50 meters upstream from the main trail crossing, where the channel divides into multiple smaller channels. If you venture off trail as you head through the upper reaches of East Creek, you will discover many gems including cirque bowl lakes, tarns (small glacially formed lakes) unseen from the trail, as well as gasp-worthy gazes down East Creek.

In the autumn, the vast broad slopes of East Creek valley are painted subtle hues of reds, yellows, and purples. As you approach the larger glacial tarns along East Creek you will see they are home to industrious beavers that have enlarged them with their dams and graced them with their lodges. This series of stream-channel-linked lakes, formed by the once scouring and then sediment- and water-depositing retreating glaciers that formed U-shaped East Creek valley, are known as Paternoster lakes.

About 2 miles past the saddle between the Summit and East Creek drainages, the trail makes a hard left up a tributary of East Creek. Hike gradually uphill for about 1 mile along the side slope across the tundra, keeping an eye open for resident willow ptarmigan birds as well as sign of bear, moose, and wolves here. By the way, most of these large wild animals, including wolves, would rather avoid you, and will do so if given a chance. If you encounter one, behave and speak calmly, stand tall and back away slowly . . . then enjoy them from a distance.

Hike to the second saddle and drainage divide at about 3,400 feet, the high point of this trail. From here you actually look down onto the top of Resurrection Pass over 800 feet below. Stop to enjoy the tremendous views east and west. There is some good ridgeline hiking north and south from the saddle if you're so inclined (I usually am). From the second saddle the trail heads down again to its intersection with Resurrection Pass at mile 8.4.

SPECIAL NOTES

Summit Creek is of course a terrific stand-alone hike; however, you can also combine it with the Resurrection Pass Trail and/or the Devils Pass Trail to form any number of loops. In addition to the obvious ones north and south along the Resurrection Pass Trail and down the Devils Pass Trail, there are numerous cross-country routes available throughout this area. Consult your topo map to plan a route or two, such as a course that links the glorious amphitheater cirque at the top of Summit Creek with Devils Pass Lake. You might also consider ridge routes from the saddles between the Summit Creek, East Creek, and Resurrection River drainages. These offer easy access to outstanding hiking across seemingly endless tundra. So if you're planning a hike up the Summit Creek Trail, give yourself lots of extra time for some marvelous side trips. And for heaven's sake, don't leave your camera and binoculars at home or back in your vehicle. In addition to the gorgeous glacial geology, you will find lots of wildlife, including a gazillion marmots, also known as whistle pigs because of the high-pitched sounds they make when you pass—listen for them. They are also known as bear burritos, since brown bears and grizzlies chase them for snacks across the grey scree slopes. Sometimes, you can see the bears, their thick coats rippling like massive bunched carpets, galumphing at 20 miles an hour after something darting you can't see. That little darting thing is a marmot, running for its life. Just be thankful it's not you.

Since it's all tundra, keep your eyes open for caribou too. Caribou, while large, are perhaps the most docile of the the big wild animals you will encounter. While you typically hear about caribou traveling in large herds, you will more likely encounter solitary beasts while hiking the Kenai highcountry. Caribou prefer the highcountry because they like to eat the lichen that is so readily available there . . . and I'll bet they like the easy walking and good views, just like we do!

And remember, when treking cross-country, try to step on rocks instead of the vegetation whenever possible.

7

Crescent Creek & Lake

Total distance: 6.5 miles to the western edge of Crescent Lake, then back again; 18 miles from trailhead at Crescent Lake to trailhead at Carter Lake (Hike 8)

Hiking time: 4 to 5 hours for Crescent Lake Trail round-trip, 2 to 3 days for the entire traverse from Crescent Lake trailhead to Carter Lake trailhead discussed below

Elevation change: 1,000 feet for the traverse

Rating: Moderate

Best season: Mid-June through September

Maps: Kenai National Wildlife Refuge by National Geographic Trails Illustrated; Alaska Road and Recreation Map; USGS Seward B-7, C-7, and C-8

Special features: A pleasant 6.5 mile round-trip hike along Crescent Creek through a pleasant spruce, aspen, and birch forest and subalpine wildflower fields to the edge of glorious Crescent Lake. Add on access to a beautiful low slope open view 8-mile traverse around beautiful Crescent Lake, with plentiful wildlife and wildflowers around the entire lake.

The Crescent Creek and Carter Lake trails (Hike 8) connect via an overgrown, primitive trail around the outside of the crescent of Crescent Lake to create a U-shaped cross-country traverse through the subalpine region of the north-central Kenai. The Crescent Creek (this Hike 7) and the Carter Lake trails are separate hikes and are treated so here.

GETTING THERE

There is only one Crescent Creek trailhead, which means that once you've done the hike, you will turn around and return to where you started, unless you want to connect this hike to the Carter Lake Trail and come out much farther north, at the Carter Lake trailhead after curving around Crescent Lake on the primitive path. The path is overgrown, unmarked, and treacherous in spots. Do not attempt it with children, who may be shorter than the overgrowth along the shoreline. Dogs too may have trouble. For those wishing to connect the two hikes, it's wise to establish a pickup at the Carter Lake trailhead at mile 33 on the southwest side of the Seward Highway, which is where you will end.

To reach the Crescent Creek Trail trailhead, start at about mile 45 on the Sterling Highway. Drive 7 miles west of the Seward and Sterling Highway intersection on the Sterling Highway to where the Sterling Highway reaches Kenai Lake. Turn south onto Quartz Creek Road. Drive 3.5 miles on the gravel road following the signs to the Crescent Creek trailhead. One-third

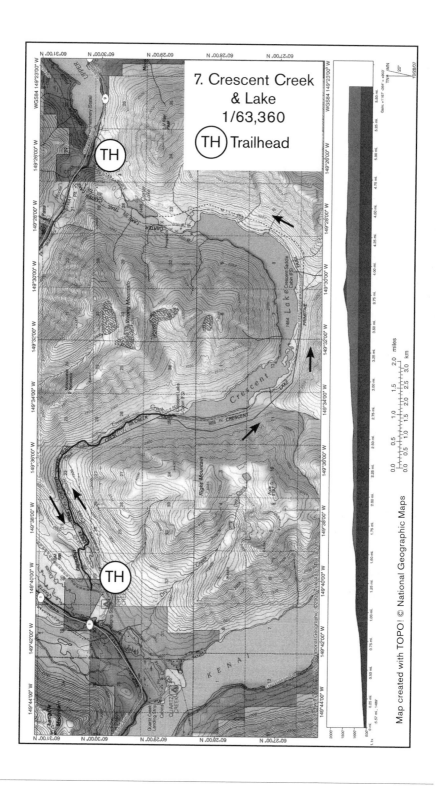

7. Crescent Creek
& Lake
1/63,360

(TH) Trailhead

Map created with TOPO! © National Geographic Maps

Crescent Lake surrounded by towering alpine tundra-covered peaks

mile from the trailhead, you will pass the Crescent Creek Campground. Park on the left; the trailhead begins on the right (south) side of the road.

There is plenty of parking at the trailhead along with toilet facilities. Slather on the bug dope before you begin.

Though this hike can certainly be done in one day, there are two campsites and two cabins you can use. The first, Crescent Creek campsite is a short one-third mile down the road from the trailhead and is not part of the advance reservation system. It is used far less than the reservation campsite closer to the Sterling and Seward highways. I have always been able to find a campsite here, even on the highest traffic weekends. The reservation cabin is 6.5 miles in at the western end of Crescent Lake. There is a second cabin along the two linked hikes, at mile 11.5. If you intend to use the cabin,

be sure to reserve it well in advance (see Information Resources pages 33–35).

THE TRAIL

The hike begins heading up immediately on a moderate slope through a forest of spruce, birch, poplar, and aspen trees on a well-maintained trail. The overstory canopy provides a shaded, cool hiking environment even on warm days. The trail follows a small stream channel as it rises through the forest on its way to a saddle and drainage divide leading over into the Crescent Creek drainage. Along the trail you will enjoy fireweed, shrouded deep purple monkshood, and large birch and aspen trees as well as a few interspersed wildflower meadows. After about one-half mile, the trail rises more steeply through a series of long switchbacks as it nears the drainage divide, then levels out as it

50 Hikes in Alaska's Kenai Peninsula

enters the Crescent Creek drainage at about mile 1.

As you enter and climb up the Crescent Creek drainage, the forest canopy begins to open to views of the surrounding mountains. Hemlock trees become more common as do the size and frequency of the grass and flower fields. One of the nice characteristics of this section of the trail is the consistent serenade provided by Crescent Creek. The slope of the stream channel is nearly always easy as you make your way along the creek. You will encounter some of the largest and most impressive birch trees, over 2 feet thick, at about 2.5 miles. Tall larkspur, wild geranium, blue bells, northern bedstraw, fireweed, and wild roses cheer your journey. The trail gradually moves closer to Crescent Creek until it meets the channel at about 3 miles. This a terrific stop, rest, and snack stop.

The trail follows Crescent Creek between the steep, high slopes of Right Mountain to the southwest and Wrong Mountain to the northeast. Both peaks top out at over 5,000 feet on either side of you, so you're hiking through a pretty dramatic canyon, which only a few thousand years ago was completely filled with glacial ice all the way up.

The trail continues on the north slope of Crescent Creek to about the 3.5-mile point. Here it crosses over a bridge and continues on the south side of the creek. You will notice that there are more side stream channels flowing down from the cooler, moister, more forested north-facing slopes of Right Mountain than there were on the other side of the creek, before you crossed that bridge.

Look southwest up onto the slopes of Right Mountain to see avalanche chutes that are clear of vegetation. Snow and ice become unstable on the higher slopes and

slide down these chutes, carrying debris to the base of the cliff. This debris is often strewn across the trail, and sometimes into Crescent Lake itself. Most of the open areas along the trail are the result of these slides, which also make winter travel hazardous. Look for similar avalanche chutes on steep slopes throughout the Kenai Mountains.

Near mile 4 the trail breaks out into the open and travels mostly across open wildflower-strewn, sloping meadows dotted with hemlock and aspen stands, but nearly always stays within listening distance of the melodic rushing of Crescent Creek. Look northeast up onto the high ridges of Wrong Mountain and you will likely see remnant snow patches well into August. These residual south-facing snows are the result of massive accumulations deposited on the southern lee slopes by the persistent north winds that blow throughout the winter.

As you approach the western edge of Crescent Lake and the end of this hike, the trail once again moves close to Crescent Creek. Here the stream is lazier and slower-moving as it meanders across the creek's floodplain graced with wildflower meadows and stands of large, white-barked aspen and cottonwood trees. From the creek bank, you can see the milky, silt-rich waters of the snowfield-fed streams that originate on the high slopes of Wrong Mountain.

The trail climbs 1,000 feet from just over 500 feet at the trailhead to over 1,500 feet at the west end of Crescent Lake at mile 6.5, where the public-use fee cabin and campground are both located on the north side of the creek and accessible via a bridge. The maintained trail stops here at the lake, where the land opens up at tree line into subalpine brushy meadows studded with spruce, hemlock, and aspen.

THE PRIMITIVE CIRCUIT AROUND CRESCENT LAKE

From the cabin and camping area at the western edge of Crescent Lake, you can follow the primitive trail around the south (longer, outside) rim of U-shaped Crescent Lake for 8 miles. The trail alternates between open wildflower meadows and open-canopy forests dominated by hemlock and spruce. By mid-summer, this trail is overgrown and slowgoing, so I recommend wearing long-sleeved shirts and long pants. The views around the lake are open and expansive. You will likely see a lot of bear sign and moose tracks, as very few people ever attempt this circuit. At mile 5—or 11.5 miles into the total trek from the Crescent Lake trailhead—there is a reservation cabin, called the Crescent Saddle Cabin.

Glaciers scoured the lake bottom as they moved through the double passes between Right and Wrong mountains and between Wrong and Madison mountains. The retreating glaciers, a diminutive remnant of which can be seen high up in the bowl along the southwest ridge of Madison, partially filled in the valley bottom with ground moraine sediment (thick sheets of sediment deposited beneath a glacier over a large area, shaping the lake and surrounding flatlands).

From the Crescent Saddle Cabin, you continue another 3 miles to the end of the traverse, where the primitive trail joins the Carter Lake Trail. Another 3.3 miles down the forested Carter Lake Trail, through the largest concentration of goatsbeard in midsummer I have ever seen, finishes the hike. When you exit at the Carter Lake trailhead, you've lost the 1,000 feet in elevation you gained on the way up the Crescent Creek Trail to Crescent Lake.

SPECIAL NOTES

The 6.5-mile Crescent Lake Trail and the 3.3-mile Carter Lake Trail make pleasant day hikes to Crescent Lake. Be sure to watch for moose and bear all summer. My favorite time of year here is the fall, when the gorgeous colors and low-angle sunlight make this a photographer's paradise. The wildflower fields along the primitive trail on the longer, western rim of Crescent Lake have some of the most intense displays of purple with dense growths of wild geranium, tall larkspur, and monkshood you will see anywhere.

8

Carter Lake

Total distance: 3.3 miles one way

Hiking time: 3 to 4 hours

Elevation change: 1,000 feet

Rating: Easy to moderate

Best season: June through September

Maps: Kenai National Wildlife Refuge by National Geographic Trails Illustrated; Alaska Road and Recreation Map; USGS Seward C-6 and C-7

Special features: Carter Lake and Crescent Lake. These beautiful, flower-surrounded glacially carved lakes are within one-half mile of each other. The hike up to the lakes is about half the distance of the Crescent Creek Hike. This a good, manageable hike for families in cool, crisp air that makes you think of the Sound of Music.

GETTING THERE

The Carter Lake trailhead is easily accessible directly off the Seward Highway at mile 33 on the south side of the road. Plenty of parking and bathroom facilities are there, and the parking lot is canted off the highway enough that overnighters in campers don't feel like they're sleeping on the side of the road. The parking area can accommodate small to medium rigs.

THE TRAIL

From the trailhead parking lot, you climb first on rocky, rutted dirt along switchbacks that take you higher and higher, and then through the densest, most beautiful white feathery goatsbeard on any mid-summer hike on the Kenai. I got a report of porcupines with enormous quills from one hiking family. As you move higher, the trees surround you, with birch and aspen and spruce and cottonwoods as the trail itself becomes narrower and narrower. Be sure to wear long pants, as the pushki can reach out and grab exposed legs wearing only shorts. After climbing for about 1.5 miles the trail begins to moisten as you reach the flood plain and approach Carter Lake. Here the forest drops away and grassland begins in a high mountain valley removed from the rest of the world. This is really a remote, unpopulated, special place, and quite a memory for families. The only other people one set of hikers met all day were a father packing a pistol and carrying his young daughter on his shoulders.

Around Carter Lake you will hike for about three-quarters of a mile through broad, open, expansive fields of wildflowers featuring wild geranium, tall larkspur, monkshood, ever-present pushki and fireweed, as well as an uncommon amount of Indian paintbrush and northern bedstraw.

Puski looks like huge Queen Anne's lace. We Alaskans worry that it's invading the plant life, having been introduced here from outside the state some years ago and taken root. But it's pretty, standing with arms outstretched and capped with white bouquets. Just don't touch it, or let it near

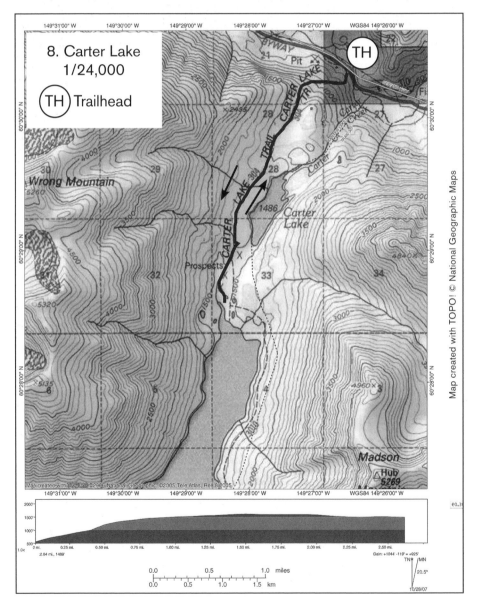

50 Hikes in Alaska's Kenai Peninsula

Crescent Lake view from the primitive trail end near Carter Lake

your exposed legs, as it stings.

The large rocks you see strewn around these fields are glacial erratics that were transported here from the surrounding peaks by the glacier that carved this valley, then dumped these big boulders here as it melted and retreated.

The main trail is offset from Carter Lake by a couple of hundred meters. Several side trails lead you down to the lake itself. There is a primitive tent camping site off the main trail near the south edge. As you stand looking at the lake, notice the wind that cuts ripples as it moves across the surface. There is more wind here than you would imagine, and more than you have probably noticed walking up.

The place has a dreamy quality, as if no one has ever been here before. The fields are pristine and untouched, high in the hills with vast swaths of green against grey mountains and snowy peaks in cool, clear air that makes you feel like singing.

Once you pass Carter Lake, it is about one-half mile of pleasant walking over to Crescent Lake as you pass through open stands of hemlock and grassy wildflower fields. This section of the trail is the drainage divide between Carter and Crescent lakes. Carter Lake drains north via Carter Creek into Moose Creek, while Crescent Lake drains the other way, via Crescent Creek, located at the other end of Crescent Lake, into Quartz Creek.

As you approach Crescent Lake, the trail diverges into several small paths into the hilly area overlooking the northeast end of the lake. Be sure to venture down . . . seeing Crescent Lake is well worth the effort. There are several pleasant overlooks on top of grassy knolls that make excellent lunch and snooze spots. Young children love to scream their heads off from them, beating their chests and listening to the wind take their voices.

THE PRIMITIVE PATH AROUND CRESCENT LAKE

If you are feeling just a bit adventurous, access to the primitive trail is about one-quarter mile from where the path terminates at the overlook area of Crescent Lake. Even if you do not want to hike the entire path, which is described in more detail on the Crescent Lake Hike (Hike 7), I recommend at least a short foray down this trail for a half mile or so to see the wildflowers and to enjoy interesting views of Crescent Lake.

You hike over a small hill through open stands of hemlock and grassland for 200 meters until you reach an unnamed stream that drains the upper north slope of Madison Mountain. Particularly in the spring and early summer, this channel can be wide and fast flowing and the cobble channel bed very slippery. Be prepared to don your stream-crossing footwear and use your hiking poles to help with balance.

After the steam channel crossing, you will hike around the east end of Crescent Lake through mostly open flower-strewn grasslands. The trail follows the lake edge for 3.5 miles to the Crescent Saddle Cabin with mostly easy hiking along less than 100 feet of elevation change, unless the path is overgrown. It is also rocky in places. You cross several stream channels, including a large cascading waterfall/stream channel about one-half mile from the cabin.

Past the cabin the trail traverses 5 miles through alternating open fields of wildflowers and open canopy stands of hemlock. The entire length of the primitive path can be quite overgrown, with the grasses over 6 feet tall, and tough going in July and August. It is not recommended for young children, who may go on strike and will be shorter than the vegetation anyway, and therefore easily lost.

Dogs, too, may have a tough time. On the upside, the wildflower fields have some of the most intense display of purple with dense growths of wild geranium, tall larkspur, and monkshood you will see anywhere. Plus, you get bragging rights for having gone where so few have gone before.

Johnson Pass

Total distance: 23 miles one way

Hiking time: 2 to 4 days

Elevation change: 750 feet

Rating: Moderate

Best season: June through September

Maps: Kenai National Wildlife Refuge by National Geographic Trails Illustrated; Alaska Road and Recreation Map; USGS Seward C-6 and C-7

Special features: This is one of the long hikes on the Kenai. Unlike the Resurrection Pass Trail that takes the high road and heads toward the highcountry, the Johnson Pass trail stays deep in the downlow next to the water. Bench and Johnson lakes are exquisite and filled with rainbow trout and grayling. The northern half of the trail is packed with treasures including a booming waterfall, lake and streamside camping, wildflower-filled gravel bars, and varied glacial topography.

This is a 23-mile forested traverse through two drainages and across an alpine pass containing two glacial lakes. You will find plenty of wildflowers and spectacular scenery along this portion of the original Iditarod route. Before the train tracks were put in between Seward and Anchorage, dogsledding along this Iditarod route was the only way to travel during the winter between these two cities. Johnson Pass also is the only low elevation pass through the northern Kenai Peninsula to central Alaska, Turnagain Arm, and Anchorage.

GETTING THERE

There are two trailheads for the Johnson Pass Trail. To reach the northern one near Granite Creek, turn south at mile 64 off the Seward Highway on the road for Johnson Pass and drive 0.4 mile to the parking area. The south trailhead is located off mile 33 of the Seward Highway near the western end of Upper Trail Lake. Both trailheads offer ample parking and toilet facilities.

THE TRAIL

You can hike this trail in either direction. In fact, it's possible to make day hikes from either trailhead to Johnson or Bench Lake, although my favorite direction is north to south. The north to south sequence of first Bench and then Johnson lakes offers much more open, sunny, and interesting views, as well as access to stream channels along the way. Plus the road noise at the northern end stays with you much longer as it travels across Trail Lake than at the southern

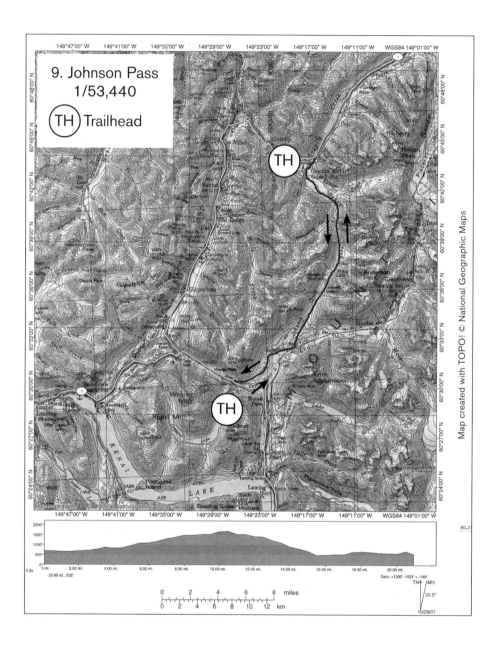

9. Johnson Pass
1/53,440

(TH) Trailhead

access. If you intend to hike in and out from the same trailhead, do so from the north trailhead near Granite Creek. Even if you are starting in Seward, I recommend the northern approach.

From the Granite Creek trailhead on the north end, you begin the hike at about 750 feet of elevation. The trail starts in a moderate canopy forest of aspen, cottonwood and spruce and winds its way through alternating grasslands and wildflower-filled meadows and stands of aspen, spruce, and cottonwood forests. In the first few miles, the trail crosses several streams, including Center Creek, which is a beautiful, milky glacier and snowfield steam at about 2.2 miles and a tributary of the larger Bench Creek that you cross at about 3.0 miles. Both these stream crossings make good stopping points for easy, pleasant day hikes.

The trail continues gradually up the west side of the Bench Creek drainage alternating between more fields of wildflower and stands of hemlocks. Between the Bench and Porcupine Creek stream crossings, there is a primitive campsite nestled among bushy and often gnarled, dark green, flat-leafed hemlocks.

The flatter valley sections through which Bench Creek flows were formed by glaciers and the ground moraine sediments (thick sheets of glacial sediment) they deposited as they retreated. The creek is making some progress in cutting a V-shaped channel into the flat valley. This process is in its nascent stages; it will take millennia for the glacially formed features to be completely modified. And long before that happens another glacial advance may well occur, undoing all that creek's hard work. As you hike along, see if you can locate V-shaped sections where the stream

has already cut deeply into the glacially deposited sediments.

Stand on the bridge where the trail crosses booming Groundhog Creek and look east up and across Bench Creek valley to see Gleason Creek cascading down the east wall. Gleason Creek drains an unseen—from this location—remnant glacier that's so high above you cannot see it. The upper Gleason valley is a beautiful glacially carved U shape whose bottom is in the process of being recarved into a classic "V" by the downward erosion of Gleason Creek.

As you gain elevation, the size and frequency of the trees overall decrease as the hemlocks become more common and the views open up providing sweeping panoramas up and down the broad glacial valley.

The trail crosses Bench Creek again at about mile 6.5 and then follows the east side of that creek for the remainder of the trek to Bench Lake. Note: On most maps the trail is shown as continuing on the west side of Bench Creek . . . this is incorrect. The map provided with this hike in this book is the correct one.

Soon after its second crossing of Bench Creek, the trail rises steeply through a slanted rocky section where Bench Creek forms a giant, gorgeous waterfall. This step-up in the trail takes you into the upper valley of Bench Creek, where your views explode as you walk in nearly constant contact with the beautiful, meandering stream channel. Here Bench Creek strolls lazily across the ground moraine. In summer, its gravel bars are replete with wildflowers. Look for moose in the shallows and backwaters.

On your way to Bench Lake, you will pass through many fields and meadows of wildflowers. In July and August these sections can be overgrown, so be prepared for

View over white-flowered pushki across Bench Lake near the high point on Johnson Pass.

some slow going in places and keep your long-sleeve shirts and gaiters handy.

The trail arrives at Bench Lake at 8.9 miles. Just north of the lake is a primitive campsite out in the open fields west of the trail. Also near the north end, Ohio Creek meets the lake as it flows down from a glacier in the cirque just northeast of Anderson Peak to the east. There is a pretty waterfall near where the trail crosses Ohio Creek.

As it then follows the eastern shoreline of Bench Lake, the trail affords many access points to the water as well as terrific views of the surrounding peaks. If you brought your fishing pole . . . you must stop here to fish! And, yes, the fish you catch are edible.

From Bench Lake the trail climbs gently through mostly flowered grasslands to 1,500-foot Johnson Pass at mile 10. If you are not paying close attention, and if you miss the sign indicating Johnson Pass, you might not notice the pass at all. This is a low pass between the Johnson and Bench Creek drainages. Both have lakes at their headwaters, so they are semimirror images. Unlike highcountry passes, which are obvious high points between two drainiages, low passes like Johnson's are subtle and easy to miss.

Johnson Lake and the beginning of the Johnson Creek drainage is just past the Johnson Pass signpost. You then follow the eastern side of Johnson Lake down into the Johnson Creek drainage.

The area around Bench and Johnson lakes is above tree line. There are camping areas on both ends of Johnson Lake with the northern end being more on open fields and the southern campsite nestled in among large cottonwoods. Access to Johnson Lake from the trail is more restricted than the trail access along the Bench Lake section.

If you are hiking past Johnson Lake toward the far south trailhead, once you pass the lake heading south you are back on a more forested stretch intermixed with grasslands and meadows. In July and August the amount of encroaching overgrowth, and particularly the towering pushki, can be quite daunting. As I say everywhere in this book, do not rub against this plant, for it stings unexposed legs and arms.

As you hike through the Johnson Creek drainage, you will have more restricted views than you did on your hike through the Bench Creek section. In addition you will have little access to Johnson Creek. For these reasons I renew my recommendation of hiking in and out from the northern trailhead if you are not hiking the entire trail.

The trail remains east of Johnson Creek until just after mile 16, where it crosses over at Johnson Creek Bridge. As you approach Trail Lake this is primarily a forest trail with some lovely sections. The higher elevations feature lovely stands of hemlocks.

Also, when you can see through the canopy, look high up on the slopes of the eastern peaks and you will see two excellent examples of hanging glaciers. These have been left hanging by the retreat of the valley glacier that used to fill the valley with ice more than 1,000 feet tall as it carved the Bench and Johnson Creek areas.

At the bridge, the current Johnson Pass Trail diverges from the original Iditarod Trail that continues farther south along the eastern side of Upper Trail Lake. The slope of this section of spruce, aspen, and birch-forested trail is mostly very shallow and easy to hike with a few steeper sections as the trail follows the slope-side topography. Using wooden plank bridges, you will cross several stream channels draining the upper western slopes. Look for dwarf dogwood, wild geranium, and monkshood along the lower sections of the trail, as well as some more encroaching areas of alder, pushki, and grasses.

You begin to closely follow the western shore of Upper Trail Lake at 19 miles, reaching the Seward Highway trailhead at mile 23. You might note that Trail Lake has a slightly milky appearance to it. This is due to the modest contribution of glacial sediment from stream channels draining the surrounding peaks, which sediment (called rock flour) is so fine it remains caught, suspended in the water by the hydrogen bonds in the H_2O. Trail Lake lacks the opaque aquamarine color of Kenai Lake, which has far greater contribution of glacial sediment, but one can still see the phenomenon.

SPECIAL NOTES

This trail, originally known as the Sunrise Trail, was the main route from the northern Kenai to the southern Kenai before the paved road was built, back when Seward and Hope were both gold-mining boomtowns. In 1907 this was part of a 34-mile Johnson Pass military road, which later became part of the rail line from Moose Pass to Hope and Sunrise. So you are traveling through Johnson Pass in some well-worn historical footsteps.

As you hike along the northern half of the route below Bench Lake, you can look east for glimpses of glaciers and ice fields in the high-elevation cirques. (A "cirque" is a circle bowl cut into a mountain by a glacier as it forms high on a mountain slope.) These are the diminutive remnants of the massive 1,000-foot-thick glaciers that once flowed down these valleys and carved out most of the stream-filled side canyons. All of these westward-flowing alpine glaciers merged together once, thousands of years ago, to form a single monstrous valley glacier that carved the valley through which you're now hiking.

One final note: The slopes along this trail are gradual enough to be used for winter travel, but beware of avalanches from the upper reaches of the 4,000- to 5,000-foot mountains on both sides of you. Avalanche threats tend to be greatest immediately after snowstorms when newer, looser snows are sitting on top of older, more compacted snow, which makes an excellent slide surface.

50 Hikes in Alaska's Kenai Peninsula

II. Northeast Kenai

10

Lost Lake

Total distance: 14 miles round trip to the south end of Lost Lake and back

Hiking time: 2.5 to 3 hours one way

Elevation change: 1,700 feet

Rating: Easy to moderate

Best season: July through September

Maps: Kenai Fjords National Park by National Geographic Trails Illustrated; Alaska Road and Recreation Map; USGS Seward A-7 (NE) and B-7

Special features: Great views of Resurrection Bay on the hike up to Lost Lake; wide-open tundra along the trail and around Lost Lake; spectacular alpine scenery; good fishing; and easy alpine tundra hiking. Access to some wonderful alpine tundra backcountry. This trail also leaves the forest behind sooner than the Primrose Trail.

The Lost Lake Trail is a companion to the Primrose Creek Trail (Hike 11), and both lead to Lost Lake. This approach is 1 mile shorter than Primrose, which allows you more exploration time if you're a day hiker. You can also combine these two trails to create a 15-mile hike. While there are great views of Resurrection Bay as you hike up the Lost Lake Trail, the real prize is the lake itself and the gorgeous alpine tundra and dramatic glacial features in the surrounding highcountry.

GETTING THERE

At mile 3.5 off the Seward Highway, turn west onto Scott Way into the Lost Lake Subdivision. Drive 0.2 mile to a T intersection, turn left on Heatherly Lane, and drive another 0.2 mile to another intersection. Turn right onto Hyden Berlin Road and drive about 0.3 mile to the trailhead. The parking lot can accommodate small and big rigs.

THE TRAIL

The Lost Lake Trail and Primrose Creek Trail (Hike 11) meet at Lost Lake, similar to the two ends of the Johnson Pass Hike meeting at Johnson and Bench lakes. Both Lost Lake and Primrose Creek trails are good day hikes. If you're camping overnight prior to your hike, I recommend starting at the Primrose trailhead, as this offers the beautiful Primrose Landing campsites. For day hikes, I suggest the Lost Lake trailhead, which has no established campground and is 1 mile shorter than the Primrose Trail.

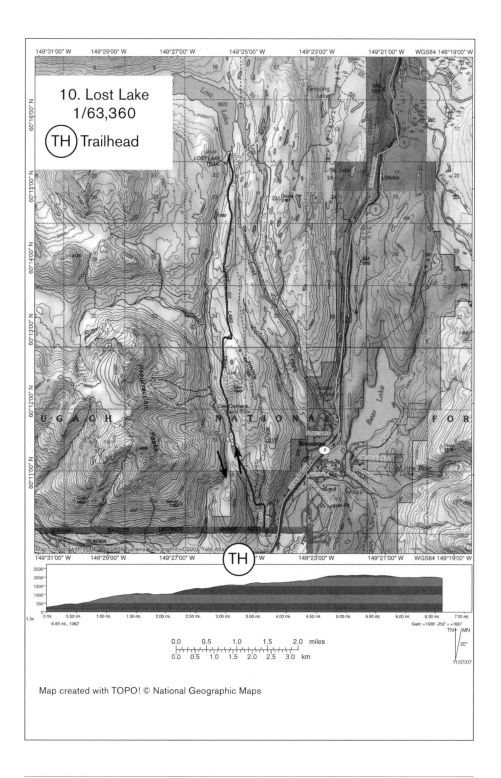

Starting at an elevation of 400 feet, the Lost Lake Trail ascends through old-growth spruce and hemlock forest cover. At about one-third mile, the trail splits into left and right trail routes: Stay left for the most direct route or take the right-hand route (marked the WINTER ROUTE), which is slightly longer but with a lower gradient via the Clemens Cabin. The sign at this split says the Clemens Cabin is to the left but this is incorrect. The right, winter route leads 1 and one half miles to the Clemens Cabin, a public-use cabin operated by the forest service (see Information Resources for making reservations), and then rejoins the left route farther up the trail in the alpine meadows. I prefer hiking the left, western route because you have views across the valley toward the Resurrection Peaks and down into the valley of the stream channel that drains this mountain front. If you are day hiking, you may want to plan to hike up the western (summer route) and back down the eastern (winter/Clemens Cabin) route to create a loop.

As you continue on the western summer route, you will hike through an open-canopy forest along first a small stream and then along Box Canyon Creek, which is the main stream that drains this valley. The forest gradually opens up as you gain elevation with more wildflower-filled grasslands emerging. Beyond about mile 2, the trail mostly crosses subalpine meadows dotted with stands of scrubby windblown hemlocks. At about mile 3, you will find a delightful copse of hemlocks off the east side of the trail large enough to offer protection and even camping.

Throughout most of the summer, there is a showcase of wildflowers and berries, which means bears. Also look for mountain goats across Box Canyon Creek on the high, rugged, glaciated slopes of the

Resurrection Peaks to the west. From afar, they look like cotton balls the size of a fingernail.

The trail begins its traverse across alpine tundra at about 5 miles. The trail up to the meadows and tundra is very moderate and often easy, with overall a lower slope than the Primrose Creek Trail. There are long sections where the trail grade is barely noticeable. The meadows offer violet blue lupine, wild geranium, goatsbeard, yarrow, Indian paintbrush, and many ferns. As you gain elevation hemlocks dominate the tree population. All along this trail you have continuous views of the high, steep and broad front of the Resurrection Peaks with their many ravines, alcoves, and avalanche shoots lined with remnant reluctant snow and moistened with luminous cascading waterfalls well into the summer.

At mile 4, the summer route you're hiking is rejoined by the winter/Clemens Cabin route. This intersection occurs where two vast fields of wildflower meadows converge. For a lovely side hike, follow the sign to a primitive tent campsite that heads east through a delightful combination of open-canopy hemlock forest and wildflower-rich meadows. This otherwise unmarked but well worn trail runs parallel to the main path heading north. You will likely have it all to yourself. You can rejoin the main trail at any time by hiking west for a short way across the meadows.

From the intersection of the summer and winter trails, the main trail begins to follow a ridge route through alternating hemlocks and wildflower meadows. The hiking is easy and pleasant with grand views of the Resurrection Peaks unfolding as you trek north toward Lost Lake.

You reach the high point around mile 6 at about 2,200 feet in elevation, where you have the first expansive view of Lost Lake.

Camping in the highcountry, alpine tundra solitude of Lost Lake

Take a rest stop here and explore the many gifts of the alpine tundra. There are several hidden lakes and remnant snow drifts well into summer. From its high point along the ridge, the trail gradually loses elevation as you continue your ridge hike toward always visible Lost Lake.

About one-quarter mile from the south end of Lost Lake, you will intersect the Primrose Trail. Continue straight north to reach the south shore of Lost Lake. This is of course an excellent lunch spot, with many opportunities to further explore the lake and the tundra slopes of the Resurrection Peaks to the west.

If you have enough time, check out the southern end of the Primrose Creek Trail, which curls around the eastern shore of Lost Lake. There are many stream channels, glacial tarns (small glacially formed lakes), and small ridges to enjoy. You will also have views and wildflowers in every direction. As you investigate, please keep in mind this is a heavily used section of trail, so step lightly, on rocks rather than the delicate tundra plants, whenever you can. And move off away from the main

trails for your side forays, please, so the immediate areas near the main trail do not become trampled.

Lost Lake is famous for its spectacular views of the glaciated alpine ridges, good rainbow trout fishing, great salmonberry and blueberry crops in the subalpine zone, lupine-rich alpine tundra, and access to cross-country treks. This is one of Taz's favorite hikes in all the Kenai.

SPECIAL NOTES

Be sure to leave plenty of extra time for exploring the highcountry around, and west of, Lost Lake. The lake is really just the beginning of your possible adventures. There are also small, accessible remnant glaciers on the peaks to the northwest, as well as southwest on Mount Ascension. Or you can hike due west into the Martin Creek drainage over the low divide in front of Ascension. From there you will have outstanding views of the entire Resurrection River valley, as well as the peaks and glaciers of the Harding Ice Field. If you love alpine rock climbing, you'll find plenty of challenges to suit you.

11

Primrose Creek

Total distance: 8.2 miles one way

Hiking time: 3 to 3.5 hours

Elevation change: 1,700 feet

Rating: Moderate

Best season: July through September

Maps: Kenai Fjords National Park by National Geographic Trails Illustrated; Alaska Road and Recreation Map; USGS Seward A-7 (NE) and B-7

Special features: A forested hike at lower elevation leads to wide-open tundra, then up to and surrounding Lost Lake, with its beautiful scenery, good fishing, and splendid alpine hiking.

The Primrose Creek Trail is one of two trails leading to Lost Lake. The other is the Lost Lake Trail (Hike 10). The lower portions of this trail are forested and the higher elevations traverse wide-open alpine tundra. The mountain meadows along the upper trail and around Lost Lake itself are the highlights of this hike. The Primrose Creek Trail and Lost Lake Trail can be combined to create a single 15-mile hike, but you will want to have a pick-up at one of the trailheads when you're done, as you will have walked a long way and over changes in elevation.

GETTING THERE

At mile 17 on the Seward Highway, just before the highway crosses the Snow River Bridge, turn left (south) onto Forest Road 953 and drive northwest 1.1 miles to the Primrose Landing Campground. This beautiful campground on the southern shore of beautiful Kenai Lake is a great place to stay the night before your hike. If you're not camping, park in the entrance area to the campground because there is no parking available at the trailhead. Walk 0.2 mile to the back of the campground to start the Primrose Creek Trail.

THE TRAIL

The Primrose Creek and Lost Lake trails are often considered one trail, with Lost Lake in the middle, much like the north and south trails for Johnson Pass (Hike 9). In fact, there is an annual Lost Lake charity run along the entire length of the trail. These two trails are presented as separate, stand-alone choices in this book, however, because either one makes a good day hike up to Lost Lake. If you drive here from Anchorage on a Friday evening, you can camp out to relax and get in the spirit of the outdoors before hiking to Lost Lake and surrounding alpine areas the next day. If in the alternative you plan to do this as a day hike without camping first, I suggest using the Lost Lake Trail (Hike 10) because it is less traveled, has no established campground to attract other hikers, is 1 mile shorter than the Primrose Creek Trail,

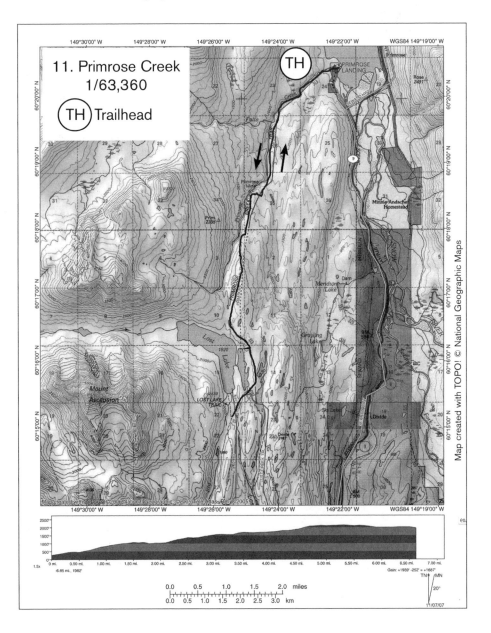

Looking north across Lost Lake from near the high point on the Primrose Trail

and allows you to take advantage of the pleasant semiloop to the Clemens Cabin trail (see Hike 10).

From the Primrose Landing Campground, the trail starts at about 400 feet in elevation and follows Primrose Creek at a fairly consistent/moderate gradient. You are hiking through a moderate-canopy spruce, aspen, and cottonwood forest at these lower elevations. You will pass several wildflower meadows in this lower section as well. At about two and one-half miles, you reach an unmarked but well-worn side trail that leads off to the west (right) side. Be sure to take this trail, which drops you first 200 meters down through a small stream channel to an overlook across from a beautiful, high, feathery waterfall on the lower reach of Primrose Creek near its confluence with Porcupine Creek far

below. Take care as you snap pictures, as the freefall is a killer.

Here Primrose Creek makes a sharp right up away from the trail into the high western peaks. It follows Porcupine Creek, not Primrose, although you seldom see or hear the creek until you break out onto the alpine tundra near its headwaters. Starting about 1 mile from the waterfall side trail, you are hiking through even-age (same-age) stands of spruce trees that form a canopy. The lower trunks are mostly branch-free, so you can see a long way through the understory. The trail here is graced with grasslands offering wild geranium, yarrow, and dwarf dogwoods. There is a historic and still currently active, although very small, private gold and copper mining claim known as the Primrose Mine near the trail at three and one-half miles. While this trail is generally closed to motorized vehicles, you may encounter a miner or two who has been granted an ATV access permit.

Primrose Trail continues gradually uphill through hemlock and spruce trees until about mile 4, when you begin switchbacks for about half a mile as the trees open up on the steeper slope and the hemlocks become the dwarf variety. Near 4 and one-half miles, the trail breaks out onto largely subalpine wildflower meadows. Once you leave the forest and grasslands completely behind at around mile 5, the trail levels out along a ridgeline covered with alpine tundra at about 2,100 feet as you approach Lost Lake (elevation 1,920 feet). The landscape opens up along this section, and your real reason for taking this trail quickly becomes apparent. The last mile of the trail provides increasingly dramatic views of first Mount Ascension and then Resurrection Peaks. Also you can look west into the upper regions of Porcupine Creek where it cuts a deep V-shaped gorge.

Lost Lake is renowned for its gorgeous views of the glaciated alpine tundra highcountry, good fishing, fabulous berry picking in the subalpine zone, and access to any number of wonderful cross-country routes across the tundra. There are many good camping spots all along the north edge of Lost Lake, as well as access to the tundra-covered saddle north of Mount Ascension and the wild tundra country of the upper reaches of the Martin Creek drainage. If you plan to camp here, camp well away from the trail. And if you venture cross-country over the tundra, walk lightly,

on rocks whenever you can, and if you are in a group try not to walk in single file so as not to start new trails.

Lost Lake has two segments: an eastern, smaller section and a larger, western one. The connector trail to the top of the Lost Lake Trial (Hike 10) continues across alpine tundra around the eastern edge of Lost Lake for about 1.5 miles. This is a fascinating section of the trail with many different views of the lake's numerous small side ponds, stream channels. and profusions of wildflowers. Big, beautiful bouquets of lupine are king here in July.

This end of Primrose Creek Trail officially meets the top end of the Lost Lake Trail about one-quarter mile from the south end of Lost Lake, where you can either turn right (north) and hike down to the lake, or turn left (south) and hike the Lost Lake Trail down to its trailhead (Hike 10).

SPECIAL NOTES

Be sure to leave plenty of time for exploring the highcountry around, north and perhaps even west of, Lost Lake. Camping around Lost Lake is a joy. The lake is really just the beginning of your possible adventures. You also have access to several small remnant glaciers on the peaks to the northwest and southwest on Mount Ascension. Or you can hike due west into the Marten Creek drainage over the low divide in front of Mount Ascension. You will have outstanding views of the entire Resurrection River valley as well as the peaks and glaciers of the Harding Ice Field. If you love alpine rock climbing, you'll find plenty of challenges.

12

Ptarmigan Creek & Lake

Total distance: 3.5 miles to the lake, plus 4 miles along the lake one way

Hiking time: 1.5 to 2 hours to the lake; 2 to 4 hours to the east end of the trail

Elevation change: 450 feet

Rating: Easy hike to lake, moderate along lake to trail's end

Best season: Late May to mid-October

Maps: Kenai National Wildlife Refuge and Kenai Fjords National Park by National Geographic Trails Illustrated; Alaska Road and Recreation Map; USGS Seward B-6 and B-7

Special features: Flower-strewn hike along beautiful Ptarmigan Creek and a gorgeous U-shaped glacial valley and family fun at Ptarmigan Lake. Some lovely protected camping spots along the lake edge.

This is an easy hike along rushing Ptarmigan Creek to a large, beautiful, glacial alpine lake with its trail extension along the shoreline for more rugged hiking and further exploration. You will find good family camping, excellent fishing, wonderful berry picking, and lots of opportunities for photography. There is also access to the Falls Creek ATV Trail.

GETTING THERE

There are two trailheads for Ptarmigan Lake. The north one is at mile 24 on the Seward Highway. This is really the access to the Falls Creek ATV route, which has a crossover access trail 1 mile up from the trailhead. The south trailhead, at mile 23 on the Seward Highway, starts the Ptarmigan Creek Trail from the Ptarmigan Creek Campground on the north side of the road and is the one I recommend using. Turn into the Ptarmigan Creek Campground and take an immediate right to locate the trailhead. There is plenty of parking and toilet facilities at the trailhead. If you are so inclined, and have two vehicles, you can use these separate trailheads to make a semicircular hike. However, to steer clear of the ATV route, go in and out on the actual Ptarmigan Creek Trail . . . that's what I always do . . . and you double your streamside hiking time along pleasant Ptarmigan Creek.

THE TRAIL

From the south trailhead, you start at about 450 feet of elevation and climb gradually for 2 miles to spruce-dominated forests.

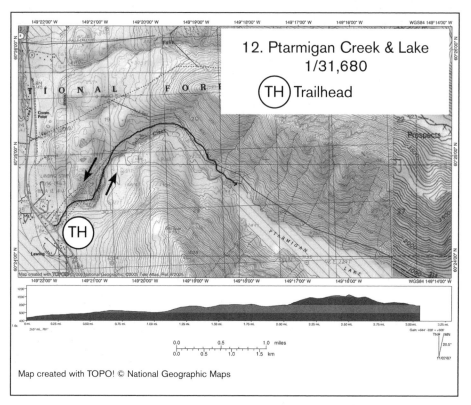

12. Ptarmigan Creek & Lake
1/31,680

(TH) Trailhead

Map created with TOPO! © National Geographic Maps

For the first mile or so, the trail hugs Ptarmigan Creek so you reap the benefits of viewing and listening to the stream. The hiking is mostly through open-canopy spruce, aspen, and large cottonwood forest, plus low willow and alder and wildflower grasslands. You will especially enjoy the wild roses along with monkshood, wild geranium, dwarf dogwood, and fireweed. You will see spruce-beetle-killed snags (dead tree trunks) with resurgent younger spruce insistently reclaiming their place in the forest.

For the next 2 miles, the trail moves up and way from the stream channel, but still mostly within view of the water, through alternating forest and grasslands. The forested sections are populated mostly by spruce and mountain hemlocks.

Along the way, Falls Creek ATV Trail will intersect from the west. As you climb higher, you will encounter more open wildflower grasslands and alders. Birch, aspen, and large cottonwoods in the moister areas become more common as you climb, since they like the higher, cooler elevation. The breeze-induced rustle of the leaves of these trees is delightful and creates a soft symphony as you hike through them.

From the trail's high point near the western end of Ptarmigan Lake, you gradually lose 150 feet to an elevation, of about 750 feet as you hike toward the lake. As you descend, notice the classic, glacially formed, U-shaped valley. Glacial valleys are U-shaped because as glaciers slowly grow and move down from where they are born in the ice fields at the highest elevations

Great family/honeymoon campsite on the south side of Ptarmigan Lake

they carve out rocks and sediments across the entire width of their base, rounding out the bottom of the valley.

Throughout the hike, and especially along the lake, keep your eyes open for wildlife. Bear, moose, and even coyotes are common.

At the lake, there are two campgrounds near the trail. There is also a one-of-a-kind open-air potty throne kids will love! Follow the signs to the loo and give your whole family a thrill they will talk about for months.

You can also hike about 200 meters south of the trail along the shore of the lake to find a lovely—some would say romantic—spruce, alder, and birch-guarded campsite with peak-a-boo views of the lake. From this campsite, hike around to the headwaters of Ptarmigan Creek at the most westerly end of the lake, which you will notice is a bit opaque and milky. This is due to superfine glacier sediment (called rock flour) that remains in suspension in the water.

You will also find large piles of bleached driftwood crowded at the western end of the lake, transported there by the constant winds blowing east to west across the lake as they sweep down.

The ptarmigan is a bird, and in fact the state bird of Alaska. It has the coloring of a mini wild turkey, sort of, with striped feathers in a fetching little tail.

Following the main trial, you can continue up and down along the northern shoreline of the lake for about 4 miles. This section is more secluded and a bit tougher to hike than the more highly trafficked Ptarmigan Creek portion. The trail heads up over the headlands providing nice views of the lake, and then down close to the lake in the embayments. There are several primitive tent camping sites within 0.5 mile of the start of this trail extension. After about 4 miles, the currently maintained trail disappears into a flat willow-choked glacial outwash plain east of the lake.

SPECIAL NOTES

As you hike along the shoreline, notice how the retreating glaciers have rounded the valley terrain, and compare this with the very tops of the higher peaks that are more jagged because the ice never reached them. On the uppermost slopes of Andy Simons Mountain to the south, you can see tiny remnants of some of the alpine glaciers that once flowed down those slopes to form the valley glacier that now has melted. If you lay out your Trails Illustrated map of the Kenai National Wildlife Refuge, you can trace how the valleys that now contain Ptarmigan, Grant, Trail, and Kenai lakes were created as the alpine glaciers flowed together to form the one, monster glacier that carved out the valley through which the Seward Highway now runs. This larger glacier was responsible for carving out all of what is now the Resurrection Bay fjord.

The Ptarmigan Lake Trail actually continues beyond the east end of the lake—it just hasn't been maintained in years. You can go another 6 miles up along the stream that feeds Ptarmigan Lake and over Snow River Pass into Paradise Valley. This trail extension isn't shown on the Trails Illustrated Kenai Fjords map, but the entire route is covered on the Trails Illustrated Kenai National Wildlife Refuge map. At the moment, however, it's a daunting scramble and especially in July and August when you will be fighting the grasses. September would be the time to tackle this extension of the trail.

50 Hikes in Alaska's Kenai Peninsula

13

Resurrection River

Total distance: 16 miles one way

Hiking time: 2 to 3 days

Elevation change: 700 feet

Rating: Moderate to difficult (due to trail conditions)

Best season: Mid to late summer, after major deadfalls have been removed

Maps: Kenai National Wildlife Refuge and Kenai Fjords National Park by National Geographic Trails Illustrated; Alaska Road and Recreation Map; USGS Seward A-7, A-8, and B-8

Special features: Abundant bear, moose, and even wolf, solitude on the river bars, and access to the Russian River Trial and Cooper Lake. The lower trail portions offer good, easy family hiking. The middle and upper portions are wild and wooly!

The Resurrection River Trail offers a 16-mile hike through mostly thick, closed-canopy forested cover, following the Resurrection River for most of its length. It connects the Exit Glacier area near Seward with the Russian Lakes/Cooper Lake trail system. While the gradient is rarely a great challenge, downfalls, wet areas, and washed out bridges can make for slow going. The isolation and wildlife, especially bears, make this an attractive adventure, but this is not a trail for hikers seeking to make good time.

GETTING THERE

Access to the south trailhead is at mile 4 on the Seward Highway. Turn left (northwest) onto Exit Glacier Road and drive 7.1 miles to the parking area turnout trailhead on the right (north) side of the road, just before the bridge over the Resurrection River. There is parking but no facilities.

A 5-mile hike from the Cooper Lake trailhead of the Russian Lakes Trail (Hike 26) brings you to the northern end of the Resurrection River Trail. Turn south onto graveled Snug Harbor Road at mile 48 on the Sterling Highway and drive 11 miles. Look for the trailhead on the left. If you drive all the way to Cooper Lake, you've gone too far unless you want to camp. The shores of Cooper Lake are a good place for the night.

THE TRAIL

Let's start at the south trailhead on the Exit Glacier Road near Seward. At the start of the trail, there is both a sign-in kiosk

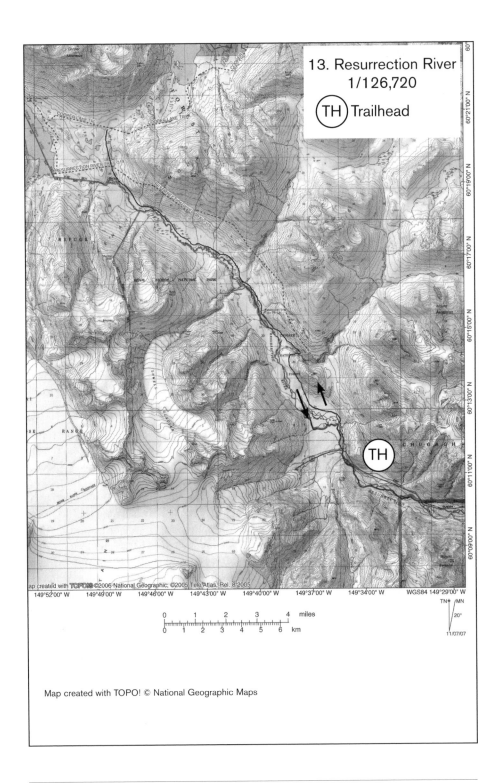

13. Resurrection River
1/126,720

(TH) Trailhead

Map created with TOPO! © 2006 National Geographic; ©2005 Tele Atlas, Rel. 8 2005

149°52'00" W 149°49'00" W 149°46'00" W 149°43'00" W 149°40'00" W 149°37'00" W 149°34'00" W WGS84 149°29'00" W

60°21'00" N
60°19'00" N
60°17'00" N
60°15'00" N
60°13'00" N
60°11'00" N
60°09'00" N

0   1   2   3   4   miles
0   1   2   3   4   5   6   km

TN MN
20°
11/07/07

Map created with TOPO! © National Geographic Maps

50 Hikes in Alaska's Kenai Peninsula

and a separate primitive trail description marker (see below). The trail runs almost entirely under dense forest cover, with a few open sections that provide views of the Resurrection River valley and surrounding mountains.

For the first mile, the trial runs close to the river bank and provides several opportunities to visit the channel itself. There are some peak-a-boo views of Exit Glacier through the trees along the early section of the trail. After about 1 mile, the trail diverges from the river as it moves inland along the edges of the flood plain and near the bottom of the eastern slope.

The trail remains mostly at low elevation along the steep banks at the edge of the river's floodplain, although it makes forays up onto the slopes, particularly where the path crosses major streams such as Martin Creek and Boulder Creek. There are not very many good camping spots along this trail, although some open meadows provide decent space in dry weather. Your best bet is to secure the single public-access cabin between Martin and Boulder creeks about 6 miles into the hike and 1.5 miles above the Martin Creek crossing.

As of this writing, the bridges over the main creeks are washed out, so take care crossing, particularly at high water.

Wildlife is plentiful in this area. Look for black and brown (grizzly) bears, moose, Dall sheep, beaver, and wolves. Large concentrations of grizzlies are reported up the Martin and Boulder drainages. Few people use this trail, so there are excellent opportunities for undisturbed wildlife viewing—and of course for wildlife's undisturbed viewing of you! Remember to be cautious, particularly around bears and moose—you are a long way from any help. Also remember that your cell phone will not work this far into the wilderness.

Particularly along the low-visibility portions of the trail, it's a good idea to make a bit of noise so the bears can hear you coming and move out of the way. If you do encounter a bear, stand tall, speak calmly, and slowly retreat.

At various points, the trail rejoins the river channel, allowing you to enjoy the bank and stream channel of the picturesque Resurrection River. These opportunities are the highlight of the hike for me. The open skies above the channel provide the best views of the Resurrection River valley and the surrounding high alpine slopes. You can even see some of the remnant hanging glaciers coming down out of the Harding Ice Field. The lower and middle sections of the river, in particular, are gravel- and cobble-strewn and braided, with lots of interesting channels, sediment, and other debris to explore. I like to lean back against my backpack and watch and listen to the river flow by. And on sunny days this is a great place to shake off some of that cold dampness you pick up hiking underneath the forest canopy. If you hang out for a while and are quiet, you're likely to see wildlife you don't normally spot right along the trail, including bears, wolves, and moose. And remember to look high on the slopes with your binoculars for Dall sheep.

From Martin Creek to the Russian Lakes Trail, this is considered a primitive trail. The description noted on the trail info marker at the beginning of the trail describes this portion of the trail well, as follows: THE RESURRECTION RIVER TRAIL IS A PRIMITIVE ROUTE FROM MARTIN CREEK TO RUSSIAN LAKE TRAIL. THERE ARE NO BRIDGES CROSSING MARTIN, BOULDER AND SUMMIT CREEKS. YOU MAY

Author, Hope, Ellie, and Zip on one of the wooden bridges on the lower portion of the trail

photo by Nancy Lasater

ENCOUNTER DOWNED TREES, HEAVY BRUSH, AND ROUGH OR MUDDY CONDITIONS. TRAVEL ON THIS SECTION OF THE TRAIL IS FOR THOSE WHO SEEK RISK AND SOLITUDE, ARE SELF-RELIANT AND WANT A CHALLENGE.

The last couple of miles open into sub-brushy alpine areas dotted with a few tarn lakes (small glacially formed lakes left by the retreating glaciers) as you approach the Russian Lakes Trail.

The trail in this last section is severely overgrown in July and August and passage can be quite daunting. You join the Russian Lakes Trail about 5 miles from the Cooper Lake trailhead or 16 miles from the Russian River trailhead.

SPECIAL NOTES

While the middle and upper sections of this hike are primitive and challenging, the first couple of miles in from the trailhead provide an easy-to-hike and very pleasant day of trekking along the forested river.

This trail can also be used as the first leg of a many-day, multitrail hike. For instance, you could start a 72-mile hike at the Exit Glacier Road trailhead, connect to and hike through the Russian River/Cooper Lake trail system, and then on through to the Resurrection Pass, Devils Creek, and Summit Creek trail systems all the way to Hope on the south shore of Turnagain Arm. (See Hikes 4, 5, and 6 for planning such a trek.)

14

Exit Glacier

Total distance: One-quarter mile on a paved path, with access to one and one-half miles of loop trails

Hiking time: 1 to 1.5 hours

Elevation change: Flat on lower trails, 100 feet on the upper loop

Rating: Easy (wheel chair accessible)

Best season: May through October

Maps: Kenai Fjords National Park by National Geographic Trails Illustrated; Alaska Road and Recreation Map; USGS Seward A-7 (NW)

Special features: Easy walk to the front of a massive glacier. A pleasant hike along the edge of the glacial outwash plain and stream channel in front of the glacier along a nature trail.

Exit Glacier is only 11 miles from Seward and is one of the easiest-to-access glaciers you'll ever find. You can drive to within one-half mile of its front. A nearly flat, paved path provides access to the area immediately in front of the glacier; wheelchairs and children are welcome. Along Exit Glacier Road leading up to the parking lot, and along the one quarter-mile paved path leading to the three loop trails, signs indicate the position of the glacier at various times in the past, demonstrating how rapidly it has been melting and retreating—like most of the world's other glaciers.

GETTING THERE

Drive 3 miles north from Seward on the Seward Highway, and turn west (left) onto Exit Glacier Road. Drive 8 miles to the parking lot. About 6 miles down the road, you cross the wild, braided Resurrection River. Beware of frost heaves along the road up to the Resurrection River bridge. One of them is nasty enough to bump your head into the ceiling of your pickup truck, even if you're driving below the speed limit. (Ellie knows this from experience!) The locals have even painted a skull and cross bones on the asphalt.

THE TRAIL

The first one-quarter mile of trail from the parking lot, ranger station, and restrooms is wide, flat, paved, and easily negotiable with wheelchairs. Near the end of the paved path is an interpretive display and shelter with information about glaciers and local

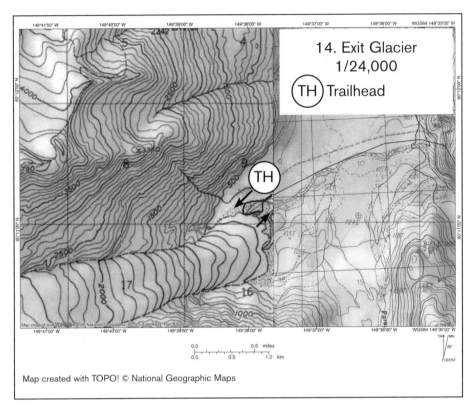

Map created with TOPO! © National Geographic Maps

animals. Three loops begin where the paved path ends.

The middle loop is one-half mile and leads out across the outwash plain in front of the retreating glacier. You have spectacular views of the front of the glacier and up across the top toward the Harding Ice Field from which it flows. You can hike right up to the stream channels being created by the melting glacier. All the rocks and sediment you hike across were deposited right out of the melting ice. Many people don't appreciate just how much sediment there is in a glacier. The ice contains a huge range, from house-sized boulders to rock flour so fine it remains suspended in still water and provides the distinctive blue-green color so commonly found in glacier lakes and streams. Some glaciers have so much sediment the ice isn't even visible.

The upper loop, also about one-half mile, climbs about 100 feet or so up the slope on the right (west) side of the glacier. Bring a hat and windbreaker when you hike this section, because even on warm days you can feel a definite chill from the cold air that blows off the ice nearly all the time. Along this path you hike directly up to and along the front of the glacier itself. Take time to step off the path and walk across some of the solid rock surfaces. Look for and feel the ones with striations—long parallel lines of scratches in the rocks. These were formed as the retreating glacier dragged rock fragments across the surface. Notice how smooth the rock feels as you move your hand along the grooves. The glacier not only carved and

Even in its diminished state, Exit Glacier is massive when you hike up next to it

scratched the rocks, but polished them as well. You also witness the glacier's melting process and will likely see and hear pieces of ice and sediment drop off the front of the glacier. Be careful not to venture too close, as overhanging sections can easily drop off—you'd become part of the glacially formed debris on the outwash plain.

The third loop is a nature trail starting at the far side of the middle loop and winds its way along the outwash plain more or less parallel to Exit Glacier Creek, which flows from the front of the glacier. You are entertained with a variety of erosional and depositional features such as numerous channel and gravel bars along the braided stream channel of Exit Glacier's outwash plain. At times of high water, this entire

braided stream channel can be filled.

SPECIAL NOTES

Exit Glacier is melting and retreating so rapidly you can easily see changes to its front from one year to the next. My favorite time to visit is in the spring, when the greatest amount of melting water is moving through the system and the action is most dramatic. Along the drive to the Exit Glacier parking lot and along the paved path leading to the glacier, the Park Service has placed date markers back to the late 1800s showing you the position of the glacial front in the recent past. You will be surprised at how fast Exit Glacier is retreating.

There is also a nice bookshop maintained by the Park Service here.

15

Harding Ice Field

Total distance: 4 miles one way

Hiking time: 3 to 4 hours depending upon fitness level

Elevation change: Roughly 3,500 feet, although you could hike higher

Rating: Moderate to difficult

Best season: July through mid-September, although new snow possible at the higher elevations year-round

Maps: Kenai Fjords National Park by National Geographic Trails Illustrated; Alaska Road and Recreation Map; USGS Seward A-8

Special features: The wondrous world of the massive Harding Ice Field, glacial features, beautiful wildflowers, snow hiking, and great views of Exit Glacier.

This is a strenuous hike into the high-altitude land of perpetual ice that is the Harding Ice Field. It is certainly the most direct access you will ever have to this strange and wonderful landscape where glaciers are born. Traveling from the lower nonglaciated environment in front of Exit Glacier up into the ice field so quickly is a fascinating experience. I always feel drawn to this surreal scenery and the fast passing of so many ecosystems along this one steep hike.

GETTING THERE

Drive 3 miles north of Seward on the Seward Highway, and turn west (left) onto Exit Glacier Road. Continue 8 miles to the parking lot. About 6 miles along the road, you cross the wild, braided channel of the Resurrection River. Beware of frost heaves along the road leading to the bridge. They come upon you so fast while you are driving that you might take a sudden dip, so drive slowly—well under the speed limit.

THE TRAIL

From the parking lot, walk one-quarter mile along the paved path to the interpretive center. The trailhead for the Harding Ice Field Trail is just past it on the right. This trail has four distinct sections: a lower forested section, a middle alpine meadow section, an upper tundra section, and snow field and bare rock section. Bears, particularly black bears, roam especially over the first two, dropping away as the vegetation thins out higher. Hikers routinely see them, and they even walk the trail, which is often the only

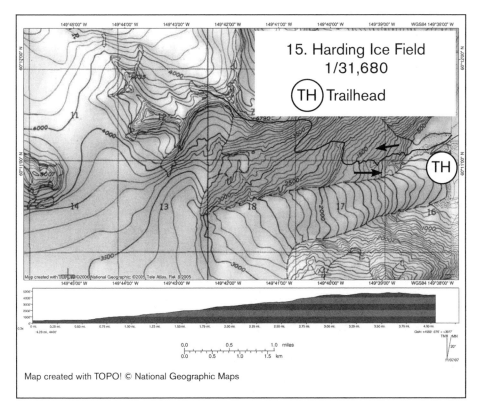

Map created with TOPO! © National Geographic Maps

cleared space across the densely forested mountain face. They also appear higher up, in among the wildflower meadows and marshy swales.

The trail begins along a flat section of closed-canopy forest of large aspen trees. After 0.1 mile, though, it rapidly ascends over moist rocks through brush and then an aspen, alder, and poplar forest directly up the west side of Exit Glacier, though because of the convex curve of the hillside you cannot actually see the glacier until you reach a much higher elevation. Switchbacks keep the trail from being too steep, though there are still several very steep rocky segments where using hands and feet is necessary. If you have hiking poles, you can move through these steep rocky sections faster. Be sure to keep your

weight back away from the rocks using your poles for balance.

There are several overlook points providing peak-a-boo views of a deeply incised side stream channel far below you, along with the lower section of Exit Glacier. One of them is clearly marked on the first section of the trail and leads to a nice catch-your-breath stop and photo opportunity.

On your return trip down this same steep section, remember basic hiking etiquette. Climbing hikers always have the right of way, so step aside to allow those laboring uphill to pass.

As you reach the second section of the trail at about the 2-mile mark at the middle elevation of about 1,000–2,000 feet, you leave the forest completely behind suddenly and pass up into wildflower meadows of

Frozen expanse of the Harding Ice Field, featuring crevasses and delicate displays of light

subalpine grasses, short alders, and wild-flowers with gorgeous violet blue lupine dominating in June and July. The fields also include the distinctive *Echinacea* plant (purple coneflower), as well as low dwarf hemlocks and ground cedar.

As you enter the open meadows, there is a short side path to a terrific overlook of Exit Glacier and its crevassed surface. As you hike across the bare rock outcrops, look for the distinctive, obvious linear stria-tions on the hard surfaces. These are evi-dence that a much-larger Exit Glacier once ground over these rocks, carving these grooves with stones it carried. Rub your hand parallel to the striation to feel how smoothly the glacier has polished these rock surfaces.

During the third section of the trial, you are still climbing, and you will not be able to see the end. One of the chief characteris-tics of this path is its segmentation visually, so that only short stretches are visible at a time, even in the wide-open tundra and then icy sections approaching the survival cabin. (Yes, there is even a survival cabin.) Each segment seems to be the last, but it is not. The trail continues, turning away from your view around another corner, higher up.

Through the third section, the subal-pine grasses and alders recede and finally disappear as you climb finally into the alpine tundra zone. The maintained trail disappears, but the well-worn path is still obvious. As this is a high-traffic area, try to stick to the main path marked by orange flags rather than meandering randomly over the ground, which can also be quite wet in spots. The grasses and lichens are fragile and easily damaged. I suggest you hike up to the rock outcrops that provide sweeping panoramas across the Harding Ice Field. If you brought your binoculars—and you'd be crazy not to—search the rocky slopes for mountain goats and the lower slopes for brown as well as black bears, particularly in summer. Even caribou are sighted here from time to time.

At about mile 3, you tackle a one-quarter-mile-long snow-covered traverse that crosses a broad slope in front of you that you can see as you approach it. Beneath it, there are big patches of wet snow you must traverse, and some of the up-hiking can be treacherous, as unaccustomed feet can slip on the sudden thick winter iciness. Children especially love to play here, since it may be their first shot of snow all sum-mer. Take care that they don't use up all their energy or get too wet, for the trek still has a long way to go!

There are numerous snow-source fresh-ets of delicious-tasting water draining this slope. On the way back, this is a terrific hill to boot-ski down . . . just remember to keep your weight forward! (Or, if you need to slip and slide down on your derriere, don't worry. You're not the first to do it, and you won't be the last even that day.)

The fourth and final segment of the trail begins at the top of the traverse at the higher elevation of 3,000 to 3,500 feet. Here you hike mainly across snow fields and mostly bare rocks. As you cross the snow, look for patches of snow covered with red algae, which blooms in patches that are unmistakable once you notice the first one and realize what it is. The areas not covered with snow are exposed scree and rock intermittently supporting spare communities of lichen and a few pioneer-ing plants, such as blue forget-me-nots, the Alaska state flower. These high slopes are too recently uncovered from the smoothing ice to support much new life yet.

This is a stark and beautiful landscape you may never see anywhere else. It feels primordial, just as one feels at the lip of a volcano. This is nature at her most extreme and un-human, showing herself at one end of the earth. The views here can hardly be described. "Astounding views of the massive expanse of the Harding Ice Field" just doesn't cut it. Standing at the top, I always find myself speaking in hushed tones, if I speak at all. Plan to devote at least an hour to simply sitting and watching the alpine light as it plays across the sea of ice before you. Also take the opportunity to explore the rocky landscape at the edge of the ice field, careful to avoid trampling the delicate plants clinging courageously to their tenuous existence. Take care also to cling to yours, by not getting too close to the edge.

This is where you also want to have lunch, carve your name in the survival cabin, and rest up for the return. Be sure also to ask other hikers if they want you to take their picture, since they will be as proud of their accomplishment as you are of yours. Few people on earth see this, as few make it up this far. You will notice how the crowd thins as you keep going.

On your return trip down through the alpine tundra section, look across the Exit Glacier valley to see a keen hanging glacier. This used to be a side glacier that flowed directly into and contributed to Exit Glacier but which has now been left high and dry by the reduction in Exit Glacier's thickness as it has retreated. This hanging glacier is proof of the glacier's thinning as well as its retreat.

Regardless of the prevailing weather around Seward, local conditions and temperatures at the glacier and up at the top of this long hike can vary wildly at any given moment—warm sunshine to fog to

penetrating rain or cold falling snow and back to sunshine again in just a few minutes. The interaction of the cold glacial ice, the mountain slopes, the winds, and the sun creates a very dynamic weather environment. Dress in layers and be prepared to put on long pants, a pullover, a windbreaker, and even gloves by the time you reach the top. Also, be absolutely sure to bring polarized sunglasses, as the light reflecting off the glacial ice and snow is polarized and strong. Up top strong winds and rapidly deteriorating conditions are common.

Near the very top, as mentioned, there is a sturdy safety cabin to which you can retreat if caught in nasty weather. Don't forget to sign the book, too. There is some wonderful glacial polish (that is, smoothing caused by glacial movement across the hard surface) in the dark rocks adjacent to the cabin.

Coming down can be very difficult, as the body is tired and knees protest above aching ankles. Some of the step-downs are big, too, jarring the legs. This is especially hard if you don't have poles. Just take your time, resting whenever you need to. Remember that injuries happen when people are tired, which you will be. You'll forget it all, though, once you develop those fabulous pictures.

SPECIAL NOTES

I am always amazed when I stand and gaze across the Harding Ice Field to the peaks beyond that stick up through the ice. The entire Kenai Peninsula looked much like this 12,000 years ago. You can see crevasses, long narrow V-shaped gashes in the glacier, which form when the glacial ice moves over a high point or bump, known as a nick point, in the landscape far underneath the ice. These crevasses can be hundreds of feet deep, and they change constantly. If you sit quietly on a calm day, you'll actually be able to hear and see the ice moving as it grinds slowly through the ice field toward the Exit Glacier terminus below. New snow often covers large areas of the glacier, and where it melts you can easily see the aquamarine blue glacial ice below and all its structure. By the way, that distinctive color is the result of the longer wavelengths, reds and yellows, being absorbed by the hydrogen bonds in the ice crystals. This leaves only the shorter green and blue wavelengths for us to see.

Although you'll be tempted, as I always am, please do not hike on the glacier. As beautiful and inviting as it seems, the ice field is a very dangerous environment. Glacier travel should only be attempted by teams of people who are skilled at using ropes, skis, crampons, and ice axes. Enjoy the Harding Ice Field from a close, yet safe distance.

Taking pictures in a snow- and ice-dominated environment can be challenging because of all the bright white snow. Automatic exposure settings on cameras sometimes result in too-bright, blown-out images with little detail. The good news is that with a digital camera you can immediately see a preview of the pictures you're taking. If they appear too bright, switch to a manual setting or set your camera to record the images 1.5 to 2.0 f-stops darker than normal. Take a few experimental shots at different f-stop settings to get the hang of how your camera's exposure system and software handle the ice and snow, and then have at it.

If you camp along the trail, make sure you set up well away from the path both to ensure your own privacy and to protect the area near the trail from damage due to overuse.

16

Mount Marathon

Total distance: 2 miles (one way) for the race route, 3 to 4 miles (one way) for the hiking trail

Hiking time: 4 to 6 hours up and back

Elevation change: 3,022 feet

Rating: Moderate to difficult on the hiking trail, very difficult to dangerous on the race trail

Best season: Summer mid-June through mid-September

Maps: Kenai Fjords National Park by National Geographic Trails Illustrated; Alaska Road and Recreation Map; USGS Seward A-7

Special features: Spectacular views of Resurrection Bay and the surrounding glacially carved alpine landscape from the race trail. Wonderful waterfalls, a beautiful cirque basin and stream, and exhilarating ridge hikes on the hiking trail.

Mount Marathon is the location of the single most Alaskan place to be on the Fourth of July every year—the famous July Fourth Mount Marathon Race, an event that has been going on since 1915. There is a race trail and a hiking trail, although neither actually goes to the summit, which is 1,600 feet higher and a mile west of the top of this hike. Instead, both routes go to a false peak, whose top is at just over 3,000 feet, which is visible from the cheering, partying crowds in downtown Seward. Winning times in the Mount Marathon race are, believe it or not, under 45 minutes—and that's up and back. There is also a women's race, as well as one for youngsters. The women travel almost as fast as the men, and what an inspiring race for girls to see, what with very fit, painted, muddy runners in all shapes, sizes, and ages. Men and women compete well into their seventies.

You will want to go at a more leisurely pace in order to both survive and enjoy the scenery. If hiking and scenery are your forte, then I recommend the hiking trail rather than the race trail, even when it's not the Fourth of July.

GETTING THERE

Downtown Seward provides access to both trails. To reach the runner's trail, take Jefferson Street west toward the base of Marathon Mount. Jefferson becomes Lowell Canyon Road as it crosses First Avenue, just before the picnic area at the trailhead. From the parking area at the picnic tables, follow the road to the base of the moun-

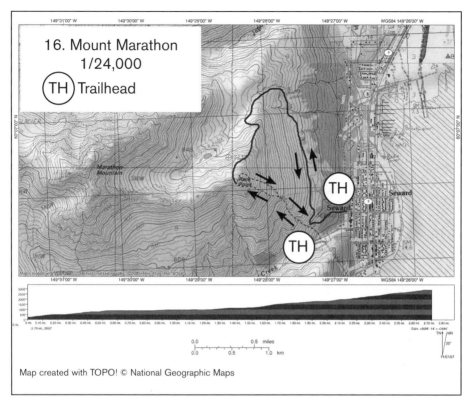

Map created with TOPO! © National Geographic Maps

tain, where you find a sign marked MOUNT MARATHON RACE TRAIL. For the hiker's trail, take First Avenue north to Monroe Street. Where Monroe Street ends at First Avenue, cross First Avenue and park at the yellow gate at the trailhead for the hiking trail.

THE RUNNER'S TRAIL

This trail is very steep, with lots of sections that require all four paws to maintain balance. There are also lots of slippery sections, made so by the passage of hundreds of pairs of running shoes over the years. If you are not in excellent shape and don't have good balance you shouldn't be on this trail. If you have good balance but are in poor shape you still shouldn't be on this trail, because fatigue will diminish your coordination. Even for

those who are prepared, this route is a great challenge.

The path traces a figure eight: You hike up the right (east) side of the lower loop and the left (west) side of the upper loop. The return trip follows the right side (east) of the upper loop and the left (west) side to the lower one. The steepest and most dangerous sections are in the bottom half. The lower trail divides into several paths across what can best be described as a sheer cliff, so just pick the paths that best suit you. Test your hand and footholds to make sure they'll support you without giving way. If you are hiking in a group, I recommend leaving ample space between each person and/or taking slightly different routes on the steepest sections to prevent injuries due to rock falls. Above tree line, the up and down paths merge into one trail as you move up the ridgeline.

A little over halfway up, you cross over to the upper loop. This intersection is a great place to take a break and enjoy the view. From here on up the trail is a bit easier and a lot less dangerous, and the views continually improve. Break out your binoculars to scan for mountain goats and Dall sheep on the surrounding hillsides. You are likely to be in the company of lots of marmots (which look like fat prairie dogs wearing carpets), as well as ground squirrels and ptarmigan (the Alaska state bird). The high point of your hike is just over 3,000 feet at Race Point.

The trail down the second half of the figure eight heads off to the east. Much of the downslope is on scree, which slides as you stride through it. Take long steps, lean forward, and keep your knees bent. Remember that it's just as easy to get hurt going down, and because it's so steep and unstable it can be very tough on your knees. My solution to help prevent sore, damaged knees is to wrap them with Ace bandages prior to starting down. They may not be sexy or cute, but they sure help protect your knees on steep slopes.

THE HIKER'S TRAIL

The hiker's trail is almost twice as long as the runner's trail, and therefore half as steep, but it is still a challenging climb, and especially up the scree slope leading to the ridgeline that will take you to Race Point and beyond, as you are gaining 3,000 feet over 4 miles. Start by taking a look at the map posted on the bulletin board near the entrance at the yellow gate. The lower portion of the trail below tree line is really a jeep trail wide enough to drive on. As you head up the jeep trail, take note that you are hiking through a lush old-growth spruce

forest with a supporting cast of hemlock and alder. ("Old-growth" means the trees are hundreds of years old and have never been felled. What you're walking through has never been logged.) Take time to enjoy the large, well-spaced stately old spruce trees and the soft, mossy forest floor duff layer below.

As you walk up the jeep trail, you reach several intersections. When in doubt, look for the arrows posted conspicuously on trees to help guide you. At the first main split, one-quarter mile up, the main trail follows the arrows to the left. The lesser-traveled, right-hand path is 100 meters long and leads to a pretty stream channel. At the second major split, another one-quarter mile up on the main jeep trail, stay to the right, for the left path takes you over to the runner's route—above the death-defying lower cliff sections. Continue along the forest road until you reach the tree line where the road-trail ends in a clearing.

After the end of the jeep trail, the way becomes a narrow path, more like a trail, which you will hike for about one-half mile along the transition zone between the lower forest and the upper alder thickets. Like many transition areas, this one too is rich in plant species, including mountain ash, ferns, horsetails, grasses, and wildflowers such as wild purple geranium, red columbine, mauve primrose, red Indian paintbrush, white Queen Anne's lace, fuschia fireweed, and the ever-present, invasive, non-native pushki, which looks like Queen Anne's lace on steroids. Beware of this stuff, since it stings exposed arms and legs. You are following a stream channel draining the alder thicket upslope.

The trail continues up an easy to moderate slope trending northwest along the boundary between the forest and the alder thicket to a saddle, which is just what it

Mount Marathon race runners with Resurrection Bay and glaciated high Kenai peaks behind

Mount Marathon

sounds like—the high ground linking two separate peaks. From this saddle, the trail turns west and begins a steeper climb up to and over a ridgeline into the stream drainage of the Mount Marathon cirque basin and its remnant glacier.

As soon as you enter this drainage, you will be near a series of waterfalls that form where the stream leaves the cirque basin and begins its race and tumble down to Resurrection Bay far below. From the falls, the trail follows the stream channel up in a southwest direction into the cirque bowl basin. You leave the alders and grasses behind and are soon hiking along beautiful alpine tundra as you are serenaded by the nearby burbling stream channel. The underlying rock types on this hike are primarily metamorphic rocks (those cooked under great heat and pressure) of mica and graphite shists (that is, flat rocks that look like big fish scales), as well as banded rocks called gneisses with some intermittent bull (big) quartz veins.

There are many side opportunities to access the stream. Once you are into the middle of the cirque basin, which has been carved by the once huge glacier that filled and gouged out this whole valley, you have many options. You can continue along the stream. You can cross the stream and head up and across the open tundra to the northwest. You can keep climbing into the cirque bowl basin to visit the lake there and the remnant glacier beyond. On the upper slopes, you will likely find remnant winter snows that are reluctantly yielding to the insistent warmth of summer . . . I call this "reluctant snow." These are all fascinating and worthy destinations that have nothing to do with Race Point.

If Race Point and the high ridgelines and maybe even Mount Marathon's real, actual peak itself are your destinations, you will want to gain the ridgeline that is prominent to the east. There is not one specific trail up the ridgeline, but you will want somehow to get to the ridgeline on the mountain's lower, northern end. The farther west you try to hike, the tougher and more dangerous the ascent. This is where the runners go.

As you prowl the north end of the ridgeline, look just to the right of the last alder bushes and you will see an unmarked, but well-worn, zigzag trail (you'll have to be up fairly close to the base of the grey scree slope to see it) that leads up to the ridgeline through the scree. Once you have gained the ridgeline, you will continue to hike southwest through alpine tundra, enjoying dramatic views east down into and along Resurrection Bay and west into the cirque basin. Follow the ridgeline to the top of the runners trail at Race Point. From Race Point, you can continue west along the narrow ridgeline that leads to Mount Marathon Peak. Hike this narrow ridge with care and enjoy the puckering near-vertical views south down into Lowell Creek and north into the cirque basin that still contains the remnants of the glacier that carved this face of Mount Marathon.

On the return route, you can either retrace your steps on the hiker's trail or opt for the runner's trail, which is faster but more dangerous. If you hike back down the ridgeline you ascended, stay just west of the ridgeline to enjoy some fun and safe glissading on the several large patches of snow that remain well into the summer.

SPECIAL NOTES

The annual Fourth of July race weekend is a grand time. Prior to the race you can hike partway up the trail and cheer the racers on. Or you can take the hiker's trail over to the runner's trail above the steepest, nastiest lower sections to stake out a dandy race viewpoint and cheering platform at the top. Journalists from all over Alaska and beyond claim out good spots at the top literally hours before the first runner appears. After the race, continue with your own challenge to the top of the mountain, and then return to participate in the postrace festivities in Seward. There are booths, bars, merchandise, food, drinks, sit-down restaurants, a Sea Life Center, and commemorative t-shirts in this remote old seasport, with its actual storefronts still in use from long ago. This is no movie set of Alaska, but the real thing, with the mountains towering behind you and enormous white cruise ships moored in the harbor. Just be sure to make your hotel or campground reservations well in advance, as nearly the whole state will be there on July 4th along with you. Oh, and be sure to get there the night before, since the town launches its fireworks right after midnight on the 4th, rather than waiting until the evening after the race is concluded. The reflection of the bright colors on the water is spectacular, along with the loud booms that echo off the snow-capped mountains.

17

Caines Head

Total distance: four and one-half miles to North Beach, six and one-half miles to Fort McGilvray one way

Hiking time: 2 days, one out and one back due to tidal restrictions

Elevation change: 600 feet, with a lot of up and down

Rating: Mostly easy, with short, moderate climbs to North Beach and Fort McGilvray; slippery footing on rocky beaches

Best season: May through September

Maps: Kenai Fjords National Park by National Geographic Trails Illustrated; USGS Seward A-7 (SW and SE) and Blying Sound D-7; Alaska State Parks Brochure Caines Head State Recreation Area

Special features: Amazing coastal scenery, lots of marine wildlife, delightful coastal camping, two public-use cabins, a World War II fort for history buffs, and access to the Caines Head Alpine Trail.

This is a wonderful, isolated coastal hike along the west side of Resurrection Bay, offering fantastic scenery and many opportunities to see marine wildlife. You will be hiking on a trail and along the beach through the western end of the Caines Head Recreation Area.

GETTING THERE

Follow the Seward Highway south into Seward and continue on Third Avenue through town to the T intersection. Turn right onto Railway Avenue, which becomes Lowell Point Road, and go 2 miles south along the edge of Resurrection Bay to Martins Road. Turn right and drive 0.1 mile to the trailhead. It is best to arrive at the trailhead an hour or two before low tide, so you can reach the coastal beach between Tonsina Creek and Derby Cove near low tide. Tides must be at a maximum of +3 feet or below in order to hike this section of beach. If you miss this window of time, you must wait until the next low tide. If you miss it coming back out, you will be stuck, possibly overnight, so beware. (You could also kayak down the west side of Resurrection Bay to Derby Cove or North Beach, which allows you to avoid the tide issue near Tonsina Creek altogether.)

There is ample parking as well as restroom facilities in both an upper and a lower (beach) parking area. While you can find the trail from the east end of the beach at lower parking area, I recommend you either park in the upper lot or, if you park at the beach, take the connecting trail to the

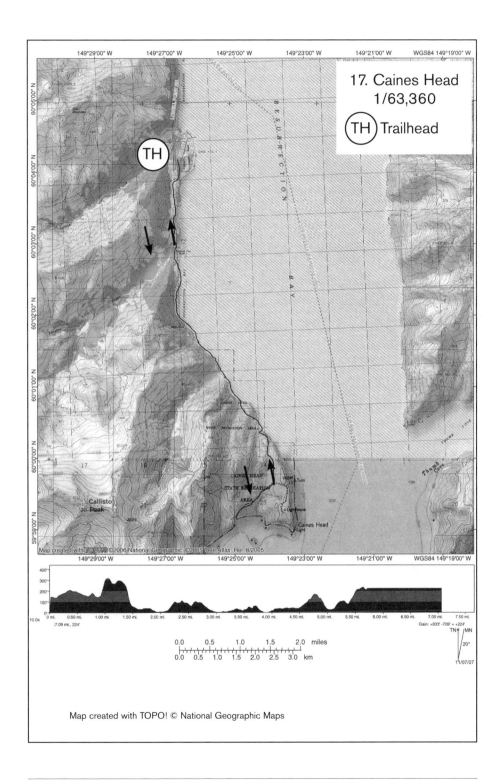

17. Caines Head
1/63,360

(TH) Trailhead

Map created with TOPO! © National Geographic Maps

upper parking area and behind the restrooms to begin your hike. This is because the lower trail off the east end of the beach is a bit difficult to find and it's steep and gnarly.

If you are camping, either tent or RV, you can also stay close to the trailhead at Millers Landing, which offers a wide variety of services, including cabins and land and water taxi services (see Information Resources pages 33–35).

THE TRAIL

Unless you plan to stop at Tonsina Creek (which is less than 2 miles in), remember to arrive at the trailhead one to two hours before low tide. From the upper parking area trailhead, the path starts on a series of gravel road segments (follow the signs to the trail) and climbs 1.5 miles up through an alder and spruce forest onto a hillside between Spruce Creek and Tonsina Creek. Here, you can still see evidence of the flooding that occurred during a massive 2006 rain.

The trail then drops rapidly through a spruce forest into the drainage and out onto the gravel delta of Tonsina Creek. The creek has two outlets separated by about one-quarter mile of wonderful open-under-story hemlock forest. There's a terrific driftwood-strewn beach, as well as beach camping in among coastal grasses (look for gorgeous wild irises here) between the two outlets. From the beach, you have some spectacular views across Resurrection Bay to the glaciers residing in the high cirque valleys on the north side of the bay. This is a great destination in itself and an opportunity to turn around after a nice hike. Tonsina Creek is also a nice stopover if you didn't arrive close enough to low tide to cross it.

The bridge over the first Tonsina Creek channel is intact. The 2006 flood wiped out the second bridge, which the State Park is planning to rebuild in 2008. If the bridge is not repaired when you arrive, simply follow the stream channel down to the beach and make your crossing where it fans out across its delta at Resurrection Bay.

From the Tonsina Creek area, hike two and one-half miles along a steep gravel and cobble beach to Derby Cove. If you are a rock skipper you have just entered heaven, as the beaches surrounding Resurrection Bay are covered with fabulous rock-skipping stones. The slate and shist metamorphic rocks weather into flat, cobble-sized pieces that have just the right heft and dimension for skipping. There is also good fishing from these beaches for salmon and Dolly Varden.

There are public-use fee cabins at Callisto Canyon and Derby Cove, the latter of which is a terrific base of operations for hikes to North Beach, Fort McGilvray, South Beach, or the Caines Head Alpine Trail (Hike 18). The weather around Seward is often rainy and windy, particularly close to shore, so the cabin is a nice perk on a multiday visit to the Caines Head area (see Information Resources for cabin reservations).

From Derby Cove, you head up and over a small headland one-quarter mile to North Beach, which is a good base for campers, with shelters for cooking so you're not stuck in your tent all the time. The trail continues down to Fort McGilvray and South Beach, splitting 1 mile south of North Beach. Take the left trail 1 more mile down to Fort McGilvray; take the right trail 1.5 miles to South Beach.

Fort McGilvray was built during World War II to protect Seward from invasion. There are all sorts of things to investigate here, including gun emplacements, an old rotting pier, and the old fort itself. If you

Enjoy spectacular views across Resurrection Bay into the northern Kenai Mountains

Caines Head

plan to nose around, I suggest bringing a flashlight and wearing your raingear.

South Beach is my favorite beach on this hike because it's the most isolated, stormy, and wild. I love to just hang out here all bundled up in my fleece and raingear and watch the goings-on out on the open south end of Resurrection Bay. The marine wildlife around Caines Head is spectacular—otters, porpoises, seals, sea lions, and whales. Killer whales are commonly seen in close, as well as out in deeper water, and humpbacks can often be seen from the beaches. If you are a birder, you've also come to the right place. You will likely see murrelets, cormorants, oystercatchers, and a variety of ducks, guillemots, eagles, and even puffins.

If you have extra time to linger, plan to stay another day or two and explore the highcountry that you can access via the Caines Head Alpine Trail (Hike 18). Though your hiking access to Caines Head is tidally controlled, there are two other alternative methods of reaching Derby Cove and beyond. Miller's Landing offers very reasonably priced water taxi rides to and from Derby Cove and points south. You can also paddle a kayak (your own or a rental) to remove your dependence on the tides. The kayak paddle along the west shore of Resurrection Bay is delightful.

SPECIAL NOTES
While it's certainly possible to do Caines Head as a day hike, you would have a very long day because of the tidal restrictions for passing along the beach between Tonsina Creek and Derby Cove. Plus, one day just doesn't give you time to enjoy North and South beaches, explore the fort, and take a hike up the Caines Head Alpine Trail (Hike 18), which you absolutely must do. So plan on making this an overnight affair, and I really actually recommend two nights. One other thing to keep in mind as you hang out along the coastline of Caines Head is that it wasn't too long ago—just a few thousand years—that all of Resurrection Bay was filled with a massive glacier that carved and filled the channel of the bay and poured ice out into the Gulf of Alaska. Imagine the size of the icebergs that must have been calving into the gulf and choking it up—cool, huh?

18

Caines Head Alpine

Total distance: 3 miles plus (one way)

Hiking time: 2 to 4 hours (one way)

Elevation change: Over 2,000 feet

Rating: Moderate

Best season: July and August

Maps: Kenai Fjords National Park by National Geographic Trails Illustrated; USGS Seward A-7 (SW and SE) and Blying Sound D-7; Alaska State Parks Brochure Caines Head State Recreation Area

Special features: Easy and rapid access to alpine tundra and spectacular, sweeping views of Resurrection Bay. Note: Be sure to bring your camera and binoculars.

One good reason to visit the Caines Head Recreation Area is to take the terrific Caine Head Alpine Trail. This hike provides quick access to delicious views of the alpine and marine environments of Resurrection Bay. The Caines Head Trail (Hike 17) covers the hike down to the trailhead for this alpine trail, which is really an extension of that other hike. They are treated as separate hikes in this book, however, because they cover very different ground, with the Caines Head Trail being beach and water-oriented and this one climbing high in the hills.

GETTING THERE

Follow the Seward Highway south into Seward and continue on Third Avenue through town to the T intersection. Turn right onto Railway Avenue, which becomes Lowell Point Road, and go 2 miles south along the edge of Resurrection Bay to Martins Road. Turn right and drive 0.1 mile to the trailhead. There are two parking areas—one upper and one lower, each with restroom facilities. The trail starts from the upper one. If you are camping, either tent or RV, you can also stay close to the trailhead at Millers Landing (see Information Resources pages 33–35).

It is best to arrive at the trailhead two hours before low tide, so you can reach the coastal beach between Tonsina Creek and Derby Cove near low tide. Tides must be at +3 feet or below in order to hike this section of beach. You could also kayak down the west side of Resurrection Bay to Derby Cove or North Beach, which allows you to

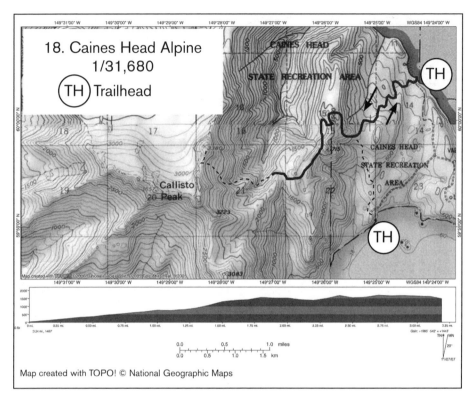

18. Caines Head Alpine
1/31,680
(TH) Trailhead

Map created with TOPO! © National Geographic Maps

avoid the tide issue near Tonsina Creek.

Please see Hike 17, Caines Head Trail, for instructions on hiking to North Beach, where this trail begins. A clearly visible sign posted about 0.25 mile north of North Beach marks the trailhead for the Caines Head Alpine Trail.

THE TRAIL

Like the Summit Creek (Hike 6) and the Hope Point (Hike 3) trails, the Caines Head Alpine Trail is underappreciated and underused. The first 1.5 miles run through a beautiful, dense, cool spruce-dominated forest with big trees and several stream crossings and waterfalls. The trail climbs steadily, but a series of switchbacks keep the gradient at a reasonable level. Large hemlocks become more common as you climb. Soon the forest drops away and views open up as you hike

first through wildflower grasslands and then open alpine tundra. The spectacular scenery includes not only Resurrection Bay and its many beautiful islands, but all the high, glaciated peaks of the Resurrection Peninsula and a whole series of separate, identifiable, named glaciers including Prospect, Spoon, and Porcupine. You can also see well out into the Gulf of Alaska. As you climb higher, you have great views on this side of the bay of Callisto Peak, Callisto Canyon, and the whole Caines Head area. If you haven't brought your camera and binoculars, shame on you.

The trail continues on, though less distinct, above tree line, and follows a series of cairns (rock piles set up as obvious trail markers) up toward the base of Callisto Peak. This is a lovely section of open alpine terrain drained by small streams and dot-

Caines Head Alpine Trail provides sweeping views of surrounding mountains, glaciers, and sky

ted with tiny glacial tarns (small glacially formed lakes). If you enjoy macro photography this is an easy place to set up and photograph the tundra.

If you have the time, energy, and inclination, there is another great prize to be won: a spectacular view of mammoth Bear Glacier, with its vast system of crevasses and recessional moraines (sediment ridges deposited by retreating glaciers), as well as the terrain to the southeast just over the ridgeline that leads down from Callisto. There is no trail or system of cairns to guide you, but you should be able to see to the ridgeline. Just pick a path across the tundra and head to it. Whenever you can, step on rocks to protect the fragile soil and vegetation. If you have a compass or GPS you can shoot a bearing to your destination, and then just follow the back bearing on your return route to the top of the Alpine Trail.

SPECIAL NOTES

You can also hike up onto the Caines Head Alpine Trail from South Beach. A pleasant 1.5-mile access trail from there intersects this trail about 1.25 miles up from the North Beach trailhead. In fact, you can use this South Beach access to turn the Caines Head Alpine Trail into a loop trail. Hike up this trail from North Beach and noodle around the alpine zone as long as you like. When you are ready to continue the loop, hike back down to the intersection with the South Beach access trail. Take this trail to South Beach, where you rejoin the Caines Head Trail. Hike back along the main trail to the intersection with the Fort McGilvray turnoff and then head back to North Beach. All these hiking opportunities represent one more reason why you need to stay more than a single day at Caines Head.

If you have limited time and want to concentrate on hiking the Caines Head Alpine

Trail's high alpine tundra country, you might consider taking a water taxi or paddling a kayak from either Miller's or the state beach located near the parking areas. For where to rent kayaks, see Information Resources pages 33–35. If you have a bit more time and enjoy the coast, hike or kayak to one of the cabins, or tent camp, near Derby Cove. Then use your cabin or tent site as your base camp. From there, you can head up the Caines Head Alpine Trail with a day pack and roam less encumbered.

III. Central Kenai

19

Hideout

Total distance: 1.5 miles round trip

Hiking time: 1 to 3 hours

Elevation change: 850 feet

Rating: Moderate

Best season: Late May through September although best views are in September color season.

Maps: Kenai National Wildlife Refuge by National Geographic Trails Illustrated; Alaska Road and Recreation Map; Kenai Lake and Vicinity USGS Kenai B-1 (NW)

Special features: Best bang-for-the-hiking buck in the Skilak Lake area. Within a scant 0.75 mile and 850 feet of elevation rise, you are gifted with spectacular, sweeping 300° views of the undulating, milky lower Kenai River and its valley, Skilak Lake, the Skilak River delta fed by the Skilak Glacier, the Kenai Mountains east of Skilak Lake and even the flats of the Kenai Peninsula. Across Skilak Lake, you can see the Harding Ice Field.

This is my favorite hike in the Skilak Lake area because I can access such terrific views in short order. I often stop here on my trips between my home in Homer and Anchorage or Seward when I want a quick hiking and view fix! To quote Nancy Lasater, who was visiting from Washington DC, "The panorama from the top of Hideout Trail is alone worth the ticket from the lower 48." This is a great view trail for a family to take even with kids six or seven years old.

GETTING THERE

The Hideout trailhead is located on Skilak Lake between the Hidden Creek trailhead (Hike 21) and the Skilak Lookout trailhead (Hike 22) 0.8 mile southeast of the intersection of the north end of Skilak Lake Road and the Sterling Highway. There is a small pullout on the south (lake) side of the road, enough for two or three vehicles. Note: There are no facilities at this trailhead. Also there is no water along this trail, so be sure to bring water with you and don't forget your mosquito repellent.

THE TRAIL

The trailhead is on the north side of the road, opposite the parking turnout. It begins with a moderate climb through an open-canopy forest of mature spruce, large cottonwoods, aspens, and some alders. Grasslands carpet the area between the well-spaced trees and offer a near-continuous riot of wildflowers dominated by the fuschia spires of fireweed along with purple monkshood, bright yellow yarrow, red Indian paintbrush, and

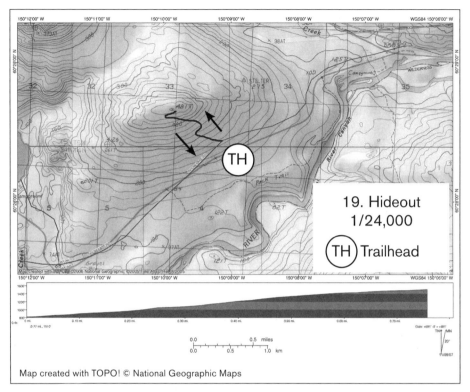

Map created with TOPO! © National Geographic Maps

tall violet larkspur. Unlike many trails that require you to hike some distance before granting any serious views, this one offers wonderful scenery south over Skilak Lake country within just a few minutes. The trailside wildflowers provide a nice foreground, too, for all the pictures you will immediately be snapping.

The great views here are a function of two things: one, the topography, which the trail planners used in choosing this superb location, building a path up a mound that rises in the center of everything, with breathtaking views all around; and two, the convenient natural lack of much tall vegetation along the trail, which means you don't have to wait until things open up at the top before you can see the clouds, glaciers, mountains, lake, river, and river delta. This is truly the view of a lifetime.

Nature helped with the lack of vegetation. Notice the many charred, charcoaled snags (dead tree trunks) that dot these lower slopes. This area forms the northwestern edge of the 7,900-acre 1991 Pothole Fire. Eventually the forest will return to these lower slopes, but until it does we get to enjoy more of the view!

The gasping panorama continues all the way to the top of the trail. Along the upper slopes, you will see larger spruce, alder and cottonwood trees not affected by the fire. These are part of the old-growth forest that exists in stands along the upper portion. "Old-growth" means these trees have never been logged. They are likely 150+ years old. An example of an old-growth forest in the Lower 48 is the Redwood Forest in California. They are exceedingly rare and becoming more so

---

Hideout

every day. Be reverent as you walk through this living history.

The views stay open as you climb due to the steeper slopes, higher elevation, and exposure to winds. As you hike, the southern aspect expands to include even more of the Kenai Mountains and the north end of Skilak Lake, as well as more glimpses of the meandering Kenai River and its forested valley.

The trail maintains its moderate uphill slope across several long, lazy switchbacks over rocks, then breaks out to cross grassy, sunny meadows open to the sky. You can almost hear the Von Trapp family singing as they swing picnic baskets . . . oh, that's you! The path ends at a rock outcrop overview, from which you can see down into these same meadows and track the progress of the rest of your party coming up. The top is achieved after only 0.75 mile and at only 850 feet above where you've started. You haven't scaled Denali, but it feels good, and the children you're with will thrill with accomplishment.

At the top, do what I did the last time–sit and mentally memorize the entire arcing view. When you're back home in traffic, you'll be able to conjure it up and take a deep breath because your soul will be back in Alaska. There is plenty of room to spread out at the top in order to do this. The views are simply amazing, especially in the fall when all the colors are at their peak and the low-angle sunlight bathes the landscape in a blanket of soft, warm yellow light. This place looks like the painting God made for His living room, above His sofa.

Enjoy sweeping views of the Skilak Lake country from the perch at Hideout lookout

SPECIAL NOTES

Standing at the Hideout lookout above the rounded lowland topography, you can easily imagine all the mountain valleys to the south being filled to overflowing with alpine glaciers. You can further imagine how all the alpine glaciers merged at the bottom of the landscape to form larger ice sheets that flowed over all the lowlands before carving and wearing them down as they ground slowly by. When they retreated not so long ago, these ice sheets left behind the beautiful rounded topography you see before you today.

If you look due east, left of Skilak Lake, across the lower valley of the Kenai River, you will see the twin peaks of Russian and Bear mountains. In the high alpine gulf between them, you will see the near perfect U shape so characteristic of glacier-carved valleys.

20

Kenai River

Total distance: 6 to 8 miles round trip

Hiking time: 4 to 6 hours

Elevation change: 250 feet

Rating: Easy

Best season: May through October

Maps: Kenai National Wildlife Refuge by National Geographic Trails Illustrated; Alaska Road and Recreation Map; Kenai Lake and Vicinity USGS Kenai B-1 (NW)

Special features: Easy hike through woods and meadows along the beautiful Kenai River and its gorge.

This is an easy 3- to 4-mile one-way hike along the Kenai River in the Skilak Lake area. The Kenai, with its famous milky aquamarine water and rapids, is a real gem, and there are fascinating views into the Kenai River Canyon.

GETTING THERE

Drive 0.7 mile south from the eastern intersection of the Sterling Highway and Skilak Lake Road. Turn left on the gravel road at 0.2 mile and head down to the river and the start of the trail. An additional 1.7 miles down Skilak Lake Road, at mile 2.4, is another trailhead with a 0.5-mile access spur to the Kenai River Trail, but the first trailhead is much easier. There are bathroom facilities here as well as a parking lot big enough to accommodate large RVs and turn them around.

THE TRAIL

The starting elevation of this trail is about 300 feet on the banks of the Kenai River, and you will be hiking southwest more or less parallel to the Kenai as it flows toward Skilak Lake. The first 0.4 mile takes you along a short dirt road to the beginning of the trail and a bluff overlook of the Kenai River Canyon. Here the river has carved a deep channel into poorly consolidated tertiary sedimentary rocks and their cap of glacial sentiments. "Poorly consolidated" means they aren't stuck together very well, and tertiary sedimentary rocks are rocks that are only a few million years old, much younger

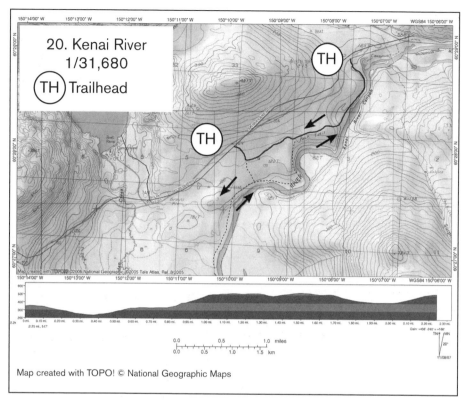

Map created with TOPO! © National Geographic Maps

than the rocks that make up most of the mountains.

This overlook is a great place to see the canyon and the aquamarine water and rapids. From here the trail descends to the river, where you can enjoy the pebble and cobble streambed. (A cobble is about the size of your palm.) Head up and away from the river channel across rolling forested hills, partly charred by the 7,900-acre Pothole Fire that burned through here in 1991. In the unburned sections, you are hiking primarily through spruce, cottonwood, birch, and aspen trees. The burned sections afford broader views across the river valley and slopes. Acres of wildflowers grow in the grass and brushlands that are regaining a foothold around the silvered snags and stumps left by the fire.

About a mile into the hike, the trail splits into a 2.5-mile loop section. Take the left path to go back toward the river, where you can see a section of rapids. The right-hand path takes you away from the river to open meadows and across another section of the burn area. These two segments of the loop trail join back up about one-half mile downriver. (A small section of the one-half mile, west-side access trail from the second trailhead completes the loop of these two sections.) You might want to hike along the river on the way out and take the middle section on the way back.

After you leave the small loop trail behind, the path continues for another mile or so downstream. Exiting the Kenai River Canyon, it drops down to the water again.

There is no distinct end to this hike,

Early winter view of Kenai River Canyon

50 Hikes in Alaska's Kenai Peninsula

which slowly peters out into fishing trails along the river. There are many good resting and lunch stops along the entire hike, so take your pick. Keep your eyes open for the plentiful moose and black bear, as well as eagles and a variety of water birds, including terns and gulls. If you have two vehicles, you could park one at each trailhead and finish at the second one to avoid hiking all the way back upriver to your starting point. If you would like to further minimize your slight elevation gain, you can start at the west trailhead, which is about 200 feet higher than the east one.

SPECIAL NOTES

The Kenai River and Kenai Lake are famous for their distinct blue green color, which results from the interaction of superfine particles, called rock flour, with sunlight. This rock flour is glacial in origin, formed by rocks and sediment grinding together as the glaciers move. It is also the smallest known sedimentary particle. In fact, they're so small they remain suspended–and interact with sunlight–even in still water. There is a continual supply of rock flour from the melting and retreating glaciers that feed the Kenai River system.

The Pothole Fire that burned through this area in May 1991 opened up some pretty spectacular vistas along this trail and other nearby trails such as the Skilak Lookout (Hike 22) and Hideout Trail (Hike 19) that were previously unavailable. It also reset the sequence of local ecological succession, so as you hike along this trail, particularly the loop portion that heads away from the river, you are gifted with a wide variety of colonizing grasses and flowers like fireweed, lupine, wild geranium, rose, and other early succession pioneers. Without the fire, this same ground would now be host to tall trees rather than these youngster plants.

This trail is also accessible in the winter by hiking and snowshoeing. The forested sections of the Kenai Gorge are especially beautiful all covered with snow. The Kenai River itself takes on an entirely different, artistic character when it is rimmed and partially covered with ice.

21

Hidden Creek

Total distance: 1.5 miles (one way)

Hiking time: 1 to 2 hours, or all day if you hang out at the lake

Elevation change: 200 feet

High point: 500 feet at trailhead

Rating: Easy, suitable for families with young children

Best season: Year-round, snowshoes in winter

Maps: Kenai National Wildlife Refuge by National Geographic Trails Illustrated; Alaska Road and Recreation Map; Kenai Lake and Vicinity USGS Kenai B-1 (NW)

Special features: A guaranteed positive outdoor experience for youngsters along a secluded section of Skilak Lake.

This short little gem of a trail offers one of the few accesses to Skilak Lake without a roadway.

GETTING THERE

Drive 4.7 miles south on Skilak Lake Road from the east intersection of the Sterling Highway. The trailhead for the Hidden Lake Trail is on your left.

THE TRAIL

The path heads gradually down and away from the trailhead through an open-canopy aspen, birch, spruce, and cottonwood forest typical of this area. Much of the middle portion of the trail is through a section burned by the 1991 Pothole Fire, which offers views to the east of the Kenai Mountains. As you can see, the burned sections show evidence of much new growth, where young spruce trees already are sprouting among the charred snags (dead tree trunks) along with wildflowers such as fireweed and bushes of alder and young aspen trees all making a comeback after the fire.

At about 1 mile the trail splits, with the left (east) and slightly longer section heading off toward Hidden Creek. It leads though the wetlands surrounding the lower portion of Hidden Creek and eventually leads to Skilak Lake as well.

The right section travels more directly down to Skilak Lake one-half mile away, re-entering unburned woods as you near the lake. The real prize awaits you at the water. You stand on the small gravel delta of Hidden Creek and enjoy sweeping views of

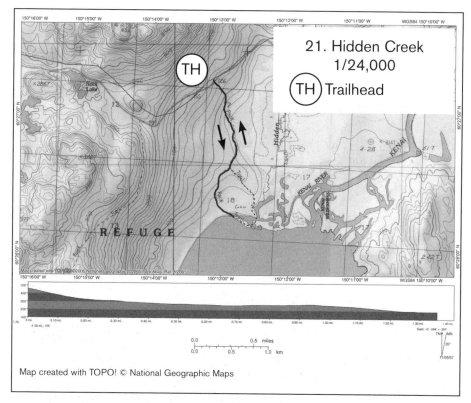

the east end of Skilak Lake and the Kenai Mountains beyond. You can also see and visit the mouth and delta of the Kenai River. If you're an angler, that may well be where you want to go.

Perhaps the greatest prize of all is the access this trail provides to the shoreline west of Hidden Creek along Skilak Lake. The real hiking and exploring begins at the mouth of the creek. Hike west along the shoreline for as long as you like. You could literally spend the entire day exploring along Skilak Lake. The lake's beach offers good hiking and treasure hunting, and there are many picnicking and camping sites along the shore, as well as plenty of driftwood.

If you look to the west as you stand on the beach, the high knoll you see on the north side of the lake in the middle distance is the lookout point of the Skilak Lake Lookout Trail (Hike 22).

SPECIAL NOTES

If you have visited Skilak Lake before and have wished for an easy lake access that was devoid of motorized vehicles, both wheeled and ruddered, then the Hidden Creek Trail is your wish come true. But be aware that the shore of the lake is likely to be windy, even if the parking lot isn't. Winds continually blow up off the Kenai Mountains and their glaciers from east to west across the lake, so be sure to bring a sweater and windbreaker, and even a hat and gloves if the weather is cool. If you have children or elderly companions, they will thank you.

The burned sections with their mix of

plant types and old and new growth provide an excellent opportunity to discuss ecological succession with children. You can show how the fire has killed the individual trees but not the forest. The forest soil is supporting growth of pioneering plant species such as the fireweed and alders as well as the beginnings of the next generation of the spruce and aspen forest.

As long as the trailhead is accessible, this trail is also great in the winter and a good location for snowshoeing. The snow-covered trees at the beginning and end of the trail create a beautiful winter wonderland effect. The snowy, ice-covered beach offers many natural ice sculpture treasures. Bring hot dogs and build a driftwood fire on the beach while you enjoy the views of Skilak Lake country in the winter. This makes a wonderful winter wilderness outing not too far from the trailhead.

Dramatic views of the surrounding high Kenai Mountain peaks from Hidden Creek Trail

22

Skilak Lookout & Bear Mountain

Total distance: 2.5 miles one way to Skilak Lookout; 0.8 mile one way to Bear Mountain

Hiking time: 2 to 4 hours

Elevation change: 750 feet, Skilak Lookout; 500 feet, Bear Mountain

Rating: Moderate

Best season: May through October

Maps: Kenai National Wildlife Refuge by National Geographic Trails Illustrated; Alaska Road and Recreation Map; Kenai Lake and Vicinity USGS Kenai B-1 (NW)

Special features: Both knobs are composed of resistant rock types that weren't worn down as much as the surrounding rocks when this whole area was covered by grinding glaciers. Skilak Lake Overview in particular offers stunning views across all of Skilak Lake country . . . bring your binoculars.

I have grouped these two trails together because they are similar in nature and close geographically. Skilak Lake Road leads to both of these short but vigorous hikes to summits with sweeping views–360-degree in the case of the Skilak Overlook–of the Skilak Lake area.

GETTING THERE

Turn south off the Sterling Highway at mile 58 onto Skilak Lake Road. The Skilak Lookout trailhead is on the south side of the road at 5.5 miles. There is a parking area on the opposite (north) side of the road that can accommodate up to 10 vehicles including small RVs. The Bear Mountain trailhead and parking is at mile 6 on your right, in a small pull-off on the same (north) side of the road from Rock Lake (an easy to locate landmark).

SKILAK LOOKOUT TRAIL

The trail begins by crossing a small stream channel flowing through a small section of spruce and birch forest. After only about 100 meters, the trail breaks out into the open as it begins to traverse a large fire-scarred section created by the 1991 Pothole Fire. Here, the trail begins and maintains for a while a moderate slope that levels out to a more gradual climb through the midsection.

You're hiking mostly through open (that is, no-canopy) forest with only silvery fire-scarred snags (dead tree trunks), which are often quite beautiful in their own way.

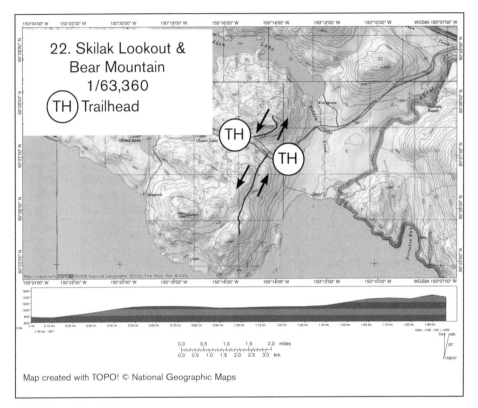

22. Skilak Lookout & Bear Mountain
1/63,360
(TH) Trailhead

Map created with TOPO! © National Geographic Maps

These snags are all that remain from the prefire forest. Notice you are now hiking through young, replacement willows, aspens, and alders. One of the fire's benefits to us is a much more open view of the surrounding countryside.

Another fire benefit is the multitude of wildflowers, including fireweed, lupine, and wild roses, as well as raspberries and mountain ash berries. If you have hiked the Hidden Lake Trail, the lower half of this trail is very similar. There are some boggy areas but most are crossed by way of raised wooded boardwalks.

Where there are berries, there are bears, so keep a sharp eye out for our ursine cousins.

About one-half mile from the summit, the trail steepens again. The going gets

a bit rough, with plenty of roots and some wet areas, so watch your step. Hiking poles help. Higher up on the trail you will encounter a few stands of large old-growth spruce trees that escaped the fire. These offer some respite from the climb on hot days with some shade and coolness.

The best views along the trail and from the summit are toward the south and east across Skilak Lake. You also have excellent views of the Kenai and Skilak rivers. The Skilak is fed directly by Skilak Glacier, which flows down from the Harding Ice Field in the upper reaches of the Kenai Mountains.

Notice the huge gravel delta and the braided Skilak River channels. The massive, wide, gravel channel that you see from here was left behind by the retreating

Skilak glacier, now far upstream having retreated into its alpine homeland. During periods of high glacier runoff, this channel can be filled with water from bank to bank. These huge flows were more common thousands of years ago, when the glacier was larger and farther down the valley. Such volume is less common now, but not unheard of. At lower flows, the multiple channels weave their way across and down the wide gravel riverbed to empty their load of glacial sediments and water into Skilak Lake. The coarser sediments drop out early to form the river delta, which continues to grow today.

Looking back to the north, you can see the alpine country of the Fuller Lakes Trail (Hike 25). You also have a nice clear, high-angle view of the Hidden Creek country, including the Hidden Creek Delta, crossed by the Hidden Creek Trail (Hike 21). The higher you climb, the better the views. At the high knob, which is the end of the trail and forms the Skilak Overview, and which is composed of resistant metamorphic rocks (layered gneisses), you have a 360-degree panoramic view of the Skilak Lake country and even all the way across Cook Inlet to the Alaska Peninsula.

There are several places to sit in order to take in the view. If the wind is blowing, there are some protected nooks as well. You will be glad if you brought your binoculars . . . you can devote a lot of time to scanning Skilak country close-up from up here.

The Bear Mountain Trail is about half the length and half the climb and altitude

Sweeping panoramas of Skilak Lake country greet you at the end of the Skilak Lookout Trail

Skilak Lookout & Bear Mountain

of the Skilak Lookout Hike. This trail is mostly through unburned forest with large spruce and birch trees along its entire length. Larger cottonwood trees up higher in some of the moister environments. So if you are looking for a short forest hike that offers some big birch trees and some good views at the top, this is a good hike to consider. You will find some maps, including the one at the kiosk at the trailhead showing the Bear Mountain Trail circling the top of the mountain. It should—it would certainly expand the view and make this an even better hike—but it does not actually circle the mountain.

This trail climbs steadily with intermittent lower-slope segments. The more mature forest offers a cooler, more shaded climb than the Skilak Lookout Hike, but it does not provide the same along-the-trail viewing opportunities. Overall this trail is steeper than the Skilak and Hideout trails, but the footing is generally good.

The hike ends abruptly at a granite outcrop, which provides excellent views of the Kenai River country and its delta from a different perspective than you have from the Skilak Overlook Trail. Both views are glorious. The Bear Mountain viewpoint, however, does not offer the same panorama as the Skilak Overlook and Hideout trails.

SPECIAL NOTES

Of the two hikes described here, the Skilak Lookout View offers better views. The Bear Mountain Trail offers more forest hiking. You could try the Bear Mountain Hike if you don't have the time for the Skilak Overview Hike. But an even better choice than the Bear Mountain Hike is the Hideout Trail (Hike 19) that is even shorter and offers finer vistas.

If you are looking for some good family hikes that can be traversed by children as young as six, the quartet of Hideout, Hidden Creek, Bear Mountain, and Skilak Lookout, in that order, would make a nice, progressive sequence in terms of length and difficulty.

23

Seven Lakes

Total distance: 4.5 miles one way

Hiking time: 2.5 to 3 hours, plus 1 to 2 hours for Hidden Lake side hike

Elevation change: 400 feet

Rating: Easy

Best season: All seasons, snowshoes in winter

Maps: Kenai National Wildlife Refuge by National Geographic Trails Illustrated; Alaska Road and Recreation Map; Kenai Lake and Vicinity USGS Kenai B-1 (NW)

Special features: Quintessential Kenai National Wildlife Refuge lowland lakes habitat with untold kinds and numbers of birds, as well as a splendid home to moose.

This is an easy lowland traverse that visits four glacially formed lakes: Kelly, Hikers, Hidden, and Engineer. Okay, so where are the other three lakes on this Seven Lakes Trail? They are north of the Sterling Highway along the no-longer-maintained trail extension (and therefore not part of this hike) that existed before the highway was constructed, back when the Skilak Lake Loop Road was the only roadway.

GETTING THERE

You can drive to either end of this trail, and it's a pretty short drive to stash a second vehicle at the far end so you can hike one way rather than doubling back on yourself when you're done. The Kelly Lake access is located at mile 69 on the Sterling Highway, approximately 10 miles west of the intersection with the east end of Skilak Lake Road. Since Skilak Lake Road intersects the Sterling Highway at two points many miles apart, and since the trail access is just off the Sterling Highway between these two distant points, it can also be said that the Kelly Lake turn-off is 6.2 miles east of the west intersection of these roads. I've included both in order to guide you no matter where you're coming from. Turn south off the highway at the sign for Kelly and Peterson lakes and drive for about 0.7 mile through a spruce and aspen forest along a good gravel road, following the left fork at 0.4 mile to Kelly Lake. The trail begins by the boat launch area.

To access the other trailhead at the Engineer Lake end of the trail, drive about

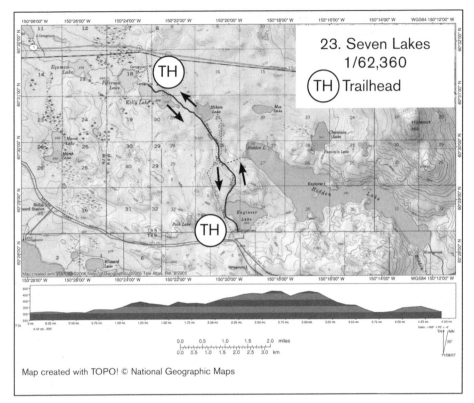

Map created with TOPO! © National Geographic Maps

9.5 miles from either junction (it just happened to be midway along the Skilak Lake Road) with the Sterling Highway and Skilak Lake Road. Then turn north and continue for 0.3 mile to the Engineer Lake trailhead.

There are toilet facilities, drinking water, and camping facilities at all three lakes—Kelly, Peterson, and Engineer—as well as boat ramps at all three.

THE TRAIL

The trail crosses lowland forests of mostly spruce and aspen. The four lakes—Kelly, Hikers, Hidden, and Engineer—are fairly equally spaced and appear in that order from north to south along the trail, with a bit more separation between Hikers and Hidden. Starting from Kelly, the trail follows the north side of the lake. In the fall, the con-

trast between the bluish dark green of the spruce and the deep saturated gold of the aspen is striking. Look for toothy evidence of beavers being busy along the trail. Wood boardwalks keep you above the moist muskeg (marshy bogs) and over a few stream channels. As you walk, listen to your boots pounding in the silence.

From the east end of Kelly, you will hike away from the lake up and over a slight rise across ancient glacial moraine deposits, then through the spruce forest providing nice views back toward the water. The higher morainal ridges, deposited by the glaciers that not long ago covered this area, support larger aspen and birch. These glacial sediment ridges provide the better-drained soils favored by these trees and a bit of distance from the maraud-

Stately aspen and birch trees basking in low-angle sunlight against crystal-clear skies

ing beavers. The spruces fare well in the moister areas closer to the lakes.

About one-quarter mile from Kelly, you pass the south shore of Hikers Lake as you hike on the slope above the lake. There are several side trails taking you down to the water.

Midway along the trail, and about halfway between Hidden and Hikers, you find yourself on a low ridgeline, the remains of the now-obscure glacial moraine. This slightly elevated vantage point offers 360-degree views through the aspens and the best photo opportunities in the area, with good views of Hidden Lake over the tops of the trees. You will likely also see bear and moose sign along the trail.

Soon after this low ridge, you encounter a little-used, one-half-mile side trail that heads east to a dead end at Hidden Lake. If you want a lake all to yourself, except for the moose, of course, then take this side trail, which continues from the Hidden Lake turnoff toward Engineer through spruce, aspen, and birch forests across both slightly elevated dryer sections and lower boggy areas that offer a most delightful journey, especially in the autumn. Finally, about one-third mile from the end, you come to the northwest corner of Engineer Lake. The last segment of the trail follows first along the western end of Engineer and then rises slightly to the parking area south of this third lake.

SPECIAL NOTES

My favorite time to hike here is in the fall, when the aspen trees have all turned gold, and they contrast so beautifully with the dark green spruce, especially in the low light of early morning and evening. All this creates a spectacular visual playground if you're a photographer.

This trail may be one of the most accessible wildlife areas you've ever visited, with moose, bears, and wolves all plentiful. Bring binoculars to extend your viewing range significantly and watch wildlife up close while at a safe distance. If you are a birder, you'll think you've died and gone to heaven. The list of birds here is astounding—loons, cranes, scoters, terns, and a wide variety of other water-loving members of the avian community.

If you want to hang around for a few days, there are campsites at all the lakes except Hidden. Fall is also the best season for camping, as the mosquitoes are far less rampant than in the summer.

As you hike through the forested uplands, keep a sharp eye out for narrow, elongated ridges, known as eskers, which are built-up sediment deposits from streams running underneath the glaciers that once flowed over this land. Interesting isn't it that the glaciers left deposits called moraine sediments, and that the streams running beneath them did too, and that each distinctively shapes the landscape? The retreat of the glaciers and their underlying streams left behind all the rocky ridges that divide the lakes.

24

Skyline Trail & Alpine Traverse

Total distance: 1 to 1.5 miles for Skyline; 9 to 9.5 miles for the Traverse to Upper Fuller Lake

Hiking time: 1.5 to 2 hours one way for Skyline, 8 to 10 hours for the Traverse

Elevation change: Over 2,300 feet to the Skyline saddle, 3,300 feet to peak 3520 on the Traverse

Rating: Difficult for both Skyline and the Alpine Traverse

Best season: June through August

Maps: Kenai National Wildlife Refuge by National Geographic Trails Illustrated; Alaska Road and Recreation Map; Kenai Lake and Vicinity USGS Kenai B-1 (NW)

Special features: Rapid access to astounding views from the alpine zone in the middle of the Mystery Creek section of the Kenai Wilderness. Special note: Be sure to bring plenty of water on this steep, thirst-producing hike, as there is no water along the trail until you reach a spring near the top.

This is a short, steep, thigh-busting hike —2,000 feet in 1 mile—to a glorious vista. The Skyline Trail is perhaps the fastest way to the alpine zone on the Kenai, and the views from the top are legendary. Do not attempt this hike unless you are fit. Even the slowest pace won't change the straight-up elevation.

GETTING THERE

The Skyline trailhead is located northwest of the Sterling Highway at mile 61. Pull off and park on the south side of the road then cross to reach the trailhead 100 meters to the west.

THE TRAIL

The trail begins at around 200 feet in elevation and heads northwest steeply up the fall line (the steepest slope downhill) through an open-canopy spruce forest on the southeast slope and ridgeline of the Mystery Hills.

As you start the trail, you immediately cross into the northeast sector of the Kenai Wilderness area, which is renowned for its roadless remoteness and unspoiled terrain. You continue climbing along switchbacks under spruces and some good-sized cottonwood, aspen, and birch trees interspersed with grasses, elderberry bushes, and fireweed. The trail is very steep so keep your body weight out away from the earth of the trail. It's counter-intuitive, I know. We all want to lean into the hillside to maintain our balance, and it's especially what we naturally do when we are winded,

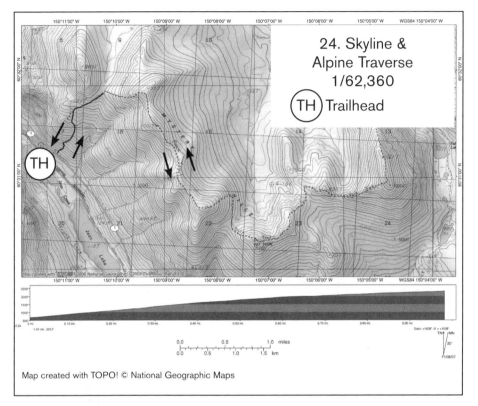

Map created with TOPO! © National Geographic Maps

but leaning outward as you climb actually helps you maintain good frictional contact with the slope. You are pressing your body weight down through your feet into the hillside, rather than causing yourself to slide parallel with it.

Look east for good glimpses of Long Lake through the trees as you hike. The dark rocks you see outcropping along the trail are ancient volcanic rocks that have been cooked for eons below the surface under high heat and intense pressure to become metamorphic rocks, which then got shoved up by Mother Nature. Look closely for patterns of smooth-surfaced striations on some of the rock faces. These are called slikensides (it's German) and are fault surfaces along which the movement of these gigantic boulders occurred.

So much heat is generated by this movement that the rocks actually melt and reform, creating the super-smooth surface. The direction of striation lines shows the direction of the movement.

Because the trail runs up a sundrenched south-facing slope, conditions are generally dry and clear with good footing. At about one-half mile, the trail turns left (west) for a couple hundred yards as it crosses down into and through a stream channel, and then heads right to resume its northwesterly course up the ridgeline. The trail can be a bit muddy. As you gain the tree line, you are hiking through beautiful groves of aspen as well as small stands of spruce and willow. And delightfully, you can feast on the many blueberry bushes that greet you at the tree line and above.

Your only competition is the bears, who also love them.

After about 1 mile and 2,000 feet of elevation gain, the trail levels out some as you reach a saddle between two peaks along the ridge in the western half of the Mystery Hills. (There is no real, distinct end to the trail, and you can continue to climb up into the Mystery Hills to elevations approaching 3,000 feet.) Near the top of the trail as you gain the saddle area, there is a copse of mountain hemlock trees whose tops have been flattened by the wind that blows pretty constantly through this saddle pass. Duck in under the hemlock canopy to find a nice protected resting/camping area. This would serve as a good base camp before assaulting the high peaks traverse farther above you.

June and July are the best months for wildflowers. Look for lupine, wild geranium, woolly lousewort, wild rose, and the state flower of Alaska, forget-me-nots.

As you hike back down the Skyline Trail, be sure to extend and use your hiking poles. Two are much better than one. Reach forward with your poles to keep your weight forward and into the slope to help prevent you from slipping on the steep and often muddy inclines. The use of the poles will help save your knees as well.

Once up in the alpine zone, you can move cross-country in just about any direction. The trail continues on through the saddle and eventually disappears in the brush as you hike back into the wilderness of the Mystery Hills lowlands. From the saddle, you can also hike up the shoulder and ridgeline to the western peak for great views across the Kenai lowlands and Cook Inlet to the Alaska Range on the other side of the water. Hike east to find a steep, switchbacking path leading to the top of the eastern peak and a ridgeline trek that will take you across from peak to peak at around 3,000 feet and eventually to the top of the Fuller Lakes Trail (Hike 25). From this high-country traverse, there are spectacular views back across the Skilak Lake region and all of the central Kenai Peninsula to the south and west, as well as a terrific panorama north and west across the lake-dotted flats of the Kenai National Wildlife Refuge and the mountainous Kenai Wilderness.

SPECIAL NOTES

If you are interested in cross-country travel, you can hike west across the alpine zone to Mystery Creek, which drains the area north of the Mystery Hills. You can also join up with the top of the Fuller Lakes Trail, although no distinct trail links it with the top of this Skyline Trail, so some good map-and-compass or GPS skills are in order. The distance between the two trail tops is about 6 miles. It's a wonderful peak-to-peak cross-country ridgeline traverse through the Mystery Creek section of the southern portion of the Kenai Wilderness that you'll almost certainly have to yourself. The next hike in this book, Fuller Lakes (Hike 25), contains a description and map of this traverse. From the saddle at the top of the Skyline Trail, you begin by hiking east up the switchback trail to access the ridgeline to Peak 3250.

Views from Skyline and the Traverse offer a splendid array of lakes and peaks

50 Hikes in Alaska's Kenai Peninsula

25

Fuller Lakes & Alpine Traverse

Total distance: 3 to 4 miles, plus 9.5-mile traverse

Hiking time: 4 to 6 hours for Upper Fuller Lake, 8 to 10 hours for the Traverse

Elevation change: 1,400 feet to Upper Fuller Lake, 3,400 feet to peak 3520 on the Traverse

Rating: Moderate for Fuller Lakes, Difficult for the Traverse

Best season: June through August

Maps: Kenai National Wildlife Refuge by National Geographic Trails Illustrated; Alaska Road and Recreation Map; Kenai Lake and Vicinity USGS Kenai B-1 (NW)

Special features: A moderately challenging, medium-length trail through forested mountain slopes to a delightful alpine lake. Note: Be sure to carry plenty of water, as none is available along the way.

Like the Skyline Trail (Hike 24), the Fuller Lakes Trail heads north toward the alpine zone of the Mystery Creek section of the Kenai Wilderness. But unlike that trail, which zooms straight up, the Fuller Lakes Trail is less steep, less demanding, and remains lower along the stream channel that drains Lower Fuller Lake, although it'll still get your heart pumping. The top of the trail ends in a basin between the Mystery Hills and Round Mountain at the beautiful, fish-filled Fuller Lakes.

GETTING THERE

The trailhead parking lot is at mile 57 off the Sterling Highway. There is plenty of parking but no toilet facilities.

THE TRAIL

The trail begins with a fairly steep, one-quarter-mile "wake-up" section with a set of railroad tie stairs followed by a few switchbacks. In the next mile, you cross from the Chugach National Forest into the Kenai Wilderness area as you head up moderate gradients through fairly open-canopy spruce, birch, hemlock, and aspen, along with grassy wildflower meadows featuring violet blue lupine, fuchsia fireweed, blousy mauve wild rose, lavender geranium, tall larkspur, and deep purple monkshood. The trail is up to a meter wide and well maintained. One of the great treasures of this trail is the many giant birch and aspen trees that have made their home here. As you hike, take time to notice the grandeur and beauty of some of these

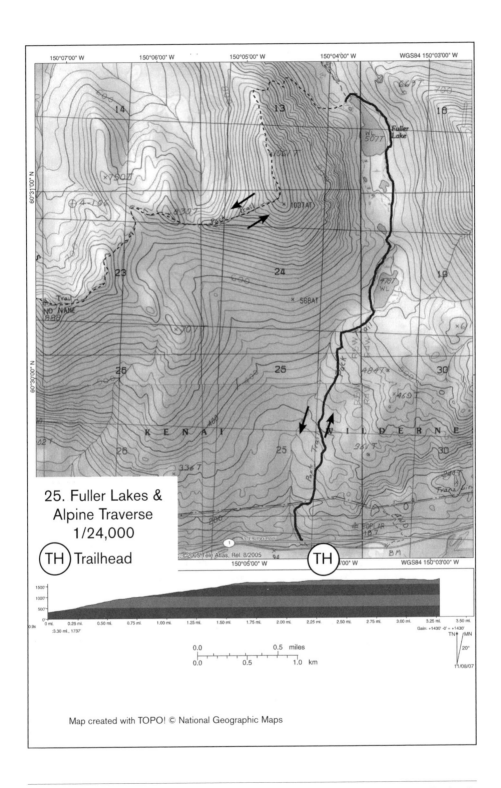

25. Fuller Lakes &
Alpine Traverse
1/24,000

(TH) Trailhead

stately, ancient deciduous monarchs. You are walking in an increasing rarity—an old-growth forest.

The trail is not right next to the stream channel that drains Lower Fuller Lake, but rather along the eastern slope above the water. However, there are several overlook turnouts that provide views of the lush stream channel and one path that leads down to the rushing water. The trail alternates between steeper and lower slope sections providing plenty of respite opportunities. You will also encounter stands of mountain hemlock including a particularly beautiful one near the upper section of the trail just before you reach Lower Fuller Lake.

At about one and three-quarter miles, you reach the south end of Lower Fuller Lake and cross the stream near its mouth, where there are two beaver dams. One dams the main lake itself and the other forms a small pond at the outlet. Lower Fuller Lake would exist without the main beaver dam, but its presence makes the lake larger and deeper.

The trail crosses the lower, smaller beaver pond on a wood beam bridge. This rounded-edge plank bridge is a sweet spot along the trail, a terrific place to stop, rest, change socks, dangle your hot feet in the cool beaver pond, and bask in the sunshine. I always stop here.

From the south end of Lower Fuller Lake, you have great views across the glassy, wind-rippled, grey water to the home of the beavers responsible for the dams at the far northern end of the lake.

An unmarked but well-worn footpath continues along the east side of Lower Fuller Lake and is used as fishing access to reach the grayling for which this lake is famous. A grayling is a small gray and very tasty fish.

Just west of the wooden bridge, climb the small knoll to find a nifty lookout, from which you have an surprise view of Skilak Lake and a camping spot large enough for horses. There is even a tie rail.

From the south end of Lower Fuller Lake, the trail wraps around to the west, following the western coastline. At the far end of the lake, you can see the residents' beaver lodge. You will also find a small, sweet camping spot right on the edge of the water down from the trail.

From the north end of the lake, the trail trends away from the water as it penetrates farther into the Mystery Hills crossing through sky-reaching stands of spruce, cottonwood, and aspen trees before opening into wildflower-filled meadows of wild rose, Indian paintbrush, dwarf dogwood, tall larkspur, red columbine, monkshood, and dwarf fireweed.

As the trail then passes several smaller lakes, you enter low thickets of alder, willow, and dwarf birch. It levels out as you approach Upper Fuller Lake, and at about 2.5 miles you reach the south shore. There is a small campsite here, but if you intend to camp I suggest hiking on to the campsite at the northern end of the lake, which is more picturesque and remote.

Past the campsite, the trail continues along the right (eastern) shore, gaining about 50 feet of elevation as it traverses mostly open and low dwarf birch and willow fields with a complete complement of wildflowers and excellent views up and down the lake.

The Fuller Lakes Trail ends at the north end of Upper Fuller Lake, where the stream outlet flows north, which is the opposite direction from the stream flowing out of Lower Fuller Lake. As you hiked between the two lakes, you crossed over a subtle drainage divide. The stream channel that

Serene surroundings of the campsite on the north end of Upper Fuller Lake

flows out of Lower Fuller Lake drains into the Kenai River that in turn flows into Skilak Lake. The outlet to Upper Fuller Lake flows north into the drainage of Mystery Creek.

Cross the outlet stream channel and hike up onto a rocky knoll surrounded by mountain hemlocks that overlooks the northern end of Upper Fuller Lake. This is the prime camping spot. (During the summer, the lake is surprisingly warm. After all, the surrounding snow has melted, so you might even consider a swim. If you do, wear your crocks, as the lake bottom is rocky.) From this rocky knoll campground, look and hike west where you will see the tight switchbacks of the trail leading to the highcountry peak-to-peak traverse that takes you over to the top of the Skyline Trail (Hike 24).

One note about camping: Please do not chop the local hemlock and spruce trees for firewood. These trees are near the limits of where they grow, and they grow very slowly. Also remember this is bear country and there are no bear boxes, so completely contain your food and clean up well after your meals . . . keep it simple to cook and clean.

THE TRAVERSE

If you are adventurous and would like to gain elevation for some better views, you can continue on the Fuller Lakes Trail to the northwest around the north side of the Mystery Hills on a cross-country, peak-to-peak traverse to the top of the Skyline Trail (Hike 24.) Some good map-and-compass or GPS navigation skills are helpful here.

You can start this traverse from either end (that is by hiking up the Skyline Trail to begin with, or by hiking up this trail at first). I myself prefer to hike up the steep Skyline Trail and down the Fuller Lakes Trail for two reasons: I love the heart-pumping challenge of hiking up steep slopes (I know, it's a sickness), and I always when given a choice opt to go down the more moderate trail in deference to my knees. You may prefer to travel up the Fuller Lakes Trail and down the Skyline, so I've included the traverse description and map here.

One note: If you decide to tackle this route from Fuller Lakes to Skyline, you should stick to the high ridgeline slopes of the Mystery Hills, as the lower elevations are overgrown and difficult to negotiate.

Another note: The traverse linking the Fuller Lakes and Skyline trails is accessed on both ends via switchbacks that climb steep slopes. The Skyline switchbacks are easier to locate than the Fuller Lakes-end switchbacks, which is another good reason to take the traverse from the Fuller Lakes side the first time.

The base of the switchbacks at the Fuller Lakes end begins about half a mile past the crossing of the stream channel that drains the north end of Upper Fuller Lake. From the north end of the lake, look northwest to locate the switchbacks that climb the mountain face up to the traverse, which follows the Mystery Hills ridgeline beginning near the base of Peak 3520, the highest point on the trek. (Notice that you are so remote now the mountains don't even have names.) Once you gain the ridgeline, you will hike for about one-half mile southeast up to Peak 3520. The views all along this stretch

are spectacular, so take plenty of time to enjoy the scenery. Continue southwest down the ridge toward the saddle between Peaks 3520 and 2912, also known as No-Name Peak. Climb up to No-Name and then turn northwest down to another saddle before ascending to Peak 3308. Continue northwest along this ridge through a series of saddles and peaks, including Peaks 3150, 3100, 3295, and 3250. From Peak 3250 you head due west down a ridgeline to meet the top of the Skyline Trail. This traverse is one of those grand, top-of-the-world hikes, so don't pass it up if you have the time and energy.

SPECIAL NOTES

Both Upper and Lower Fuller lakes were formed by a glacier that flowed down this valley as little as 10,000 years ago. As it retreated, the melting water filled the scoured-out depressions, which are now maintained by rainfall and high groundwater levels. As you hike between the lakes, look for the subtle drainage divide between Upper and Lower Fuller lakes. Remember, Upper Fuller Lake is actually part of the Mystery Creek drainage flowing northwest into the Swanson Lakes area, whereas Lower Fuller Lake drains south toward the Kenai River.

To facilitate your logistics, you can park vehicles at both the Skyline and Fuller lakes trailhead parking areas. Alternatively, you can stash a bike at the Skyline trailhead parking area and hike the traverse from the Fuller Lakes end to the Skyline end. This will leave you with a 4.1 mile *downhill* coasting bike ride to your vehicle at the Fuller Lakes trailhead.

26

Russian Lakes

Total distance: 22 to 24 miles for entire traverse, but shorter hikes possible. The official length is 21.5 miles, but you will want to add at least another 0.5 mile for a visit to the Barber Cabin and the shoreline of Lower Russian Lake, and perhaps a 2-mile jaunt down to the Russian River waterfall and back along the way.

Hiking time: 2 to 3 days for traverse, or shorter day hikes

Elevation change: 1,100 feet

Rating: Easy to moderate

Best season: June through September; best before mid-June and after mid-August to avoid the fishing hordes if you want to hike the trails near the Russian River.

Maps: Kenai Fjords National Park by National Geographic Trails Illustrated; Alaska Road and Recreation Map; USGS Seward B-8

Special features: Easy access to great fishing on the Russian River including a nice waterfall, gorgeous Lower and Upper Russian lakes; hikes of different lengths appropriate for individuals, couples, small children, teenagers, and groups; trails generally well maintained and easy to negotiate, although some meadow sections are very overgrown with tall grasses and pushki in July and August.

This trail offers a series of hikes of different lengths. There are two 2.3-mile trails to the Russian River Falls and the Barber Cabin at Lower Russian Lake, a moderate 9.5-mile hike to Upper Russian Lake, and a complete 22-mile traverse to the Cooper River trailhead. The entire trail is an easy walk past beautiful lakes through open-canopy forest and meadow terrain. You can hike this terrific path in either direction, though I prefer hiking west to east and then camping at the more secluded, and less populated, Cooper Lake. Early morning hikers may want to bring gaiters to fend off the dew above Lower Russian Lake. Also be sure to bring binoculars.

There are three public-use Forest Service cabins along the way, which should be reserved in advance, located at Upper Russian Lake, Lower Russian Lake, and Aspen Flats. There are also six primitive campsites (containing fire rings and bear boxes) located en route at mile markers 2.8, 5.7, 7.7, 10.9, 16.7, and 19, which are available on a first-come, first-served basis. In addition, the largest campground complex on the Kenai is located at the Russian River end (that is, the beginning) of the trail, and good locations for primitive (no designated sites) vehicle and tent camping are available at the far, Cooper Lake end.

GETTING THERE

From mile 52.5 on the Sterling Highway, take the access road south toward the Russian River Campground. The trailhead is about 1 mile past the campground entrance

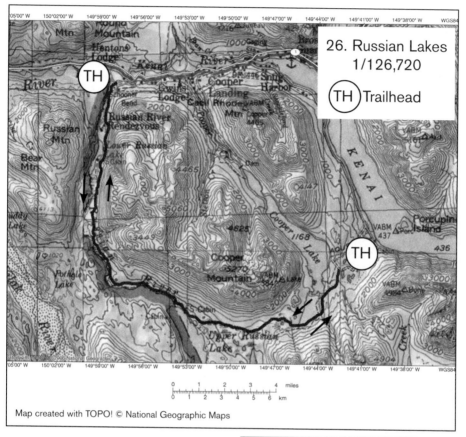

Map created with TOPO! © National Geographic Maps

and one-quarter mile short of the main campground complex. Obtain a free trailhead parking permit at the station.

If you prefer to start at the Cooper Lake trailhead at the other end of this hike, access is via Snug Harbor Road at mile 48 on the Sterling Highway. Drive south 11 miles on the gravel road looking for the trailhead on the left. If you drive all the way to Cooper Lake, you've gone too far.

If you intend to stash a bike at one end and bike back, definitely stash it at the Cooper Lake end so you are biking *downhill* for the 10-mile trip back to the Sterling Highway.

THE TRAIL

Although this trail can be hiked in either direction, let's start from the Russian River trailhead, which sits at 500 feet in elevation, as that is where most people are and you may likely begin. As you can already tell, this is a very popular and populated part of the Kenai every summer.

There are two accesses to the Lower Russian River trailhead separated by a couple hundred meters. The main trailhead with the best parking is the first one you see on the right (east) side of the road as you drive in. Park here if you can. If you can't, continue two hundred meters to your right and park in the overflow area, where the second trailhead is located.

You begin the hike parallel to, but a bit away from, the Lower Russian River. Note that a connecting, 2-mile trail known as the Anglers' Trail stays closer to the river. It is a pleasant alternative if you hike here any time but fishing season.

The first 1.7 miles of the trail are on a hiking highway of smooth gravel over 2 meters wide, which trends gradually uphill along low, open-canopy forest with small spruce, alder, and aspen trees punctuated in late July and August by spires of fuchsia fireweed in willow grasslands to add color to the trail. The small size of these trees is the result of two events. The first was a 1969 forest fire evidenced even today by the many silver snags (dead tree trunks) standing in the rejuvenating forest. The second was a spruce bark beetle kill in 2001/2002, which devastated the spruce population of the Kenai. As you hike, look up and to the south for good views of Russian Peak.

At mile 1.7, you reach the turnoff to Russian River Falls, whose great round trip adds about 2.0 miles total to your hike. It is an easy detour for just about anyone and is even wheelchair-accessible. The hike up and back to the Russian River Falls from the Russian River trailhead makes a pleasant, 5.4-mile, easy-grade day hike.

Back on the main trail once again, you will see many short side trails leading down to the Russian River, which is rushing, rocky, and snow-fed for much of the year.

Take the left turn over a stream channel, which supports some large cottonwood trees, toward the Upper Russian Lake to continue the main hiking trail. It remains a wide gravel path. From the spur trail turnoff, hike another 0.9 mile across willow, alder, and wildflower meadows (good moose habitat) toward the 0.7-mile side trail to the Barber Cabin on Lower Russian Lake. On the early part of this trail as you starting heading for the Barber Cabin turnoff, look due south into the distance directly up the Russian River and Skilak River drainages, which are the valleys the water has cut into the mountains opposite. You will enjoy some of the best views of the front of Skilak Glacier on the far horizon. Orienting yourself and your trail map to the glacier and these other topographic features is an excellent map-reading exercise that will help acclimate you to all the surrounding landscape.

As you continue toward Lower Russian Lake you gain a bit of elevation up the hillside hiking through a dense birch forest with some northern bedstraw, tall larkspur, and wild geraniums. Also look for ptarmigan along the trail. They are our Alaska state bird.

Take the right (south) turnoff to Barber Cabin, which is the first of the three public-access fee cabins. (See Information Resources pages 33–35.) Hiking to the Russian River Falls and then up to the Barber Cabin and Lower Russian Lake is a good full day's hike encompassing some 4.5 miles one way; the 3.3-mile return trip to the trailhead makes it about 8 total miles.

I definitely recommend taking the side trip down to the cabin and the Lower Lake . . . it's beautiful. The trail to the cabin, which is named in honor of Dave Barber (a Seward district ranger instrumental in developing this cabin and providing the physically disabled access to it), starts in flowered grasslands and then alternates with canopied birch forest scattered with spruce. After about one-quarter mile, the trail traverses a clearing scraped by winter snow avalanches. Take a look at all the felled trees running parallel to the fall line . . . now

Reflections off Lower Russian Lake by the Barber Cabin

Russian Lakes

look up slope and image that avalanche in action!

The trail continues through forest and open meadow with spectacular fireweed displays in August, down to and along the lake to the second public-use cabin on a small beach on Lower Russian Lake. Hang at the lake for a while and explore the coastline and then continue on toward Upper Russian Lake. The good news here is that you need not hike all the way back to the turnoff in order to proceed on the main hike. About 100 meters west of the lakeside cabin back along the access trail, look up the steep, grassy slope to find an unmarked but well-worn trail that joins the main trail to Upper Russian Lake.

From the Barber Cabin turnoff, it's 6.5 miles to the Aspen Flat Cabin, the second public-use cabin. The trail toward Upper Russian Lake narrows here and becomes more of a primitive hiking trail. If you are hiking in the morning, you will want to don your gaiters to fend off the copious amounts of early morning dew in the high encroaching grasses.

The trail roughly follows the path of the Russian River and its flood plain through alternating sections of flowered grasslands and aspen, birch, and spruce forest. As you leave the Lower Russian River behind, note how the southern end of the lake is gradually filling in with sediment, foretelling the time when this lake will become a flower-filled alpine meadow. As you hike, you will have good views into and across the boggy willow-spruce muskeg that surrounds the Russian River. This flat-floored valley across which the river flows was formed by the deposit of a thick ground moraine (that is, layer) of sediments as the glacier that once carved and filled this valley retreated at the end of the Pleistocene.

About 3.5 miles from the Barber Cabin turnoff, the trail moves away from the river and gains several hundred feet of elevation up and over a small ridgeline before returning back down. This is the steepest up-and-down section along the entire trail, through beautiful, mature, old-growth birch, spruce, and aspen forests as you cross several perennial stream channels. The high points offer some narrow but beautiful views down into the Russian River.

The turnoff to the Aspen Flat Cabin is about 9 miles from the Russian River trailhead. Take this side trail for about one-quarter mile to a nice beach along the river where you can rest. And what kinds of trees do you see all around you at Aspen Flats? You guessed it. Spruce trees! Nary an aspen to be seen!

From Aspen Flats, continue another 3 miles through forest and wildflower grasslands (with daunting, trail-encroaching, skin-stinging, invasive pushki, which looks like mammoth Queen Anne's lace) to Upper Russian Lake at mile 12. This is the largest lake on the trail at 3 miles long and up to nearly a mile wide, and it's the source for the Russian River. The third public-use fee cabin is located here in a grove of large cottonwood, aspen, and spruce trees (newly renovated in the summer of 2007), and there are also good camping sites. If you are attempting the entire traverse, this is a good destination for the end of day one. I hear the rainbow trout fishing is excellent here.

The gravel beach at Upper Russian Lake is one of the snoozy sweet spots along the trail with excellent views of some glacier-carved cirque bowls on the high peaks opposite.

You might note the lake's southeast-to-northwest orientation, which is similar to Cooper Lake and Kenai Lake. This orientation follows the flow of the retreating glaciers that once covered this entire area during the Pleistocene. Upper Russian Lake was under 1,000 feet of ice about 12,000 years ago. That's 167 of you if you're about 6 feet tall, with each of you standing on top of the other's shoulders!

From the lake, the trail heads west on a moderate grade uphill across alternating open canopy forests and grasslands. There are a lot of bear along this section of the trail, so practice your REALLY LOUD singing. Do try to avoid the pushki, which is not indigenous and has invaded Alaska to annoy and irritate exposed hiker arms and legs with its scratchy, stingy branches.

Where the trail begins to levels out, you leave the Russian River drainage and enter that for the Resurrection River. You will meet the upper end of the Resurrection River Trail (Hike 13) 4.5 miles from the Upper Russian Lake Cabin and 16.5 miles into the traverse. From that intersection, you are then hiking through a broad low-slope upland between Cooper Mountain to the northwest and an unnamed Kenai Mountains peak to the southeast. Look to the south and high on the slopes to see glaciers hanging on the edge of the Harding Ice Field (Hike 15).

Two miles east of the Resurrection intersection, you reach the high point of the traverse at 1,500 feet on the drainage between Resurrection River and Cooper Lake. The slopes are so low in this upland divide that the change is easy to miss. As you hike through, look up and southeast to the high slopes to see several hanging glaciers. The many lakes you see throughout the forest and valley are small kettle lakes (small pot-shaped glacially formed lakes) in the thick sheets of glacial ground moraine sediments left behind by the retreating glaciers. The glaciers really have defined the Kenai, even though they abandoned more than 10,000 years ago the particular spots where we are standing.

From the drainage divide, it's a mere 3 miles gently downhill to the Cooper Lake trailhead. You will cross several small stream channels draining the hanging glaciers above, which then merge into the main stream flowing into Cooper Lake.

SPECIAL NOTES

Hike this trail in early June or after mid-August if you want to avoid the crush of anglers looking for salmon, Dolly Varden, and rainbow trout. My favorite season here is early fall—late August and particularly early September—when there are few people and you are treated to autumn colors and crisp air. Regardless of when you visit, remember that you're in bear country and that bears don't follow any fishing timetables.

IV. Southeast Kenai—Homer & Anchor Point

27

Bishops Beach & Homer Spit

Total distance: 5 miles one way

Hiking time: 2 to 3 hours

Elevation change: None

Rating: Easy

Best season: Year-round

Maps: Kachemak Bay State Park by National Geographic Trails Illustrated

Special features: Dynamic beach with lots of marine wildlife, birds, and tide pools at low tide, as well as spectacular views of Kachemak Bay and the surrounding Kenai Mountains along with a fascinating boat harbor.

This beach hike extends from the tip of the Homer Spit near Land's End Resort about 5 miles to Bishops Beach, which is quite broad at low tide. In fact, you can walk along the beach in all but the highest tides and enjoy grand views of Kachemak Bay, southern Cook Inlet, and the Kenai Mountains. On clear days you may even see the Alaska Peninsula and Mount Augustine, our most active local volcano. The Spit and the beach are also favorite bald eagle hangouts. In winter, they seem like sea gulls, there are so many.

GETTING THERE

You can begin this hike from the Bishops Beach end or from the tip of the Spit. I suggest starting at Bishops Beach, which allows you to hike 5 miles to the end of the Spit, have lunch at one of the restaurants and cruise the shops, and then hike back after a rest.

From the intersection of the Sterling Highway and Pioneer Avenue, go east on the Sterling Highway for about 0.25 mile to Main Street and turn right, then take the first left onto Bunnell Street. The Bunnell Street Art Gallery is on the near corner to the right. Continue 100 yards and turn right onto Beluga Place just before the Two Sisters Bakery. This is the access road to Bishops Beach. You should have no problem finding a parking space. Picnic tables are available here as well.

For those wanting a shorter version of this hike, park on the Spit itself, near Mariner's Park, which has a statue of a

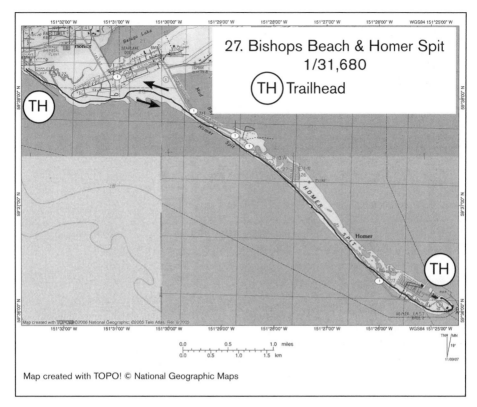

27. Bishops Beach & Homer Spit
1/31,680
(TH) Trailhead

Map created with TOPO! © National Geographic Maps

sailor on the east side of the road and parking nearby. You could then hike up to where the Spit joins the mainland and walk as much of connecting Bishops Beach as you want before returning to your car.

THE TRAIL

Bishops Beach extends from the parking lot east toward Kachemak Bay to the next point of land. Sand for this beach is mostly supplied by the eroding cliffs to the west and transported by the prevailing longshore current flowing west to east along the southern coast of the Kenai Peninsula from Anchor Point all the way to Homer. This is a great area if you enjoy looking for driftwood treasures.

Sand dunes form at the mouth of Beluga Slough, which is a low-energy tidal environ-

ment next to the bay. If you care to take a side hike up into the slough area, you'll find high, waving grasses and a sandy estuary with wading birds and the occasional moose.

The area around the Bishops Beach parking lot is popular with beach walkers and their dogs, but if a bit more solitude is what you're after, it's not far away. Within a couple hundred yards, most of your fellow travelers will disappear and you will have the beach largely to yourself.

At the east end, the beach takes an almost 90-degree bend toward the north and parallels Ocean Drive at the base of Homer Spit. This back beach area changes from the dune-and-grass estuary of Beluga Slough to low cliffs, which receive the full force of the wind and

Bishops Beach view of Kachemak Bay and the southern Kenai Mountains and glaciers

waves coming in from lower Cook Inlet. As you can see, the cliffs are undergoing rapid erosion. Midway along the beach you encounter the controversial, and many think ill-advised, seawall constructed in a futile attempt to fight Mother Nature.

The beach continues for another one-quarter mile before turning east again and beginning its long path down the Spit. Along this wide beach area at the western end of the Spit, you encounter another broad, low dune and slough area known as Mariner Park. For a shorter version of this hike, you could park here and walk down the Spit or back toward Bishops Beach. You'll probably encounter other beach walkers in this area, which is also a favorite spot for people who like to fly kites, windsurf, and participate in a variety of para-glider sports—great fun to watch.

For the next one-quarter mile east from Mariner Park the beach increasingly narrows, particularly at moderate and high tides, due to huge boulders that form the roadbed and wave-protection barrier for the west end of the Spit. This large section of boulders concentrates wave energy at the base of the rocks on the beach, which causes a lot of beach sand to be deposited offshore when the tide is high and the waves are large. The sand moves back near shore when wave energy drops. At low and moderate tides this can be a beautiful flat walk on a fine sandy beach.

There is a woman who lives on the Spit who feeds the bald eagles in winter. She is the only one allowed to do it, by state law. You can tell which one is her low, wooden, old-fashioned house. It is quite distinctive, dotted in winter with eagles waiting for their next meal. They cluster too on pilings near the parking lot that faces the beach and on the skeletal remains of dock structures built here many years ago. Homer is known for these eagles, which appear in photographs around the world. Please, do not feed them and do not get close.

About one-half mile from Mariner Park beach, you reach the end of the elevated Spit roadway, and the huge boulders disappear. The beach once again widens and becomes more passable at moderate to higher tides. Three miles down the beach, you begin to encounter some of the many gift shops, art galleries, and restaurants that inhabit the far end of the Spit. Your spending money here helps the local economy, as these vendors and shop owners must survive a whole year on what they earn during our short tourist season. In winter, most of these shops are shuttered.

As you continue down the beach to the tip of the Spit, you traverse areas of sand and cobble. The easiest walking is on the sand at the base of the steeper cobble beach slopes. At the east end of the Spit you will find the Land's End Resort and the Alaska Ferry System terminal, as well as great, flat stones to skip in the water.

You can exit the beach at any point along this last section of the hike to take a break, go shopping, or just hang out. The wonderful thing about the beach here is that a short walk down the cobble-sloped top beach quickly separates you from the Spit's frenetic business environment. The constant onshore winds carry the noise away from you.

SPECIAL NOTES

The Homer Spit originally formed on top of the terminal moraine of the glacier that filled Kachemak Bay. A glacier is like a conveyor belt rolling downhill carrying tons of ice, rocks, and sediment. When it advances and retreats (melts) at about the same rate, the end, or terminus, of the glacier remains in the same position. Meanwhile, the glacial conveyor belt continues to deliver massive quantities of sediment all along the front of the glacier. Over time this debris forms a long ridge known as a terminal moraine. When the glacier finally retreats, this elongated ridge of glacial sediment is left behind.

After this glacial retreat, sea levels rose and what is now Kachemak Bay filled with water. Then, the terminal moraine began diverting the flow of longshore currents and sediments at the opening of the bay. This transportation of sediment is what led to the formation of the Homer Spit. So as you walk along the beach here, let your imagination transport you back some 15,000 years to when a huge, towering glacier dominated this area before slowly retreating to allow a thin spit to gradually form.

The fascinating Homer Harbor is located on the northern side of the Spit. It is the largest harbor, in terms of the number of boats, in Alaska. You'll see boats of nearly every description, from large commercial fishing vessels to small skiffs and dinghies. If you're up to it, take time to walk around the harbor and enjoy the boats, people, and maritime culture. Don't forget to look on the underside of the docks for thriving communities of sea anemones and starfish. In fact, you might want to return for one of the hour-long guided tours of the marine life of Homer Harbor offered by the Alaska Center of Coastal Studies. Stop in at their yurt behind Mako's Water Taxi or check the calendar in one of the local newspapers for scheduled tours.

28

Bishops Beach to Diamond Beach

Total distance: 6.5 miles one way

Hiking time: 3 hours

Elevation change: None

Rating: Easy to moderate (due to rocky winter beaches)

Best season: Year-round. Each season has its separate personality and beauty.

Maps: Kachemak Bay State Park by National Geographic Trails Illustrated; and USGS Seldovia C-5

Special features: Wild, rocky, eroding high-cliff coastline with many landslide and slump features as well as exposures of coal and peat layers on the soaring cliffs. This hike also offers coarse cobble areas with tide pools at low tide, so it's great to walk with children.

This beach hike has a more remote, wild, and secluded feel than Bishops Beach & Homer Spit (Hike 27). As you hike west from Bishops Beach to Diamond Beach, you'll have increasingly spectacular views of the Alaska Peninsula and the Augustine and Iliamna volcanoes across the water, with their distinctive cone shapes. You will see high cliffs and have access to good tide pooling at lower tides. In fact, it is best to only take this hike at low to moderate tides because of the narrow coastline at the first headland. If you intend to hike out and back along this same route, making a round trip, I recommend starting midway through an ebbing tide so you have plenty of time to return before the next high tide arrives.

GETTING THERE

You can start this hike from either Bishops Beach or Diamond Beach. If you intend to go one way, you might want to hike from Diamond to Bishops Beach, which allows you to hike down, rather than up, the Diamond Gulch Trail to access Diamond Beach. Also, once you reach Bishops Beach, you'll find it easier to arrange for a cab back up to the Diamond Beach trailhead, as Bishops is closer to Homer. (For information on accessing Diamond Beach, see Hike 29.)

As a round-trip hike if you prefer the all-beach hike, start at Bishops Beach to avoid the Diamond Gulch Trail altogether. From the intersection of Sterling Highway and Pioneer Avenue continue east on Sterling Highway about one-quarter mile

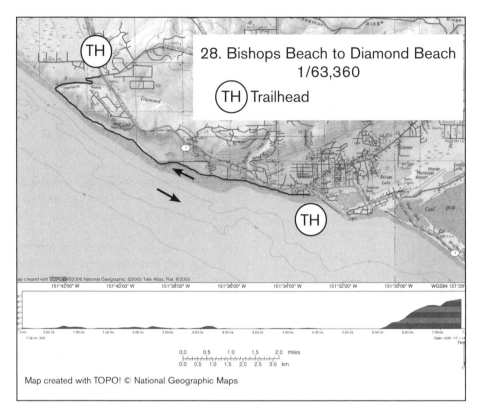

28. Bishops Beach to Diamond Beach
1/63,360

(TH) Trailhead

Map created with TOPO! © National Geographic Maps

to Main Street. Turn right on Main and take the first left onto Bunnell Street at the Bunnell Street Gallery. Continue 100 yards and take a right onto Beluga Place at Two Sisters Bakery. This is the access road to Bishops Beach. You should have no problem finding a parking space, and picnic tables are available here.

THE TRAIL

You are starting at the same Bishops Beach parking lot that takes you down the Homer Spit (see Hike 27), but this time you'll walk in the other direction, west. The first mile of this hike is along the beach, which can be sandy or rocky depending on the weather conditions and time of year. In general, this and other Alaskan beaches are sandy in summer and fall and rockier in winter and

spring when wave energies are higher. High wave energies tend to move the smaller, lighter sand offshore, leaving the coarse, rocky sediment behind.

Hike along the beach toward the first of four headlands you'll encounter on this trip. These headlands all have rocky areas where you'll typically find good tide pooling at low tides. In between the headlands, the embayment beaches tend to be broader and covered with finer sand.

At the second headland, a little over 2 miles into the hike, look up on the high cliffs at the back of the beach to view distinct coal beds. These are distinguished by their dark color and the fact that they stand out in relief from the surrounding sandstones and siltstones. At about 3.5 miles, again look up at the soaring cliffs

50 Hikes in Alaska's Kenai Peninsula

Wide beaches at low tides make for great beach hiking and tide pooling

to see direct evidence of the dramatic forces that uplifted these rocks, now being eroded into high cliffs. Look carefully and you'll notice that the layers are folded and deformed and that active landslides are present. Watch for forests that have trees pointing up in different directions. This is known as a drunken forest, which forms when trees grow on land that is actually moving slowly downhill.

You encounter the third headland at about 3.6 miles. Plan to hang out here for a while near low tide as this is probably the best tide-pooling location along the entire hike. It's also a great place to take a break and have a snack and enjoy the sweeping view from east to west from the southern Kenai Mountains across lower Kachemak Bay, southern Cook Inlet all the way to the volcanoes of the Alaska Peninsula on the western and southwestern horizon . . . it's quite a panorama!

At about 4.5 miles, you arrive at cliffs that soar to over 800 feet. If you look carefully, you can see alternating layers of sandstone shale, volcanic ash, peat, and coal. This is evidence of the several million years of sedimentary deposition that occurred before these rocks were uplifted and the ocean waves began to erode them into high cliffs.

At the fourth headland, at about mile 5.2, there is a house and some cabins up off the beach in a small dune area. This is the weekend retreat of Homer doctor Ken Hahn. If he is around, he'll invite you to stop in and say hello . . . but don't overstay your welcome . . . grant the man and his family their privacy.

From the fourth headland to Diamond

Beach is a little over a mile, or 6.3 total miles in. When you reach Diamond Beach, you encounter the first major stream channel, Diamond Creek. If there has been a lot of recent rain, the creek may be flowing high and fast. At lower tides it's typically safer to cross down on the beach where the single stream channel divides into several slower, shallower ones.

Diamond Beach is a terrific place for lunch, and you'll likely find plenty of driftwood for a fire. Cook some food and lounge around on the beach to enjoy the spectacular scenery, coastal wind that whips constantly, and endless waves. It feels here as if you really are at some primordial end of land, since this is the spot where Kachemak Bay opens into Cook Inlet and the open water that connects to the Pacific Ocean. The beach is rough and gray, strewn with huge boulders the glaciers have left here.

From here, you can hike 0.7 mile, and 600 feet up to a small parking area at the Diamond Gulch trailhead or hike back down to Bishops Beach. If you're making a round trip, don't forget to leave yourself plenty of time to get past that first headland before high tide arrives. If you decide to hike up to the Diamond Gulch trailhead, you should be able to call a taxi with a cell phone. Otherwise, you'll have to hike 5.4 miles back on the road to the Bishops Beach parking area. Of course, you could also park a second vehicle here before the hike, if you have one available, to make it an easy one-way trip for at least two adults, so you can then retrieve the other vehicle.

SPECIAL NOTES

You will see numerous active examples of coastal beach erosion as you walk along. In some places waves have eroded the cliff bottoms, and the cliffs above are sliding down onto the beach. If you are hiking in rainy weather, you'll likely spot mud or debris that has recently flowed down small stream channels or right off the cliffs themselves, depositing rocks, sediment, and vegetation on the beach. Many people avoid hiking in the rain, but storms offer some of the best times for beach trekking because wind, water, and waves create so much activity—you can actually witness geologic processes in action.

29

Diamond Gulch & Beach

Total distance: 2 miles round trip, plus unlimited beach walking

Hiking time: 1.5 hours

Elevation change: 500 feet from trailhead down to beach

Rating: Easy to moderate

Best seasons: Spring, summer, and fall; winter weather can be challenging but the surf is often thrilling.

Maps: Kachemak Bay State Park by National Geographic Trails Illustrated; USGS Seldovia C-5

Special features: Beautiful, secluded beach with sweeping views, soaring coastal cliffs, and large glacial erratics. Special note: Remember to bring hot dogs to have a wiener roast over your driftwood fire on the beach!

This is the perfect hike if you don't have a lot of time but want to quickly access an isolated beach with great views. If you do have more time, you can walk for miles along Diamond Beach in both directions.

Located at the southern tip of the Kenai Peninsula, it offers dramatic vistas east across the mouth of Kachemak Bay toward the southern Kenai Mountains and west across Cook Inlet to the towering volcanoes and other Alaska Range peaks of the Alaska Peninsula.

The beach itself is decorated with driftwood perfect for sitting on, making fires, or photographing. Rock hounds will be in heaven here because the retreating glaciers left behind all kinds of prizes including boulder-sized glacial erratics, which get their name from being dragged so far out of place by the ice. So come down for the fabulous views and a quick hit of beach air or build yourself a driftwood fire and hunker down with a book or explore the beach to your heart's delight.

GETTING THERE

From the lookout rest area on top of Bay Crest Hill just off Sterling Highway on the west side of Homer, drive west 1.5 miles to the Diamond Ridge turnoff. Instead of turning right for the ridge, though, go left (south) and park in the pullout in front of the gated state park fence or continue through the gate 0.5 mile on a dirt road to the trailhead. In windy weather, dead (beetle-killed) spruce trees often are blown over across the dirt road. More than one hiker

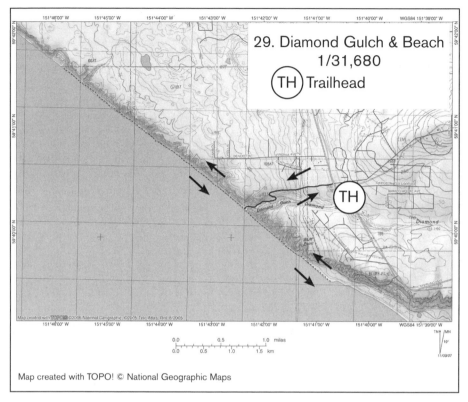

Map created with TOPO! © National Geographic Maps

29. Diamond Gulch & Beach
1/31,680
(TH) Trailhead

has been trapped behind downed trees when attempting to drive out after a hike. Park at the gate if the wind is up or come prepared with a small chain saw. (That last is no kidding.)

THE TRAIL

Start at the clearing in the trees on the east side of the small parking area at the end of the dirt road. It's about 1 mile down to the beach from here. You will begin well above Diamond Creek and descend through steep-sided Diamond Gulch. In the first one-quarter mile, the trail heads east and down toward the stream channel. Then, after the only switchback, the trail more or less parallels the creek down to the beach and the mouth of Diamond Creek, which empties

into the mixing waters of lower Cook Inlet and Kachemak Bay.

The only obstacles on the trail are some wet patches where small channels or springs create muddy areas. Minor slope failures occur occasionally from the steep uphill (west) side of the trail, usually after a heavy rain.

The walls of Diamond Gulch consist of late Tertiary—5 to 10 million years old—layers of sandstone, shale, and volcanic ash, along with peat and coal. Coal layers are easily identified by their prominent dark, often black, color and by the way they typically protrude slightly from the hillside. Also watch for folds in the rock layers, which are evidence of the relatively recent and ongoing uplift that created the high cliffs through which Diamond Creek has cut a path.

After the switchback, enjoy dramatic views down into Diamond Gulch, with its rapids and waterfalls. Wildflowers grace the trail throughout spring and summer. In July, look for pink and lavender lupine. In August, brilliant fuschia fireweed covers the steep hillsides. Its tall spires change from blossoms to cotton by late August, and then the cotton tufts fill the air.

Once on the beach you can hike east (left) toward Homer or west toward Anchor Point. As you dodge the granite boulders, think about the glaciers that deposited them here thousands of years ago. There are many rock types on the beach that aren't present in the steep cliffs facing you—further evidence of their glacial transport.

You will also find rocks that have eroded right out of the cliffs. These local sandstones and mudstones break down quickly in the surf zone because they're less resistant to weathering than the glacially transported boulders and cobbles. Also scattered on the beach are examples of the process that transforms a plant-rich swamp into compacted beds of coal: peat, red to brown semi-rocks that will someday be coal composed almost entirely of compact mattes of plants; lignite, brown to black almost-coal rocks that contain more visible plant parts; and coal, black and well layered. These forms of coal are also eroding out of the slope front. Break some pieces open to find plant fossils.

As you hike the beach, watch for small streams cutting down through the towering cliffs. From spring through early fall, these channels offer wildflowers and waterfalls. Also, some of the best rock hunting happens where these rivulets meet the beach, redistributing rocks the glaciers deposited on the cliff-top uplands hundreds of feet above you. For some boulder-hopping and other stream-channel adventures, head up Diamond Creek, whose mouth is just west of where the trail ends at the beach. The many rapids and small waterfalls offer lots of playtime opportunities, but be prepared to get your feet wet. An extra pair of dry socks can make the trip back up the canyon much more pleasant.

Be warned that in the spring and after extended rains, this channel can become a dangerous torrent, so exercise some common sense when the waters are high.

SPECIAL NOTES

If you can, time your hike to reach the beach close to low tide, when it will be wide and inviting and the sandy flats left by the retreating water are easier to walk on than the boulder- and cobble-strewn areas closer to the cliff. If you plan to hike a long way down the beach, it's best to start this hike when the tide is still ebbing, well before low tide. Also be sure to give yourself time to return to the trail before high tide, since high tides of 18 feet or more can engulf the entire beach. Tide times and levels can be found in tide-table books available at most outdoor stores and other businesses in Homer or from tide tables published in local phone books.

Also, don't forget to leave yourself enough time and energy to hike back up the trail to your vehicle. The return trip is all uphill, but the trail is wide and not overly steep. And remember to bring your hot dogs to have your wiener roast over your driftwood fire!

Peace, quiet, and contemplation on wild Diamond Beach

30

Homestead–Demonstration Forest

Total distance: 1.5 miles to Reuben Call Bench, 2.0 miles to Rucksack Drive link to Crossman Ridge Trail extension of Homestead Trail.

Hiking time: 1 to 2 hours

Elevation change: ~1,200 feet

Rating: Easy to moderate

Best season: Spring through fall for hiking; extensive groomed Nordic ski trails in winter.

Maps: Kachemak Bay State Park by National Geographic Trails Illustrated; USGS Seldovia C-5, and Kachemak Nordic Ski Club map (http://kache maknordicskiclub.org/images/maps/ bacrestmapcolor)

Special features: Trail traverses a variety of environments, from wet lowland tundra bogs to forested lowlands and slopes to dry upland ridges. Great views across lower Kachemak Bay and Cook Inlet to the Kenai Mountains, the Alaska Range, and Augustine volcano. Special Note: Whether you are hiking or skiing these trails, you will notice they often pass by private residences. Many of these landowners have graciously allowed these trails to pass through their properties, so please respect their privacy and land ownership and quietly stick to the trail as you pass by.

The Demonstration Forest area is within easy reach of Homer. If you've already done the Spit and seen Diamond Beach and Anchor Point (Hikes 27, 28, 29, and 33), and you're up for another easy to moderate hike, but this time through more diverse environments, then Homestead Trail is a great choice.

The area is known by several names. On some maps, it's designated the Reuben Call Memorial Trail. On others, it's called the Kachemak Bay Nordic Ski Club Trail System. Still others refer to this as the Homestead Trail System or the Bay Crest Ski Trials. I've decided to call this the Homestead/Demonstration Forest Hike to match the name displayed at the main trailhead on Rogers Loop Road. Other access points include two Diamond Ridge Road trailheads as well as several more informal ones from minor roads east of the forest. There are also several access points at various elevations along both Roger Loop Road and Diamond Ridge Road (see accompanying map).

GETTING THERE

From the intersection of Pioneer Avenue and the Sterling Highway in Homer, drive west on the Sterling Highway up Bay Crest Hill. About 100 yards shy of the top, turn right onto Rogers Loop Road. Drive 1 mile and park on the right near the sign for the Demonstration Forest. Although there is no designated parking area, you can pull your vehicle off to the side of the road.

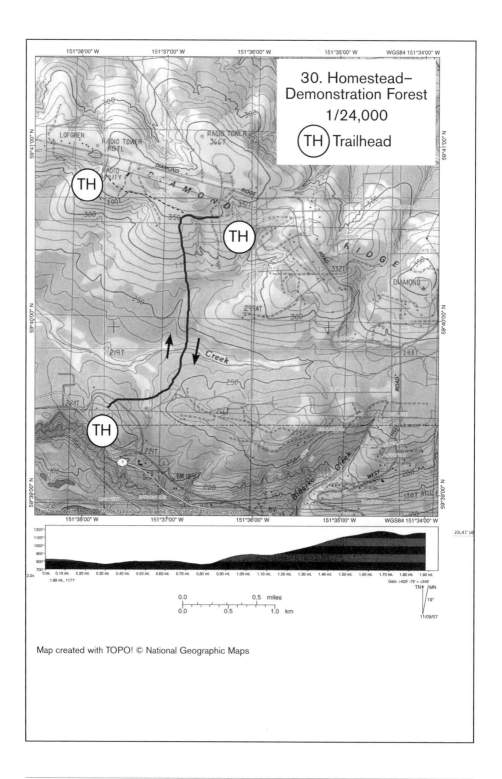

THE TRAIL

From the Rogers Loop Homestead-Demonstration Forest trailhead, walk about 200 yards slightly downhill through a meadow (that will be ripe with fireweed in August) into an open-canopy spruce forest and the first trail intersection. At the intersection, look for a kiosk offering maps and information about the Demonstration Forest and sometimes even a numbered, written trail guide.

To continue on the Homestead Trail (also known as the Headwaters Trail as part of the winter Nordic ski trail system), turn right and hike east on the wide path covered with woodchips. You will notice the trees are small along this section of the trail as this was once a logged area that is now regrowing. You will pass a sign saying this forest was replanted in 1999 and is part of the Global Reforest Project. That is where the name "Demonstration Forest" comes from, in case you were wondering.

The path continues through the open spruce forest. At about 0.1 mile, look on the right for a side loop path to the outhouse, which was built by the Nordic skiers who use these trails in winter.

The forest is open enough that you can enjoy long views into the trees, across meadows, and even up onto the higher grassy slopes to which you are heading. The trail, in places, is on slightly elevated wooden boardwalks over boggy areas known as muskeg. Here you will walk on cushy mats of ground cedar, pass stands of small spruce trees and fluttering willows, as well as enjoy a variety of grasses, flowers, and berries. The first 0.3 to 0.5 mile is flat and accessible to all including wheelchairs.

After the first 0.5 mile, the trail turns north and heads slightly uphill through a more moderate-canopy denser spruce forest as the trail leaves the boardwalk and becomes more narrow and rooty toward the upper grasslands. You will notice many beetle-killed older spruce trees being replaced by eager young spruce recruits.

As you gradually gain elevation, you leave the trees behind to climb grassy, meadowed slopes covered with a bright magenta carpet of fireweed in August.

Puski is also common. For those of you unfamiliar with this invasive, non-native plant, it looks like Queen Anne's lace that's been working out. Do not touch these strong, hard branches, and do not pick the flat, pretty flowers, for pushki scratches and stings human skin. Alaskans clearing it from roadways and paths must wear gloves and protective clothing.

At about 0.75 mile, a side trail takes off to the right across the slope to a clutch of homes located near the edge of the forest. Feel free to explore this trail, but please be respectful of private property.

To continue on the Homestead Trail, take the left trail that continues up the fall line toward the high slopes. This portion of the trail is called Master-Blaster in the winter because of the hill climbing you are invited to do on skis!

As you continue up, the vegetation's height lowers to provide wonderful views of lower Cook Inlet, the mouth of Kachemak Bay, the southern Kenai Mountains, and on really clear days a spectacular vista of Mt. Augustine and Mt. Douglas, the last two (most southerly) in the sequence of five volcanoes on the Alaska Peninsula. Also look east for some terrific views of both the Wosnesenski and Doroshin glaciers. These are fed by the Harding Ice Field on the other side of the mountains (Hike 15).

As you look across the vast fields of fireweed, you will see several derelict

Breathtaking views of Kachemak Bay, the Kenai Mountains, and glaciers from the R.C.M. Bench

cabins built during the homestead period of Homer's history, from which this trail gets its name. Early homesteaders used this trail as their primary byway to reach their 160-acre homestead plots back in the 1800s, long before any roads were built. In fact, the main road you drove in on, from Soldotna, wasn't built until the late 1940s.

At 1.5 miles you reach the high point on the trail and the Reuben Call Memorial Bench, named in honor of one of Homer's grand early settlers who was instrumental in helping to establish Homer as a community. Reuben's cabin can be found farther west of this location downslope and near the edge of the forest.

Reuben's bench is huge, built for Sasquatch to sit on I think, and a terrific place for lunch or a snack or to just sit and

gaze across the glorious landscape of the southern Kenai. From the bench, you can add the Grewingk Glacier to your lifetime glacier view list, as well as some slivers of the central portion of Kachemak Bay over the top of the forested hills to the east.

The bench is also the nexus of several trails whose intersection sports a sign. If you want to continue on the extension of the Homestead Trail over to the Crossman Ridge Trail (Hike 31), turn right here toward Rucksack Drive. You will hike about a half a mile to a road, then turn left and another half mile up and over Diamond Ridge and Diamond Ridge Road onto Rucksack and the trailhead for the Crossman Ridge Trail.

If, on the other hand, you choose to take the left-hand trail from the bench, you will hike about 0.5 mile gently up and over to the top of Diamond Ridge and an unmarked trailhead along Diamond Ridge Road. There are terrific views along the upper section of this path, so even if you are heading over to Rucksack Drive and Crossman Ridge or turning back to Rogers Loop from where you came, take a half-hour detour along this view- and wildflower-filled side trail . . . you'll be glad you did. Be sure also to look for the striking blue spruce trees gracing this upper-slope trail. (See map for trail and road locations.)

If you plan in advance, you can park a second vehicle (motor or pedal type) at the intersection of Rucksack Drive and Diamond Ridge Road, where you will find a convenient parking area.

SPECIAL NOTES

The Demonstration Forest area was originally designed to serve as an actual working demonstration forest, testing various forest management plans and techniques. However, this trail system has become so popular with Homer locals that there would be a local uprising if this forest were ever proposed for cutting. It has become the centerpiece of a cooperative patchwork of private, state, and city lands used year-round by area hikers and skiers. Contact the Kachemak Heritage Land Trust for more information on these interconnected lands (www.kachemaklandtrust.org).

There is also a Winter Ski Trail System in this area. I know this is a hiking book, but I must mention that in winter, the Demonstration Forest Loop morphs into an extensive ski trail system offering a variety of forest, meadow, and hillside ski trails to explore. There are six named ski segments including the Demonstration Forest Loop, Headwaters, College Avenue, Ravens Way, Homestead Loop, and Sunset Loop.

Because these numerous trails crisscross each other and their intersections are not always marked, it is a good idea to make a copy of the map shown at the Kachemak Nordic Ski Club Web site (http://kachemaknordicskiclub.org/images/maps/baycrestmapcolor).

If you are in Homer during the winter, this entire area, including the Crossman Ridge Trail (Hike 31), is used for annual ski events such as the Homer Ski Marathon and the Wine & Cheese Ski Tour.

31

Crossman Ridge (Homestead Extension)

Total distance: ~4 miles one way

Hiking time: 2 to 4 hours depending on trail conditions.

Elevation change: 1,200 feet at start to 1,237 feet on Crossman Ridge

Rating: Easy to moderate; the Homestead Trail includes moderate hills

Best season: Spring through fall, although you can ski here in winter; in fact, it's often part of the Homer Cross-Country-Ski Marathon course.

Maps: USGS Seldovia C-5; Kenai Peninsula Kachemak Bay Road and Recreation, Todd Communications

Special features: Spectacular views east across Kachemak Bay toward the southern Kenai Mountains, with an uncommon view of all five main southern Kenai Mountain glaciers, and west toward the Alaska Peninsula with its glorious volcanoes and fields of wildflowers. At the top of this hike, you will have a rare view of all five of the individual glaciers that surround Kachemak Bay.

The Homestead and Crossman Ridge hikes traverse upland grass punctuated with open stands of spruce forests at elevations from 700 to 1,200 feet, offering many spectacular views of Kachemak Bay and the Kenai Mountains to the east and the rugged, mountainous, volcano-dotted Alaska Peninsula to the west. Much of the Crossman Ridge portion is dirt road, so it isn't considered a wilderness hike, but it's beautiful and worthwhile all the same.

This hike can be considered a natural extension of the upper portions of the Homestead/Demonstration Forest Hike (Hike 30). Indeed, on some maps the Homestead Trail is shown as starting at the Rogers Loop Road trailhead discussed in Hike 30 and progressing through the Demonstration Forest Trail, up and over Diamond Ridge Road near Rucksack Drive, and then on through the trail discussed here.

GETTING THERE

This hike can be accessed from either end, but the trailhead for the Homestead Trail off Diamond Ridge Road is easier to find. This hike is written assuming you begin at the following trailhead. Drive 1.8 miles up Diamond Ridge Road from its intersection with the Sterling Highway to Rucksack Lane. You will find a parking area on the south side of Diamond Ridge with an information kiosk for the Homestead and Crossman Ridge trails. Walk across Diamond Ridge Road and Rucksack Lane 0.1 mile to the trailhead.

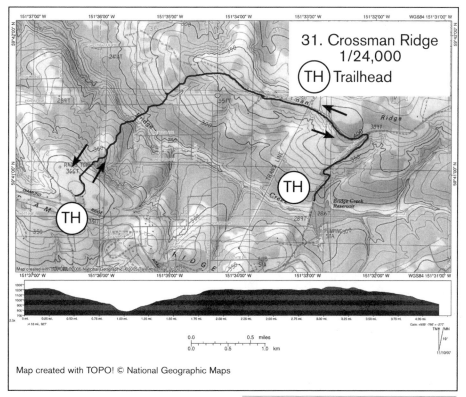

31. Crossman Ridge
1/24,000
(TH) Trailhead

Map created with TOPO! © National Geographic Maps

Alternatively, to start at the other end of the trail, you can reach the Bridge Creek Reservoir end of the Crossman Ridge Hike by driving another mile to the end of Diamond Ridge Road, where it intersects with the beginning of Skyline Drive and the top of West Hill Road. This is also a good alternative if you want to avoid the steeper up-and-down slopes of the Homestead Trail and only hike the Crossman Ridge section. To get to this other trailhead, turn left onto Skyline Drive and drive 0.5 mile, then turn left again on the unnamed dirt road that heads downhill 0.8 mile to Bridge Creek Reservoir. Drive over the dam and park on the far side. You can leave a vehicle here and catch a ride to the trailhead at Rucksack Road, so you have wheels when you are done with the hike.

THE TRAIL

Finding the trailhead can be a bit tricky. Look for a small wooden sign labeled HOMESTEAD TRAIL on the left side located in the grasses between the two driveways at the end of Rucksack Road. Walk 100 feet north down the well-worn path. Where it turns west and follows the underground gas pipline along the ridgeline (see the flat-faced orange post markers), look for a less-traveled path that continues north parallel to the driveway you have been following on the right side . . . this is the Crossman Ridge–Homestead Extension Trail.

It heads slightly downhill for about 100 yards, then turns left to follow the top of the grassy slope for another 100 yards along the edge of an alder thicket. The trail then turns right (north) again and starts downhill more deliberately into the Bridge Creek drainage.

Where you began this hike at the top of the Homestead Trail, you were at about 1,200 feet in elevation. The first mile trends gradually, and then more steeply, downhill with a drop in elevation of about 500 feet into the Bridge Creek drainage. This portion of the trail is through open meadow and fireweed grasslands tufted with stands of white and beautiful blue spruce and small thickets of alder. In August and September on the upper portions of the trail, the grasses can be so high and overgrown you have to feel your way in places.

Along the upper portions of the trail, you will enjoy sweeping views of the southern Kenai Peninsula with striking views of Redoubt and Iliamna volcanoes 100 miles to the west across Cook Inlet on the Alaska Peninsula. Keep an eye out for flattened areas in the grasses where moose have bedded down for a rest. They have a good idea!

As you progress downhill the trail becomes easier to follow as the grasses thin out and the forest thickens. Most of the older, larger spruces have been beetle killed and are being rapidly replaced with younger trees. Blueberry bushes are common through here as well. The trail is alternately high and dry and wet and muddy.

About 0.75 mile along the trail, look for a coal seam in the stream channel. As you then continue downhill after the coal seam, keep the stream channel on your right all the way to Bridge Creek. Downfalls of dead trees are not uncommon along this trail and there are a number of side paths into the underbrush that can divert you, so keep one eye on the trail at all times, and watch closely for the trail markers.

At about 1 mile you will reach the two-log bridge crossing Bridge Creek. I suggest you plan to hang out here a while to explore (be sure to bring your Crocs® or booties for this) the pools and riffles of the stream channel and floodplain of Bridge Creek. You'll find fish in the stream and lots of willows and wildflowers in the near-stream riparian zone. Take a moment to notice the whole generation of young, spruce trees growing eagerly among the older beetle-killed spruce. This is also a wonderful ski valley in the winter, and especially during spring for crunchy crust skiing!

The trail continues north up and out the other side of the Bridge Creek drainage across log steps. About 0.2 mile past the creek it levels out as it skirts a boggy meadow. Look for numerous sign of moose and bear, both scat (poop) and trampled vegetation as you pick your way along. If you have hiked over from the Homestead Trail, you will find this trail far more primitive and less well maintained with more roots and downed trees to negotiate, so the going will be a bit slower but nevertheless quite an adventure.

One mile from the Bridge Creek crossing, the Homestead Trail breaks out onto a single-lane dirt road that follows the spine of Crossman Ridge. At the cabin located at the end of the road, look west across the wildflower meadow for a breathtaking view of Mt. Iliamna volcano.

From there, you then follow the ridgeline road 2 miles along Crossman Ridge, passing older properties as well as some newer developments while you enjoy the glorious views of Kachemak Bay and the southern Kenai Mountains to the east. Throughout the summer you will be greeted by thousands of wildflowers.

Near the high point of the Crossman Ridge Trail/Road, just before you turn right to head down to Bridge Creek Reservoir,

View of Redoubt volcano across the rolling forest and meadow landscape of the southern Kenai

you will have a rare view of all five of the separately named, individual glaciers around Kachemak Bay. From north to south, they are Dixon, Portlock, Grewingk, Wosnesenski, and Doroshin glaciers.

From Crossman Ridge you have excellent views north across Ohlson and Lookout mountains into the south-central interior of the Kenai Peninsula. As you gaze north across this rounded landscape, remind yourself that just a few thousand years ago this entire southern peninsula was covered with thick sheets of grinding glacial ice that were moving east to west from the high Kenai Mountains toward Cook Inlet. The planing erosion caused by these massive ice sheets is responsible for the smoothed, low-rolling peaks and wide valleys. Current-day stream channels are just starting to change this topography through their own processes of erosion and deposition.

At 2 miles, you reach a trail-crossing with four choices: (1) turn right and hike one-half mile down to Bridge Creek Reservoir; (2) continue straight on the Crossman Ridge Road for another 2.5 miles until you reach the east end of Ohlson Mountain Road; (3) turn left and hike 2 miles northeast through the Bridge Creek drainage toward the west end of Ohlson; or (4) retrace your steps back to the trailhead for the Homestead Trail.

SPECIAL NOTES

The Homestead Trail got its name from its use by homesteaders to access their plots of land throughout much of Homer's early history and long before the current road system was constructed. For example, the main road out of Homer wasn't built until the late 1940s. So as you hike the Homestead and Crossman Ridge trails, imagine what it was like 60 years ago when you ventured to Homer by steamship or overland by foot

to establish a homestead only accessible via this trail system. Or picture the scene 15,000 years ago, when the landscape you are now walking over, including Crossman Ridge, was covered by huge alpine glaciers merging into valley glaciers a thousand feet thick, covering all of Kachemak Bay. They were in the process of carving out the bay, the rugged Kenai Mountains, and all the steep, U-shaped valleys that now separate the various peaks.

On any of the trails in this area, you'll find vast jumbled arrays of rock from sources all over the Kenai Peninsula that were dragged down and deposited here by the advancing and retreating glaciers thousands of years ago. These glacially deposited sediments are known as glacial ground moraines. Many of the rocks deposited on Crossman Ridge and the surrounding areas of the Anchor River drainage are the same type that were subsequently deposited on beaches by post-glacial stream erosion and beach bluff retreat (see Hike 33).

Both the Homestead and Crossman Ridge trails cross or skirt private property. Most owners are fine with hikers trekking their property, as long as nothing is disturbed and no one ventures too close to their homes. So just respect the land as you would your own property and everyone will continue to have free access to these wonderful trails.

A note to Nordic skiers: The system of trails beginning from the west end of Ohlson Mountain links to the Crossman Ridge and Homestead trails, then down to the Demonstration Forest Trail System. These trails are part of the backcountry Nordic ski trail system used by we locals throughout the winter. So if you return to Homer during winter or spring, make a note to strap on your Nordic skis and come back up here to enjoy the same spectacular views.

32

Calvin and Coyle

Total distance: 0.5 mile one way

Hiking time: 1 hour

Elevation change: Negligible

Rating: Easy

Best season: Spring through fall

Maps: Homer Chamber of Commerce tourist map

Special features: Easy hike for all ages with views of moose, wetlands, and mountains with a viewing platform near the halfway point.

Note: Children at least five years old can easily take this hike. Younger walkers will likely stumble over the endless exposed tree roots.

You can access this flat, short, easy hike through brushy moose habitat directly from downtown Homer. It's a good warm-up hike to knock the kinks out when you first hit town. Don't forget the bug repellent.

GETTING THERE

From the intersection of the Sterling Highway and Pioneer Avenue in Homer, drive 0.5 mile on Pioneer to the stoplight at the intersection of Lake Street. Here Pioneer Avenue changes to East End Road. Follow East End Road about 0.5 mile to Mariner Avenue. At Mariner you'll see a small brown sign pointing to the Calvin and Coyle trailhead. Turn right on Mariner and proceed about 0.25 mile to the trailhead. Currently, there is no designated parking area here, although one has been in the works for some time. Park close to the trailhead off the side of the road; just make sure you're not blocking the roadway or a driveway.

THE TRAIL

The Calvin and Coyle Trail takes you through bushy and grassy areas, offering willows, alders, sedges, and grasses, in this low-elevation wetland moose habitat. In winter this area supports over 100 moose that make their way down here from the hills to the west in search of food.

You start through some spruce trees (this area sports a special variety of spruce

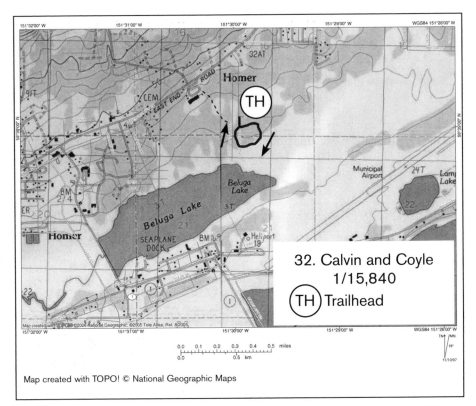

Map created with TOPO! © National Geographic Maps

known as the Lutz spruce) and then enter an open, high-grass meadow. Lupines and wild roses are common here in June and July, while fireweed dominates in August. Also look for the deep purple blooms of monkshood in late August and early September—poisonous but beautiful. Birders will also delight in finding a wide range of birds—including American bald eagles—which are plentiful around Kachemak Bay.

About 100 yards in, the trail splits: the Calvin and Coyle Trail proceeds left, while the path to the right extends for about one-quarter mile through an open meadow and along a forest edge to Joseph A. Banks Junior High School. Take this 15-minute side trip to enjoy the wildflowers throughout spring and summer.

Continue left, or north, on the Calvin and Coyle Trail, where you soon reach another trail split. You can take either branch, as this is a circular path that ends right back where you're standing. I suggest going left to hike clockwise around the loop because the return from the viewing platform will be a shorter distance on the return. You hike through alternating areas of meadow and trees for about one-quarter mile. While the trail is flat, there are numerous knotty roots and, early in the season, windfall branches and logs to negotiate. Visibility is often limited to only a few feet by the tall grasses and dense underbrush.

Remember, this is prime moose habitat. If you are quiet, you have a better chance of seeing one. In spring and early summer, when mama moose are with their newborn, be particularly careful not to walk between mother and baby. Be aware of your immediate surroundings and you'll be fine.

A little more than halfway around the circle trail you arrive at the viewing platform, which provides a nice look at the upper end of the marshy Beluga Slough, also prime moose habitat. This is a great place to rest and take in the sights and smells of this unique wetland smack in the middle of Homer. Sit quietly for a few minutes and you'll be serenaded by warblers, wrens and hear the occasional squawks of mockingbirds and local jays.

The viewing platform is about two-thirds of the way around the loop trail if you are hiking clockwise. The rest of the trip again alternates between grassland meadows and stands of trees. To gain more expansive views of the open wetlands in front of the viewing platform, there is an informal but well-worn side trail that leaves the main trail just north of the platform. This trail leads to a partially submerged wood plank walkway that takes you out onto the boggy wetlands. You can also explore other side trails that meander through the trees on both sides of the platform.

SPECIAL NOTES

Because of the tall grass all along this hike, it can be soaking wet after a rain or in early morning. So wear water-repellent or waterproof pants and gaiters over your footwear. And if you do encounter a moose on this or any other hike, your best course of action is to back slowly and carefully away. Retreat a safe distance and enjoy the experience.

Across Beluga Slough toward Grace Ridge in the Kenai Mountains from the moose-viewing platform

33

Anchor Point Beach

Total distance: As short or as long as you like

Hiking time: As short or as long as you like

Elevation change: Sea level, unless you play in the dunes

Rating: Easy

Best season: Year-round

Maps: Kachemak Bay State Park by National Geographic Trails Illustrated

Special features: Spectacular views of Cook Inlet and the magnificent mountainous Alaska Peninsula with its five volcanoes and terrific rock-hounding.

While there are many great beach hikes along the southern Kenai Peninsula, the walk south from Anchor Point Beach at the mouth of the Anchor River is one of my favorites for several reasons. The views up and down Cook Inlet are so sweeping that on a clear day you can see all five Cook Inlet volcanoes: from north to south—Spur, Redoubt, Iliamna, Augustine, and Douglas. The beach is also broad, especially at low tide, with plenty of sandy and rocky areas, as well as supratidal (above the tides) grassy dunes. On top of that, the beach south of Anchor Point offers some of the best rock-collecting around. Hike weather conditions will vary from dead calm to stormy with high winds and waves coming off Cook Inlet. This is because you are at the westernmost tip of land and beyond there is only water.

Note: Take a minute to notice the sign you've passed about Anchor Point being the end of the road in the Western Hemisphere. That's correct. There is no other connected road traveling any farther west. There are roads around ports and small towns farther west in Alaska, but you can't drive to them. They are self-contained and accessible in the first instance only by boat. As you know from geography class, the rest of the coast of the Western Hemisphere trends east, with South America far to the east of California. Be sure to take a picture of yourself at this sign, for no one back home will believe you until you get a map and show them.

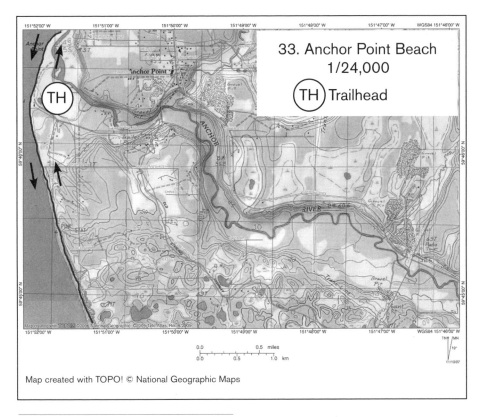

33. Anchor Point Beach
1/24,000

(TH) Trailhead

Map created with TOPO! © National Geographic Maps

GETTING THERE

From the intersection with the New Sterling Highway at Anchor Point, drive 0.25 mile downhill on the Old Sterling Highway to the bridge over the Anchor River. Turn right onto Anchor River Road after you cross the bridge and drive 1.1 miles to where it ends at Anchor Point Beach.

THE TRAIL

Don your windbreaker, hat, and shades, fill your day pack with lunch and water, and head south from the parking area at Anchor Point. (Look for that same sign noting that you are at the end of the westernmost road you can drive to in North America.) If you start your hike about two hours after high tide, you'll have an ever-widening beach. This is one of the best walking beaches around thanks to its width and relatively low slope.

Hike south for about one-quarter mile, and then start looking at the tremendous variety of rock types in the gravel and cobble. All the major rock groups are here, including plutonic igneous rocks like granites, a variety of volcanic rocks, metamorphic rocks like shists and gneisses, and a wide array of sedimentary rocks like sandstones, shales, and conglomerates. You'll even find stretched-pebble conglomerates that were heated and squeezed from round pebbles into elongated ellipsoids. If you are like me, your backpack will soon be filled to the point where you can't even lift it, never mind carry it back. This is when you flag down one of the locals who is down there with a pickup truck or four-wheeler and beg them to transport your rocks back to the parking lot for you.

So where do all these rock types come from? Well, those glaciers on the other side of the peninsula and Kachemak Bay in the southern Kenai Mountains used to be a whole lot bigger. In fact, the whole southern Kenai Peninsula was once covered with glacial ice that eventually deposited a variety of rocks here. As the winds and waves from Cook Inlet then eroded the Anchor Point coastline, finer sentiments were swept away while the larger pebbles, cobbles, and boulders were left concentrated and exposed along the beach. This process continues today.

If rock-hounding is not your thing, just keep walking. The coastline south of here is spectacular, offering sweeping views of the southern half of Cook Inlet and the Alaska Range to the west. And as you hike around the southern tip of the peninsula, you enjoy increasingly revealing views of the mouth of Kachemak Bay in the southern Kenai Mountains. It's kind of tough to stop walking, as the curving coastline entices you to continually wonder what's around the next bend.

As you move south and east, the cliffs become higher. If you are interested in geology, you'll be delighted with the variety of sandstones, shales, siltstones, and volcanic layers, as well as the peat, lignite, and coal exposed along the cliff fronts.

At some point, you should stop for lunch and just enjoy a little quiet time on the beach. If you started your hike well before low tide, you can enjoy hours of beach hiking. Just be sure to give yourself enough time to hike back. (At moderate high tide levels of 15 feet or below, you'll typically have plenty of beach to enjoy.)

Alternately, and particularly if you have fishing on your mind, you can hike north of the parking area toward the mouth of the Anchor River. This river, which drains much of the southern portion of the Kenai Peninsula, is one of the premier trout streams on the Kenai and no slouch when it comes to salmon. The mouth and delta are about 0.5 mile north along the beach, which is predictably much more heavily used than the southern section because of the great fishing.

This northern section of beach also offers dune exploration and good views of both Cook Inlet to the west and the Anchor River estuary to the east.

SPECIAL NOTES

I think the beach south of Anchor Point is one of the great beaches of the world, even though you may have to share it with a few other people, some of whom will be driving pickup trucks or four-wheelers. But on most days there are only a few of those, and the grand views, the dynamics of Cook Inlet, and the treasure trove of rocks make this a very special place.

During the winter both the north and south treks along this beach offer solitude and wonderful, often crystal-clear views across Cook Inlet. Look for lots of ice sculpture features formed by the interaction of waves, tides, and winds. There is often a cold wind blowing but dress for it and you can enjoy it. Polarized sunglasses are a good idea when beach hiking any time of year, due to the strongly polarized light reflecting off the water, but they are a must in the winter with the snow as well as the water reflecting the intense, bright light.

View across Cook Inlet toward Iliamna volcano from glacial-boulder-strewn Anchor Point Beach

V. Southeast Kenai–Across Kachemak Bay

34

Red Mountain

Total distance: 8 miles to base of Red Mountain one way; +3 miles to summit one way

Hiking time: 10 to 12 hours if hiking; 5 to 6 hours if biking and hiking

Elevation change: 3,524 feet, sea level to Red Mountain summit

Rating: Moderate to difficult

Best season: July through September

Maps: Kachemak Bay State Park by National Geographic Trails Illustrated; USGS Seldovia Quad, and Kachemak Bay State Park and State Wilderness Park Map (www.dnr.state.ak.us/parks/units/kbay/kbaymap.htm)

Special features: Spectacular and unique views both east to the southern portion of the Gulf of Alaska and west all the way to the Alaska Range; unique mantle-origin geology

This trail can be enjoyed as a hike or a bike/hike combination. Red Mountain is located just south of Kachemak Bay State Park in the northern portion of the Seldovia tribal lands. The peak is one of the highest in the southern Kenai Range and offers majestic views east into the Gulf of Alaska and west across southern Kachemak Bay and lower Cook Inlet. On a clear day you can see all the way across to the Alaska Peninsula and four of its volcanoes: Mt. Douglas, Augustine, Iliamna, and Redoubt. This is a good day hike and well worth the extra effort, water-taxi ride, and bike ride/hike it takes to get there.

GETTING THERE

Access the Red Mountain area by taking along your bike, if you want, on the water-taxi ride across the bay starting from Homer. From Homer Harbor, take a 30- to 45-minute water-taxi ride to the public dock at the head of Jakolof Bay. Most water taxis allow you to transport bicycles as well as hiking gear. From the public dock, it's a 6-mile hike or bike to the base of Red Mountain. I suggest you opt for the bike ride to give yourself more time to explore and play on the high ridges surrounding Red Mountain. Suitable bikes can be be rented in Homer (See the resources section of the Introduction.)

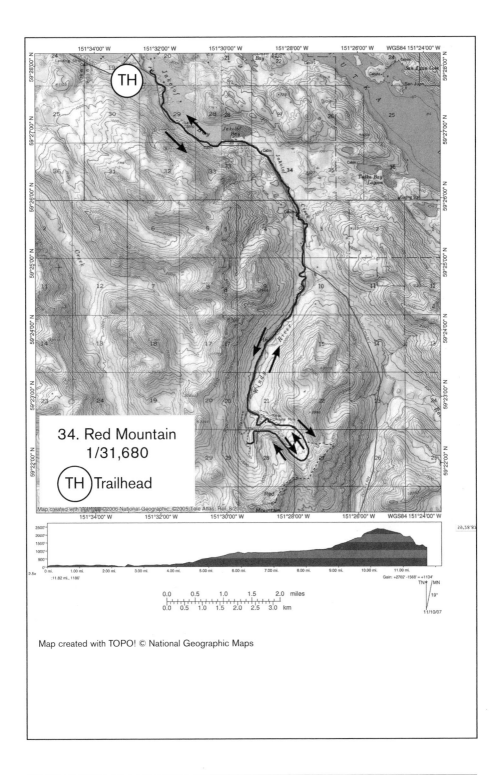

34. Red Mountain
1/31,680

TH Trailhead

Map created with TOPO! © 2006 National Geographic; ©2005 Tele Atlas, Rel. 8/2005

Map created with TOPO! © National Geographic Maps

THE TRAIL

A dirt road runs from the public dock at Jakolof Bay to the base of Red Mountain. The first 3 miles along the floodplain of Jack Clark Creek are flat, after which you begin your ascent into the headwaters of Jakolof Creek toward the drainage divide between the Windy and Rocky rivers. At 3.5 miles the road splits and the left path leads downhill through the Rocky River drainage to the far other side of the Kenai Peninsula and into the Gulf of Alaska. This Rocky River Road is a challenging bike ride/carry to the coast as the trail is often overgrown with alders and has washed-out bridges. The other, right-hand path toward Red Mountain, still a dirt road, begins a steep ascent into the headwaters of Windy Creek. This is a fascinating and beautiful section of your bike or hike, especially where the road levels out near the top as you pass an interconnected string of glacially formed ponds and meadows and the Windy Creek stream channel.

This necklace is a periglacial feature left behind by retreating glaciers only a few thousand years ago. This series of small in-line lakes linked by stream channels is typical of glacier areas and are known as Paternoster lakes, which were formed in small glacially carved depressions left by the retreating Red Mountain glacier. Take some time to explore these lakes and connecting streams, as they offer many delightful surprises such as braided streams, constantly changing gravel bars, and areas of calm quiet waters.

You can bike for about 6 miles up to the base of Red Mountain at about 1,300 feet of elevation and then stash your bike in one of the bushy areas there. Here you begin your hike up the remaining 2,200 feet to the summit. You'll see lots of evidence of the old chromite mine—a chromium source used in making steel—that was active at Red Mountain for many years. Start hiking up the old mining road that circles around the north end of the mountain.

The first one-half mile is a moderate climb that takes you to the bottom of the old cirque (a bowl-shaped area) that was the zone of ice accumulation for the glacier that slowly flowed down from Red Mountain and carved out the valley that starts with Windy Creek and continues into Jakolof Creek then Jakolof Bay. Imagine the size of it. The relatively flat floor of Windy Creek was formed by the deposit of great quantities of sediment that were trapped and then released by the glacier as its front retreated back and up toward its cirque bowl basin.

From the bottom of the cirque, you climb a steep slope for one-quarter mile to a steep path/old mining road that leads three-quarters of a mile to the summit. If it's a warm sunny day, the top of the mountain is a delightful place to have lunch and enjoy breathtaking, 360-degree views of the southern portion of the Kenai Peninsula, the Gulf of Alaska, and the volcanoes of the Alaska Peninsula far to the west. The hike from the base to the summit is above tree line, so you have little protection from driving wind and rain or, if you're particularly lucky, snow.

On the descent, consider hiking north along the ridgeline that leads off to your right from the summit. After about a one-half mile hike, you reach a saddle from which you can descend a moderately steep slope into the cirque you hiked up from earlier. This ridgeline hike offers continuously spectacular views east down into the Rocky River Drainage and west across Kachemak Bay. If you are hiking in September, don't be surprised if you are greeted by an ephemeral snowfall sent by impatient old man winter.

Red Mountain's cirque bowl basin and companion peak display their autumn light

SPECIAL NOTES

Red Mountain is composed of very dense rocks rich in iron and magnesium that were formed miles below the surface in the earth's mantle at well over 1,000 degrees Celsius/1,800 degrees Fahrenheit. All the folding, faulting, and tectonic activity in and around these rocks shoved this little slice of mantle thousands of feet into the air. The high iron content of these rocks oxidizes, or rusts, giving it the red color. For anyone interested in exotic rock types, if you bang around with your rock hammer you'll find dark green dunites that have been weathered to a dull red, composed of iron- and magnesium-rich silicate minerals known as olivine. You'll also find the black mineral chromite (often occuring in thin layers), which was the focus of all the mining here, as well as green and black peridotite, another rock common to the mantle that has a high iron and magnesium silicate content.

These rocks have been pushed to the surface by the same forces that caused the formation of the folded and faulted mountain ranges of the Alaska Range and the rest of the Kenai Peninsula mountains. It is a rare thing for we humans to see these rocks in our world.

Because Red Mountain sits on one of the narrow segments of the eastern half of the southern Kenai Peninsula, it offers one of the few hike views into the wild drainages and waters of the Gulf of Alaska. So the bike-hike up here is worth it just for that unique perspective.

35

Tutka Lake

Total distance: The longest trail runs 3.5 miles from the Sea Star Cove Cabin access to the waterfall at the terminus of the Tutka Lake Trail

Hiking time: 3 hours to and from the waterfall at trail's end

Elevation change: 300 feet

Rating: Easy to moderate

Best season: Early spring through late fall, although this is one of the few trails also accessible in winter.

Maps: Kachemak Bay State Park by National Geographic Trails Illustrated, and Kachemak Bay State Park and State Wilderness Park Map (www.dnr.state.ak.us/ parks/units/kbay/kbaymap.htm)

Special features: A short, little-used trail with a surprising amount of scenery, including moss- and lichen-draped trees in a stately, high-canopy, cool, moist, old-growth spruce forest, a lake surrounded by meadows, a stream, a canyon, a waterfall, and a lagoon; darn good berry picking around Tutka Lake in late summer and early fall.

These two short, connected trail segments are located on the south side of Tutka Bay and offer serene walks through old-growth spruce forests. They can be delightful, sheltered interludes from active days spent kayaking and fishing in the bay. One added attraction is that you'll likely have this trail to yourself because few people consider this little gem a worthy destination on its own.

GETTING THERE

The Tutka Lake trail system can only be reached by water–kayak or water taxi–yet surprisingly there are four distinct access points. One is from the Sea Star Cove Cabin located on the south side of Tutka Bay. A second is from the main trailhead a little over one-half mile to the west. The third is from the south side of Tutka Bay Lagoon via a tiny snippet of trail known as the Hatchery Spur Trail. The fourth is a stair access at the entrance to Tutka Bay Lagoon, which in turn joins the Hatchery Spur Trail before it meets the main Tutka Lake Trail at the south side of the lake. Take a look at the map to choose your route. Hiking the Tutka Lake trails is a great way to stretch your legs after kayaking the southern shores of Tutka Bay.

Note: If your goal is primarily the waterfall, the Hatchery Trail (or if the tides are too low, its spur trail from the mouth of Tutka Bay Lagoon) offers the fastest route. But be aware that access to the trailhead is via Tutka Lagoon whose access is tidally controlled, so be sure to check with your water taxi about scheduling if you

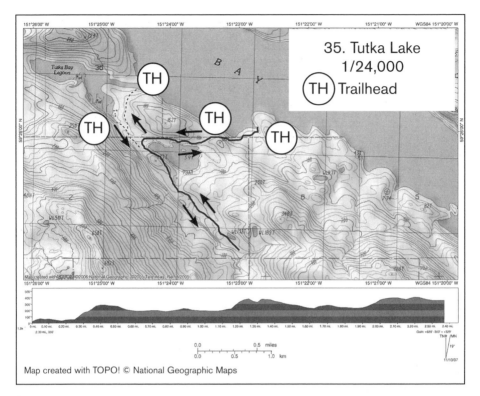

35. Tutka Lake
1/24,000
(TH) Trailhead

Map created with TOPO! © National Geographic Maps

want to use this trailhead either coming or going.

If tidal levels are not cooperative with your schedule, you can use the stair access located at the mouth of Tutka Bay Lagoon, and the taxi can pick you up there.

Also Note: If hiking and seeing forest, the lake and waterfall are your goals, I recommend hiking in from the two western trailheads at the main trailhead or the Sea Star Cove Cabin (most eastern trailhead), which are both reachable at all tidal levels.

THE TRAIL

If you start at the main trailhead and campsite, hike about 0.2 mile up a fairly steep, forested slope to an intersection with the trail from the Sea Star Cove Cabin, which is a half-mile to the northeast. The woods around the cabin are filled with old-growth

trees covered with wonderful moss and lichen, creating a gnome-forest-like feel.

The trailhead at the Sea Star Cove Cabin is on the south end of the Sea Star Cove beach. The trail climbs up about 100 feet through a few short switchbacks into the old-growth forest. You will hike for 0.5 mile to the intersection with the main access trail segment coming from the main trailhead.

From the intersection of the main and Sea Star Cove Cabin trail segments, you will continue your forested hike west and then south about one-half mile up and down but gradually climbing to Tutka Lake, which is several hundred feet above Tutka Bay. As you begin to circle Tutka Lake, you have good views up and to the south of a peak and ridge known locally as Broken Knife for its ragged appearance. The trail winds around the northern edge of the lake roughly one-half mile to the intersection with the Hatchery Spur Trail, which then leads to the right (west) and takes you down to Tutka Bay Lagoon and its fish hatchery. The left trail continues to follow the edge of beautiful Tutka Lake, dotted with boggy areas and providing views of the forest-rimmed lake. Look for irises along the lake edge.

The trail can get a bit gnarly with roots, especially when it's wet, so watch your step and use your hiking sticks.

Skirt the southern edge of Tutka Lake for one-half mile, set off as it is against the peaks and ridges of the high Kenai Mountains that rise to the north on the far side of Tutka Bay. About two-thirds of the way down the lake, the trail begins to trend up and away from the shoreline as it traverses up the steep southern shore. At the top of the traverse, the trail continues along a rolling forested upland with easy to moderate up and down trail segments. Along this final upland section, you will be serenaded by the sounds of the stream channel above and along which the trail follows. Along the way you will be treated to some spectacular, gut-clenching views far down into the gorge carved by the stream channel.

You will notice as you hike that the old-growth spruces are generally larger–up to 2 feet in diameter–and more widely spaced than trees in other forested hikes on this side of the Bay. This one area, the southern shore of Tutka Bay, was one of the few areas spared the kill of the spruce bark beetle, which eats mature spruce trees. There was an epidemic of this beetle in 2001/2002, which wiped out most all the

Tutka Lake trail system can be reached by kayak across Tutka Bay Fjord

adult spruces on the Kenai. So while most of the forested hikes are through stands of younger, shorter, more closely spaced spruces, here you can enjoy the visibility, moist coolness, luxurious spongy forest floor, and high canopy formed by large, widely spaced, stately old-growth trees. Another pleasant consequence of this lack of beetle kill is the relative lack of blown-down, weakened, or dead trees so common along many other Kenai forest hikes, particularly early in the season. On my last hike here, I encountered only one fallen tree across the path.

The trail ends at a beautiful waterfall, one you will hear long before you see it. Give yourself time to hang out here and have lunch or a snack and enjoy the sights, sounds, smells, and wonderful solitude of this forested jewel.

SPECIAL NOTES

In addition to the Hatchery Spur Trail, there is another trail access via a steep flight of stairs at the opening to Tutka Bay Lagoon from Tutka Bay. This is a good place to stash kayaks and hike up into the Tutka Lake trail system. This short access trail intersects the Hatchery Trail, which in turn joins the main Tutka Lake Trail at its western end. One word of caution about stashing your kayaks: The kayak landing area at the base of the steep stairs is rocky and not very wide, so secure your kayaks to some trees near the base of the stairs to prevent an incoming tide from whisking them away.

Like so many other lake-filled depressions along the Kenai Peninsula, Tutka Lake was scoured out by a glacier that ground into this valley until about 12,000 years ago. (This area was once under more than 1,000 vertical feet of ice.) The waterfall at the end of the trail, like most others in Tutka Bay, formed when the steep face of the mountain front was sliced off by the passing glacier.

36

Grace Ridge

Total distance: 8 miles one way

Hiking time: 8 to 10 hours, but leave a couple hours to dawdle on top

Elevation change: 3,105 feet

Rating: Moderate on trail to difficult on steeper cross-country routes

Best season: Late July and August because snow may linger on Grace Ridge through mid-July

Maps: Kachemak Bay State Park by National Geographic Trails Illustrated, and Kachemak Bay State Park and State Wilderness Park Map (www.dnr.state.ak.us/parks/units/kbay/kbaymap.htm)

Special features: A stunning variety of views across fjords, glaciers, islands, volcanoes, and wildflower-strewn tundra. On the ridgeline section, as you walk without a trail, you will also delight in dozens of pockets of mini-ecosystems of grasses and flowers.

Grace Ridge is one of my three favorite hikes on the Kenai (Summit Creek and the Harding Ice Field being the other two). If you have time for only one hike on the Kenai, this might be it. This trek takes you from a high-wave-energy, steep, gravel-and-cobble-beach trailhead located at the heads of Sadie Cove and Tutka Bay up through old-growth spruce forests, berry-laden grasslands and meadows, then across wildflower-strewn alpine tundra. You'll hike on a well-defined trail and your own cross-country route.

Once on top of Grace Ridge, there are awe-inspiring views down into Sadie Cove and Tutka Bay fjords and commanding vistas across the southern Kenai Mountains to the east and west across the Herring Islands and the southern entrances to Kachemak Bay, southern Cook Inlet to Kamishak Bay, and the volcanoes of the Alaska Peninsula. The 2-mile walk along the spine of Grace Ridge is a hiking adventure all its own. If you have time, and the weather is not going to be too windy, also plan to stay overnight nestled in one of the many grassy ridgetop nooks located along the alpine ridgetop section.

GETTING THERE

From Homer, take a water taxi to the Kayak Beach Trail access on the western end of the Grace Ridge Peninsula. You can also hike this trail from the Tutka Bay access on the east end, but I recommend starting from Kayak Beach because of the incredible views east up toward the ridgeline as

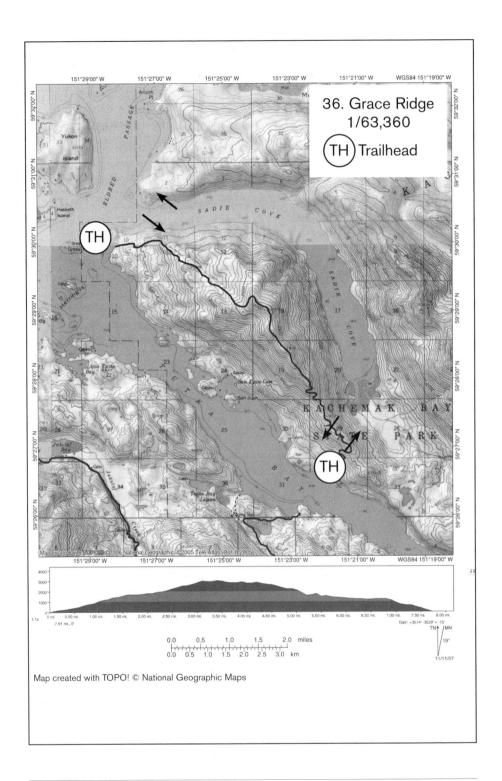

36. Grace Ridge
1/63,360

(TH) Trailhead

Map created with TOPO! © National Geographic Maps

you hike. Plan to have a water taxi pick you up at the other end of your hike either later that day or the next day if you plan an overnight stay.

THE TRAIL

The Grace Ridge Trail starts at the steep cobblestone and pebble slope of Kayak Beach. You can camp out at the top of this beach or simply arrive by water taxi early in the morning. There's actually another access point at this end of the trail, right around the corner at an old quarry at the mouth of Sadie Cove. However, the access from Kayak Beach is easier—except at very high tides and when big waves are present—and the views southwest across the Herring Islands to the grand volcanoes of the Alaska Peninsula are far better.

Sign in at the trailhead and begin your hike up a gradual slope. In a few minutes you reach an intersection with a trail from the left, the Sadie Cove quarry access. Turn right and hike through grassy areas and under a power line. In late summer the area is rich in blueberries. The trail assumes a moderate slope as you traverse a hillside of spruce and hemlock for about one-half mile. Where the trail steepens, relax against the big pine tree conveniently located on your left and take in the nifty view of the mouth of Sadie Cove and Sadie Knob to the northeast.

Over the next mile you wind your way through forests as the trail passes waterfalls on the stream that drains the north slope of Grace Ridge. The trail eventually turns into a series of switchbacks that lead up and out of the forest to subalpine meadows, where the truly gorgeous views begin. About 2 miles into the hike, you arrive at the first knob, just a little over 1,700 feet in elevation. This is a great rest stop to drink some water, have a snack, and gorge yourself on the views. If you're not up for traveling cross-country and up the ridgeline, you can turn back here. The views alone down into Tutka Bay, across the Herring Islands and across Cook Inlet to the volcano-studded Alaska Range are well worth the hike . . . but if you have adventure in your soul you'll continue on.

This first viewpoint is the end of the one well-defined trail on this hike. From here you are above tree line and can go cross-country making your own route in several different directions depending upon snow, moisture, and your desire to explore. The most sensible route takes you east up the obvious valley and then around north up the steep but broad slope toward the summit. This section is slower going, as you are hiking across rocky alpine tundra.

Throughout August, this glorious high ground is covered with wildflowers. Take some time to get down on your hands and knees to peer more closely. There are some tiny but beautiful flowers down at the level of your toes. Step on rocks, though, whenever you can in crossing the delicate terrain, avoiding as many plants as possible. Go slow and watch your step too, as it's easy to turn your ankle here.

About 500 feet from the summit, the slope becomes very steep regardless of your approach, so pant away in anticipation of gaining the ridgeline and its glorious views. If you have thighs of steel, you can hike directly up the fall line, which is the steepest line of ascent. If you prefer a more moderate incline, take a diagonal traverse and maybe a few long switchbacks across the open tundra slope.

Once on top—after hiking about 3.5 miles and gaining over 3,100 feet—take a well-deserved respite. Air out your clothes and have a snack. You could have lunch here, but I suggest waiting until you're

Grace Ridge view of Tutka Bay fjord, the Herring Islands, and the Alaska Range in the distance

a little farther down the ridge. Put your drier clothes back on now, and head out along the ridge. For the next 2 miles stay along the top of Grace Ridge. Don't walk in a straight line; wander about. There are all sorts of interesting, grassy gardens nestled between the upturned, erosion-resistant shists and quartz-rich layers that "hold up" the top of this ridgeline. If you're really adventurous you can camp overnight in one of these protected nooks . . . you will have a night you are unlikely to forget!

All along the ridge you will have spectacular views down into the Sadie Cove fjord to the north and the Tutka Bay fjord to the south. You are slowly losing elevation as you hike east along the ridgeline, but at about the 5.5-mile mark you begin to encounter steeper downhill sections. Pause for a last look around prior to heading down from this enchanting ridgeline.

The next 2.5 miles take you down through grasslands and berry patches and then into the spruce forests that blanket the near shorelines of Tutka Bay. The grasslands and brush are often populated with black bear getting their bellyful of berries in late summer. Make noise as you come down the trail and they will avoid you. Finally, at about mile 8, you conclude your descent midway along the north shore of Tutka Bay.

SPECIAL NOTES

You may want to carry a cell phone and/or a VHF band radio to call the taxi service at the beginning of your descent from Grace Ridge so the water taxi arrives to pick you up close to your estimated finish time. If that's not an issue, take your time exploring the ridgeline. Allow at least 10 hours for this hike. It is one whose beauty, subtleties, and jaw-dropping views you'll never forget.

37

Sadie Knob

Total distance: 4.3 miles from north trail-head to top of Sadie Knob; 3.7 miles from north trailhead to south trailhead, if you choose not to scale the Knob.

Hiking time: 3 hours one way to top of Sadie Knob

Elevation change: 2,200 feet up Sadie Knob

Rating: Moderate

Best season: All summer and into fall; you can hike Sadie Knob earlier and later than Alpine Ridge (Hike 44) or Grace Ridge (Hike 36) due to its significantly lower elevation.

Maps: Kachemak Bay State Park by National Geographic Trails Illustrated, and Kachemak Bay State Park and State Wilderness Park Map (www.dnr.state.ak.us/parks/units/kbay/kbaymap.htm)

Special features: The view from Sadie Knob is particularly good for glacial topography and features. A look up the Wosnesenski River drainage reveals not only the shrinking Wosnesenski Glacier itself but startling examples of glacier-carved U-shaped valleys, braided stream channels, hanging glaciers, and outwash plains.

The Sadie Knob Trail is one of four primary alpine trails in Kachemak Bay State Park, along with Alpine Ridge (Hike 44), Grace Ridge (Hike 36) and Red Mountain (Hike 34). This trail is not as long, steep, or high in elevation as those three hikes, though, so if you have less time and/or you're looking for a less-challenging trail that nevertheless ascends to the alpine zone, Sadie Knob is a good choice. It will reward you with spectacular views of Kachemak Bay and the Wosnesenski River valley to the Wosnesenski Glacier with all its periglacial (glacier-associated) features. You can feast your eyes on the wonderful braided channels of the Wosnesenski River and its delta. You also have an excellent perspective on how the muddy glacial-sediment-choked waters of the Wosnesenski River interact with the clear marine waters of Kachemak Bay. There is also a lush complement of wildflowers and berries, just like on the more arduous ridge hikes. And, if you're only up for a nice walk through some rare, old-growth spruce forest, you can hike from the north trailhead to the south without tackling the alpine section of the Sadie Knob Spur Trail at all.

GETTING THERE

As with most of the trails in Kachemak State Park, access to the Sadie Knob Trail is typically via water taxi from the Homer Spit. There are two trailheads: a northern one by Neptune Bay and a southern one by the mouth of Sadie Cove. I recommend you start at the north trailhead and finish at the south trailhead.

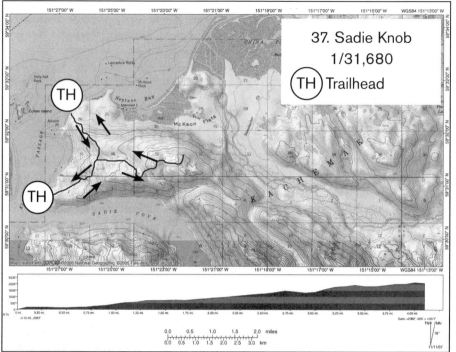

THE TRAIL

It's about 1.7 miles from the north trailhead to the intersection of the south trailhead route and Sadie Knob Spur Trail, gaining about 700 feet of elevation through dense old-growth spruce forest. The first one-half mile is an easy steady uphill climb, a good warm-up section, followed by about a mile of steeper climbing onto the first bench of the Sadie Knob Peninsula. At the intersection, turn left to head up the Sadie Knob Spur Trail, then travel through more spruce forest as you gradually gain elevation along a stream much of the way.

Once you cross the stream, the trail begins to switchback up a much steeper slope for about one-third mile. This is the toughest part of the hike. At the end of the switchbacks, the trail once again levels out to a slow, low-slope climb as you begin your hike across glorious alpine meadows filled with flowers—look for wild geranium

and roses in the mix. You will also find salmonberries, watermelon berries, and blueberries as you hike for about the next mile. One-third mile from the Knob end you reach the alpine zone where the tall grasses drop away and the sparse low tundra begins to dominate.

The top of Sadie Knob is a great place for lunch and glorious views into the west end of Kachemak Bay, Homer Spit, and across to the volcanoes of the Alaska Peninsula. But don't stop here. Take some time to explore the area immediately around the Knob or take a tour cross-country to the east and north. The topography drops away steeply on the northern edge of the Sadie Knob bench, offering the best views to the northeast up the Wosnesenski Glacier drainage. Hike east along the rim of the bench until you're looking straight up at Sadie Peak. You will be gazing across and down into a very steep gorge that you likely had no inkling was there.

Hiking cross-country is easy because there is little vegetation and many rock outcrops that make walking easier. Avoid trampling the vegetation when you can to protect the fragile tundra plants and lichens.

On the return trip, descend toward the south trailhead. From the intersection of the Sadie Knob Spur Trail and the main north–south trail, it's about 2 miles to the south trailhead. There you'll find a campsite and water. If it's open, enjoy some food and refreshments at the Otter Cove restaurant nestled in the trees and/or rest on the deck and wait for your prearranged water taxi to pick you up.

SPECIAL NOTES

Since most of this trail is below tree line in dense old-growth spruce forest, you aren't afforded the mosquito protection provided by the cool breezes that commonly blow throughout Kachemak Bay. Bring plenty of bug repellent and wear a long-sleeved shirt and pants. If it's too hot for the long stuff, slather on repellent and move fast to the highcountry above tree line where the breezes caress the tundra.

Also: There are campsites at both the north and south trailheads. If you want to combine a day of hiking and kayaking, you can have the water-taxi company stash kayaks at the south trailhead and then kayak back up to the north trailhead to be picked up again, or vice versa. Be sure to build that kayak time (about 1 hour) into your time estimate for the water taxi pick-up.

Good views up the Wosnesenski River to the Wosnesenski Glacier

38

Wosnesenski River

*Total distance: Approximately 12 miles
one way from the Haystack Rock access
to either the trialhead at Halibut Cove or
headwaters at the Wosnesenski Glacier*

*Hiking time: To the Glacier and back 2
to 3 days is best, unless you fly in and
float out. I suggest a day to hike in, a
day to hang out, and a day to hike/float
back. The hike between the Halibut Cove
Lagoon and the mouth of the Woz can be
accomplished in a long day, but an overnight along the river is nice.*

*Elevation change: About 500 feet up to
the glacier mouth, unless you scramble
up the mountainside around the glacier—a
grand idea*

*Rating: Easy along lower sections; mod-
erate along the day hike through China
Poot Lake section; difficult up toward the
glacier if a stream crossing is required*

Best season: Spring through fall

*Maps: Kachemak Bay State Park by
National Geographic Trails Illustrated, and
Kachemak Bay State Park and State Wilderness Park Map (www.dnr.state.ak.us/
parks/units/kbay/kbaymap.htm)*

*Special features: A wild and wooly jour-
ney through the lower portion of an active
glacial stream environment, with wild
stream crossings on the upper sections of
the rock-strewn Woz River.*

The trek up the Wosnesenski drainage,
known locally as "the Woz," is one of the
best wilderness hikes in Kachemak Bay
State Park. You will see abundant wildlife
along the entire hike and evidence of a
whole lot more, including lots of moose,
bear, and wolf sign. The Woz drainage is
remote and you are likely to have it to yourself, as few hikers venture up here.

Most maps of this area route this trail
around through the China Poot Trail area,
making it a shorter hike. The multiday
hike described here takes you additionally
farther up into the wilder, more remote sections of the Woz. For a long, one-day, one-
way trip you can hike from the Halibut Cove
Lagoon public dock to Haystack Rock on
the outside of China Poot Bay, where the
taxi pickup will not be so tide dependent.

GETTING THERE

As with all the trails on this side of Kachemak Bay, access to the Woz is by water
taxi from the Homer Spit. On the other side,
one access route is via an extension of the
trail to China Poot Lake/Leisure Lake (noted
on some other maps as the Wosnesenski
Trail); the water taxi drops you off at the
head of Halibut Cove Lagoon and you hike
past the base of Poot Peak to the Woz. For
a multiday hike that focuses on the Woz, I
recommend starting your hike on the beach
just inshore from a sea stack called Haystack Rock out in Kachemak Bay; the water
taxi drops you off at the base of the beach
spit hugging the southern outside edge of
the China Poot Bay tidal flats.

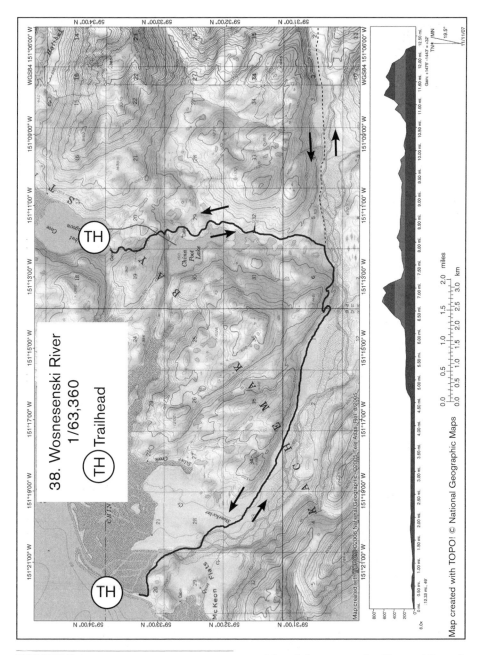

38. Wosnesenski River
1/63,360

(TH) Trailhead

Map created with TOPO! © National Geographic Maps

THE TRAIL

The initial 2.6 miles of the trail from the Haystack Rock beach runs across the southern edge of the China Poot Bay tidal mud flats, and then follows a rough utility road through a low area between the bay and the lower section of the Wosnesenski River. When you enter the Woz drainage, you have good views of the lower section of the river just upstream from where it divides on the McKeon mud flats into multiple channels at its delta on Kachemak Bay. You can bushwhack over to the delta for some bird watching, a nifty half-day adventure.

From the low divide that separates the Woz drainage from China Poot Bay, you travel gradually for 5 miles upriver along the north bank, sometimes walking across the gravel riverbed itself and sometimes along the floodplain bank under aspen and spruce trees. At about 7.5 miles, the trail detours briefly for roughly one-half mile up, over and through a rocky forested promontory that protrudes into the stream channel. The main channel of the Woz River flows directly, and forcefully, against the steep rocky promontory, so the trail must be diverted up and over. On the other side of the promontory, the trail continues along the open rocky streambed for about 1.5 miles to the intersection of the extension of the China Poot Lake Trail.

If you are doing this as a day hike to Halibut Cove Lagoon, turn left (north) and follow the trail about 2.5 miles past the base of Poot Peak to China Poot Lake. This section of the trail alternates through grassy, flower-filled meadows (with some invasive, scratchy cow parsnip—known locally as pushki—and thistles here and there so be alert to these and use your hiking poles to fend them off) and canopied spruce forests. Then continue on to the public dock at the head of the lagoon.

To continue on to the Wosnesenski Glacier, stick to the north bank of the Woz for another 5 miles to the terminus of the glacier. About 1.5 miles past the intersection with the China Poot Trail extension, you have a grand view to the southeast up the Doroshin River drainage to the Doroshin Glacier.

Things can become interesting along this section. Depending upon water levels and the position of the braided stream channels, you may have to make multiple crossings on foot. Water conditions may not allow you to hike all the way to the terminus of the glacier, but at lower levels it's usually possible. Be prepared to turn back if the water is too high, fast, or dangerous. Peak runoff typically occurs in early to mid-spring.

Along both the lower (below the China Poot Trail) and upper (up toward the glacier) sections of the Woz Trail, be on the lookout for ample evidence of large mammal wildlife including moose, black bears, and wolves. As you hike the trail you will have the sense of the wildness and isolation the Woz drainage offers. You can easily remain in Woz country for two weeks and never see another soul.

Plan to spend at least a full day and night exploring the country around the terminus of the Woz Glacier, then head back downstream.

The next time you come, consider bringing an inflatable raft (see Information Resources pages 33–35) with you, to carry you back down on a float trip to the delta, but you should get out before the water becomes too shallow and strands you on the mud flats. Then, hike up and over the low divide between the Woz and China Poot Bay to the beach at Haystack Rock.

SPECIAL NOTES

Tips for crossing stream channels:

1. Two hiking poles are better than one for stability.
2. Always have at least three points of balance, such as two poles and one foot or two feet and one pole. And,

place your poles and lean upstream when you can.

3. Always reach forward with your pole prior to reaching forward with your foot.

4. It is worth the extra weight to bring a pair of sneakers or thick booties. Another alternative is to carry and use Crocs® and heavy wool socks as your stream-channel crossing footwear. The crocks make a nice lightweight, quick-to-dry alternative to booties or sneakers that serve as good round-the-campsite footwear as well. I typically hang my wet socks on the back of my pack to dry them out and have a ziplock bag as well to store them and other wet gear.

5. Keep a waterpoof fire-making kit—wood matches or lighter and newspaper or dry tinder in a sealed ziplock bag—handy near the top of your pack.

Once you reach the terminus of the glacier, set up camp away from the face and off to the side, above the stream channel. This will protect you from the winds that typically blow off the front of the glacier, and from any increase in water levels that may occur. Take care as you hike around the glacier, and never hike up onto the glacier itself, as this is slippery and crevasse-filled and therefore very dangerous. The views from the slopes above the glacier are more revealing anyway.

The "Woz," your destination if you hike all the way up its glacial stream channel and valley

39

China Poot/Leisure Lake

Total distance: 2.8 miles one way

Hiking time: 1.5 hours

Elevation change: 300 feet up to the lake

Rating: Moderate due to gnarly roots and uncertain footing

Best season: Spring through fall

Maps: Kachemak Bay State Park by National Geographic Trails Illustrated, and Kachemak Bay State Park and State Wilderness Park Map (www.dnr.state.ak.us/parks/units/kbay/kbaymap.htm)

Special features: China Poot Lake is the highlight of this hike. It's a beautiful, quiet, serene subalpine lake surrounded by old-growth forest. Look for gorgeous irises along the trail. State Park Cabin at China Poot Lake is a great base camp for exploring other hikes such as Coalition Loop (Hike 42), Moose Valley (Hike 41), and Poot Peak (Hike 40) trails.

The China Poot Lake (aka Leisure Lake) Trail is, along with the Glacier Lake Trail, one of the best introductory hikes on the east and more remote side of Kachemak Bay. It is an easy 2-mile day hike through old-growth spruce forests and flower-filled meadows that ends in a delightful resting spot at a beautiful subalpine lake. The moderate rating for this hike is mostly due to challenging footing along the trail, created by the many roots. This is a terrific hike to get your feet wet, so to speak, in the Kachemak Bay area.

GETTING THERE

Access to the trailhead is typically via water taxi from Homer Spit, which will take you across to the east side of Kachemak Bay to the public dock at Habibut Cove Lagoon. It's even possible to directly access China Poot Lake via floatplane and then hike back to the public dock at the head of Halibut Cove. The most common approach is to get dropped off by the water taxi at the public dock near the ranger station at the southeast corner of Halibut Cove Lagoon.

THE TRAIL

The China Poot Lake Trail is one of the most frequently used, yet seldom crowded, trails in the Kachemak Bay area. From the public dock by the ranger station, the Estuary Trail leads up and away from Halibut Cove Lagoon to the south for about one-half mile. You walk through a short series of switchbacks and several sections of elevated walkway by a stream with a small waterfall,

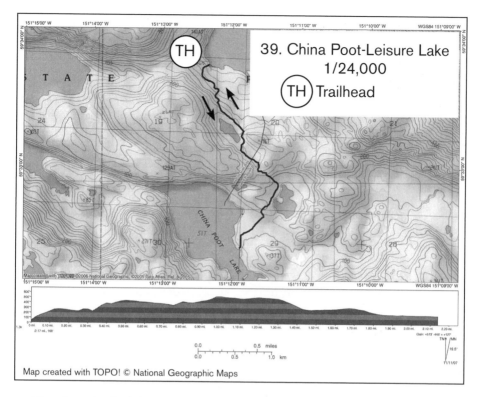

and then through a final short, steep section to intersect the Coalition Trail. At this point you have climbed to almost 200 feet, so you should be warmed up. Turn left to continue toward China Poot (Leisure) Lake. (A right turn here would take you over to the West Lagoon Cabin and put you on a counter-clockwise hike around the Coalition Trail (Hike 42).) For the next one-third mile you hike straight upslope. Many roots eagerly wait to reach out and grab your ankles in this steep section, so watch your step.

Where the trail levels out you arrive at First Lake, a lovely smaller version of China Poot Lake. You then drop down a bit through two switchbacks as the trail pro-ceeds southeast. Hike across a wetland and some elevated walkways with an eye out for birds and wildflowers, especially irises. After the marsh, you move through

an area known locally as Alder Valley, because of the small, branchy alder bushes whose leaves rustle in the wind. Here the trail takes a distinct turn to the east, and after about one-third mile you reach an intersection with the Moose Valley Trail (Hike 41.) You have come about 2 miles so far, and are finished climbing.

Turn right; for the next one-third mile you are hiking along Two Loon Lake. There are several small side trails and resting places here that offer good waterfowl viewing and some sweet solitude. Beautiful purple irises often grow plentiful in the wetland areas here, and moose are common.

About 0.2 mile past the Moose Valley turnoff, you reach an intersection with the east end of the Coalition Loop Trail. From here to China Poot Lake you are hiking mostly through grass meadows. Dew lies heavy on the grass in the morning, so rain pants and gaiters are a good idea.

At about 2.6 miles a short trail heads off to the south (right) toward the China Poot Lake public-use cabin. The lake itself is about 0.2 mile farther on. Walk out onto the gravel bar where Moose Creek deposits its sediment load at the delta on the lake. Surrounded by the serene solitude of the lake and the old-growth spruce forest, this is the place to stretch out and take a little nap or just sit and enjoy the view. One good plan is to pack and enjoy a picnic lunch while lounging on the gravel bar on the edge of the lake.

SPECIAL NOTES

There are four public-use fee cabins close to the ranger station at the public dock at Halibut Cove Lagoon and one public-use cabin at China Poot Lake. (See Resources Information for cabin reservation.) Campsites are available at the West Lagoon trailhead and the other ranger station, as well as on Moose Creek just upstream from where it flows into China Poot Lake. The public-use cabins, and especially the one located at Leisure Lake, make great base camps for multiday hiking forays, such as along the Coalition Trail, Moose Valley Trail, the arduous climb up Poot Peak, or hikes to and from the Wosnesenski Trail.

For an easier hike you can contract with a flying service to drop you at Leisure Lake for a mostly downhill 2.5-mile hike back to the public dock and water taxi pickup.

Along the high sections of the trail, you will catch glimpses of the surrounding glorious peaks

40

Poot Peak Hike & Climb

Total distance: 3.7 miles for the circle hike; add one-third mile (and at least two more hours . . . see hiking time below) for the Poot Peak summit

Hiking time: 3 to 4 hours for the circle hike (2 more hours minimum for the summit assault)

Elevation change: 1,800 feet on the circle trail; another 800 feet to the 4,600-foot Poot Peak summit

Rating: Difficult to very difficult

Best season: July and August for a summit assault; snow and ice often persist into late spring and even early summer, and winter comes early.

Maps: Kachemak Bay State Park by National Geographic Trails Illustrated, and Kachemak Bay State Park and State Wilderness Park Map (www.dnr.state.ak.us/parks/units/kbay/kbaymap.htm)

Special features: Spectacular views of the surrounding area, including China Poot Lake, Moose Valley, and the Wosnesenski River drainage and glacier.

There are really two hikes here: the Poot Peak Circle Hike, which circumnavigates Poot Peak (also known as the Chocolate Drop because it looks like a Hershey's Kiss); and the assault on the peak itself. The circle hike can be taken in either direction. These hikes are very difficult and to the description of the Poot Peak summit climb you can add the word "dangerous," especially when there is ice and snow. The trails are typically poorly maintained, often with blown down trees, and they're steep and difficult even in the best of summer weather. The climb to the summit doesn't require technical climbing gear, although it's sometimes necessary to use all four limbs—and maybe some inappropriate, or should I say appropriate, language. But the spectacular 360-degree views of the surrounding mountains, glacier, lakes, rivers, and Kachemak Bay are worth every bit of this.

Special Note: Be sure to take two hiking sticks. You'll need them.

Another Special Note: This hike is not for young children, or for the infirm or unfit. You will be on the far, other side of the bay, a long water taxi away from help with no cell phone service, no food for sale, and no shelter, but with plenty of wildlife including bears to keep you company, so *please* know what you're doing and be prepared before you head out.

GETTING THERE

Take a water taxi from the Homer Spit to the public dock at the head of Halibut Cove Lagoon, and then hike to China Poot Lake

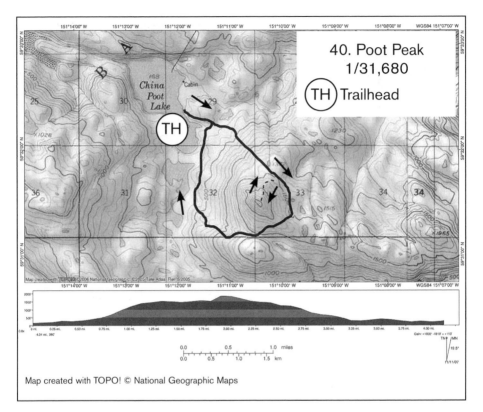

Map created with TOPO! © National Geographic Maps

(Hike 39) or follow the Wosnesenski River Trail (Hike 38). The 2.8-mile China Poot Lake option makes the most sense if your time is limited, as the Wosnesenski route covers 11 miles. Or, if you have the money, you could take a float plane to China Poot Lake rather than hiking in.

A terrific two-day plan is to hike into the public-use fee cabin at China Poot Lake, hang out at the lake overnight, and then attack the Poot Peak Circle Hike or summit bid on day two. For information about reserving the public-use cabins, see Information Resources pages 33–35.

THE TRAIL

From the campground at China Poot Lake, head east toward the Wosnesenski River drainage. At one-half mile you reach the

intersection with the northern segment of the China Poot Peak Trail. At this point you have to decide whether to go north or south on the circle hike. I suggest taking the northern route for three reasons. First, it's the fastest and most direct path to the summit. Second, I love the views across the landscape when coming down the trail around the south rim of the circle. And third, the south trail is slightly less steep, which reduces the downhill pounding on the knees.

Turn left to take the Poot Peak North Trail upslope, and I mean directly upslope. The climb is rocky and strewn with roots and may be overgrown with alder in areas. Some sections require both hands and feet, so your hiking poles will be of limited use at times. I just strap my hiking poles to my day pack on the steepest climbs to leave both hands free. A pair of leather gardening gloves is also handy here and for your ultimate scramble up Poot Peak if that is part of your destination. The leather will protect you from the ubiquitous devils club and thistle thorns.

After about 1.1 miles and 750 vertical feet, you break out into the alpine zone at the 1,000-foot mark and begin to enjoy fantastic views. Continue to climb for another 800 vertical feet to where the trail intersects with the route to the summit on the right (south) side. If Poot Peak is your goal, read on. If you're continuing on the circle trail, skip over the paragraph below.

The approach to the summit is only about one third mile, but it's steep and can be dangerous. If you want to enjoy the glorious views on your hike up, which you absolutely should, come to a complete stop before you look around. This is particularly good advice for the hike back down. On the ascent, you start by traversing an alder thicket and a scree slope. The trail steepens (help!) as you approach the summit. Once again, you need to use both hands and feet as you scramble to the top. Beware if you are hiking early in the season: You may encounter remnant ice and snow on this shaded north-facing slope that wasn't readily apparent from below. If you are hiking with companions, be sure to maintain some distance between each person as loose rocks are commonly dislodged during the approach. Once at the top, all your efforts are gloriously rewarded with spectacular views of the Wosnesenski

Part of the stunning 360-degree panorama from the top of Poot Peak

Glacier and its drainage, China Poot Lake, Moose Valley, Halibut Cove Lagoon, and beyond to Homer.

Descend back to the intersection of the Poot Peak Trail and continue on the Poot Peak South Trail, which is also part of the southwest section of the Moose Valley Trail (Hike 41). For the next 0.8 mile, the trail trends gradually downhill. You lose about 700 feet of elevation with the aid of a couple switchbacks at the end of the section, and then arrive at the intersection with the Moose Valley Trail. Here the China Poot South Trail turns right and away from the Moose Valley Trail, which heads left.

As you continue on the China Poot South Trail, it wraps around the southern slopes of Poot Peak and drops gradually to the west. You traverse a flat section along the edge of a small lake and hike through some beautiful meadows that are often filled with wildflowers. About 1 mile past the Moose Valley Trail junction, you proceed steeply down again to a series of switchbacks and downhill scrambles through alders and then spruce and cottonwood forests. The steep sections are good places to use your walking sticks for balance and to control your descent. The trail gradually moderates so you can mostly hike rather than scramble down. The entire hike down from the intersection with the Moose Valley Trail offers stunning views of the landscape below, so stop often to enjoy them.

About 1.9 miles from the junction, your route intersects with the path that comes from the Wosnesenski River Trail toward China Poot Lake. Turn right here and hike about 1 mile along the edge of an unnamed lake just south of China Poot Lake back to where you started on the northern Poot Peak Trail. Turn left here to return to China Poot Lake.

SPECIAL NOTES

In addition to nearly always wearing "knee covers," one of my favorite knee-protection techniques is to carry a pair of self-adhesive Ace bandages in my day pack. I use them to wrap my knees when traversing steep downhill sections, which pays big dividends in mitigating knee stress, fatigue, pain, and damage. I also suggest hiking sticks for all but the steepest uphill sections and find them especially useful when negotiating downhill slopes.

41

Moose Valley

Total distance: 6.3 miles (Moose Valley only). About 10.3 miles, when you combine this hike's 6.3 miles with the 2 miles each way in and out that you must hike in order to get there from the Halibut Cove Public Dock.

Hiking time: 4 to 5 hours (Moose Valley only), or overnight along the trail or at the Poot Peak Lake public-use fee cabin

Elevation change: 1,400 feet

Rating: Moderate

Best season: Summer and early fall

Maps: Kachemak Bay State Park by National Geographic Trails Illustrated, and Kachemak Bay State Park and State Wilderness Park Map (www.dnr.state.ak.us/parks/units/kbay/kbaymap.htm)

Special features: Widely varied terrain, great views of Poot Peak (also known as the Chocolate Drop because of its distinctive shape), wildflower meadows, and outstanding moose habitat. Wonderful fall color hike.

Moose Valley, located just northeast of Poot Peak, offers a colorful hike through open meadows and forested terrain on a little-used trail. Stream-crossed lowland meadows and grasslands rise to moderate-altitude spruce forests with alpine lakes. This trail offers a nice combination of intimate views of meadows and wetlands in the lower, northern areas and expansive breathtaking views from its higher-elevation, southern section.

GETTING THERE

Travel by water taxi from Homer Spit to the public dock at the head of Halibut Cove Lagoon. Hike about 2 miles toward China Poot Lake (Hike 39) to the intersection of the Moose Valley Trail.

THE TRAIL

From the intersection of the China Poot Lake Trail near Two Loon Lake (Hike 39 contains more information on this section), the Moose Valley Trail wanders near the north edge of the lake, offering good views of the water and China Poot Peak. The path then slowly winds uphill along an alder-choked stream. A side trail at about mile 1 takes you down to the Moose Valley public-use cabin, an old, renovated trapper's cabin maintained by the state park system. At about 1.5 miles you enter a large grassy meadow carpeted in wildflowers throughout most of the summer. If you hike here in early morning you'll likely end up with wet legs, so wear your gaiters or don rain pants. The high grasses sometimes make the trail

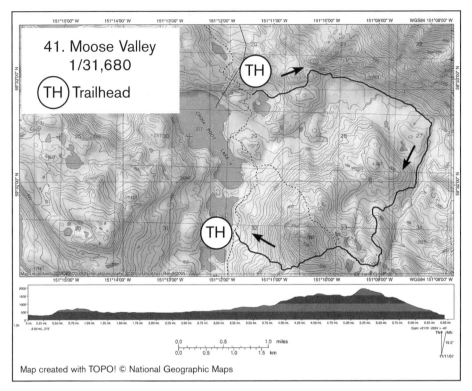

41. Moose Valley
1/31,680

(TH) Trailhead

Map created with TOPO! © National Geographic Maps

difficult to follow, so look for the orange trail markers.

The trail continues through lowlands that parallel and criss-cross Moose Valley Creek. At about 2.5 miles, across the bridge and over the creek, you have a splendid view of a 100-foot waterfall on the left side of the trail.

At about 3 miles you come to the Moose Valley campsite, an easy spot to reach on day one of a two-day hike and a pleasant place to stay for some quiet solitude. (If you are a photographer, this is a great base camp with early morning access to wildflowers and wildlife such as moose.) Continuing past the campsite for about one-half mile, you hike through spruce trees and some spectacular cotton-woods. From here you hike south and gain elevation gradually and then rapidly as you enter the alpine zone of the trail.

The trail traverses across and up the fall line of the slope, with many changes in grade. As you hike up and through the forest, you are treated to many fine views of Moose Valley and the glaciated mountain terrain to the north, as well as the Wosnesenski Glacier to the east.

For roughly the last 1.5 miles prior to the intersection with the China Poot Trail, you hike above tree line through alpine meadows and lakes. This is my favorite part of the trail. The views are breathtaking, the hiking is easy, and the opportunities for landscape photography are nearly endless.

The rounded nature of the topography here is the result of the smoothing effect of the 1,000 feet of ice that ground through and scraped the high areas clean. The lower-elevation lakes, marshes, and grasslands formed on top of the thick layer of ground moraine sediments deposited by the retreating glaciers.

When you reach the Poot Peak Trail intersection, you can turn right to hike up toward the Poot Peak Summit Trail and then down the steeper North China Poot Peak Trail, or go left to hike down the South Poot Peak Trail. I like to take the latter trail to enjoy the spectacular views of China Poot Lake and the Wosnesenski drainage and glacier areas. Both routes eventually take you back to China Poot Lake.

SPECIAL NOTES

Another option if you want to hike all of this trail in one day is to hike Moose Valley in the other direction, starting from China Poot Lake and hiking the Poot Peak section first to get the tough uphills completed in the cool early morning. This also provides you with higher-altitude, low-angled sunlight views of the whole Moose Valley, China Poot Lake, and the Wosnesenski Glacier drainage, which are great for photography.

Moose Valley in the fall is a riot of light and color among the white-tipped peaks

42

Coalition Loop

Total distance: 7 miles, total loop distance; 1.3 miles, Coalition Trail segment between trailheads; 3.7 miles, Coalition Loop main segment; 2 miles, China Poot Bay segment

Hiking time: 3 to 4 hours

Elevation change: 500 feet

Rating: Moderate

Best season: Spring through fall

Maps: Kachemak Bay State Park by National Geographic Trails Illustrated, and Kachemak Bay State Park and State Wilderness Park Map (www.dnr.state.ak.us/parks/units/kbay/kbaymap.htm)

Special features: Access to China Poot Bay, Halibut Cove Lagoon, and China Poot Lake along spruce and hemlock forest paths with great trees and lots of cool mushrooms.

This is really a combination of three trails: the Coalition Trail, the Coalition Loop Trail, and the loop back. The Coalition Trail runs between the trailhead and west campground at the head of Halibut Cove Lagoon on the one hand and the campground and trailhead at the head of China Poot Bay on the other. The Coalition Loop Trail then picks up from China Poot Bay and continues to the China Poot Lake Trail (Hike 39). Finally, the loop all the way back to the Halibut Cove Lagoon trailhead runs along the latter trail. See the map.

This low-elevation trail system leads you through dense spruce forests and connects Halibut Cove Lagoon, China Poot Bay, and China Poot Lake. It's a beautiful series of forest walks, which are also great hiking adjuncts and on-land breaks for kayakers staying at the campgrounds in Halibut Cove Lagoon or China Poot Bay.

GETTING THERE

The trailhead at the head of Halibut Cove Lagoon can be reached by water taxi from Homer Spit or by kayak paddled from multiple points around Halibut Cove Lagoon. The trailhead at China Poot Bay is best reached by kayak as water-taxi service can be limited to only the very highest tides.

THE TRAIL

At Halibut Cove Lagoon, the trail proceeds up and away from either the West Bay trailhead located at the West Lagoon Campground or the public dock near the ranger station for the China Poot Lake Trail (Hike

39). Turn right (west) from either spot to begin this trail. The hike over to China Poot Bay from the dock is about one-third mile longer than the hike there from the West Bay trailhead at the West Lagoon Campground. From either trailhead you'll head west on the Coalition Trail.

The trail climbs fairly steeply for about one-half mile to 300 feet in elevation, and then flattens out in the saddle before heading back down toward China Poot Bay. There are a couple of switchbacks before the trail begins to level out on the approach to the bay, and you have several good opportunities for viewing and photographing this beautiful notch in the shoreline. The steep sections on both ends of this trail segment become treacherous when wet, so hiking sticks are a good idea.

At about 1.2 miles you come to the access trail that leads down to the trailhead and campground at China Poot Bay.

As you continue on around the Coalition Loop from the China Poot Bay access trail, the path heads south and uphill on a moderate slope for about one-half mile, and then drops down to a small picturesque pond, a nice commune-with-nature spot. From here the trail continues southwest, trending up and down through continuous stands of wonderful spruce and hemlock trees.

In a little over a mile, the trail turns east-southeast along the steep-sided wall that forms the north slope of China Poot Creek, which drains China Poot Lake. At about 2 miles there is a steep, treacherous, and poorly maintained path you can thrash your way down to

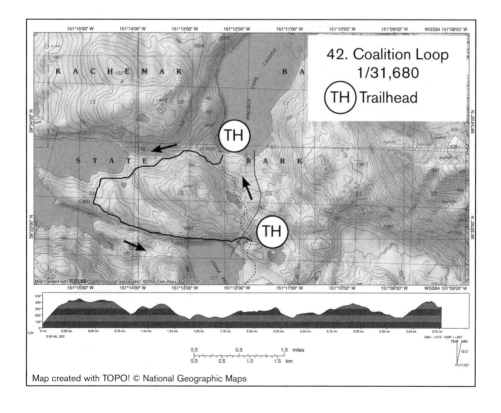

Map created with TOPO! © National Geographic Maps

get to the creek. China Poot Creek is a favorite locals dip-net area for silver and red salmon.

The Coalition Loop continues along the upper portions of the creek's ravine, reaching a high point of about 500 feet before slowly winding down to China Poot Lake. As you approach, there are several good viewpoints for taking pictures of the lake and Poot Peak beyond.

After that, the trail slants down and wraps around the lake's north end before leaving the shore behind to continue another three-quarters mile to intersect the China Poot Lake Trail.

At this intersection you can head right down toward China Poot Lake and the public-use fee cabins and campground at Moose Creek or proceed left for the 2.2-mile hike back on the China Poot Lake Trail to the trailheads at Halibut Cove Lagoon. On the latter route, you pass the access to the Moose Creek Trail along the way.

SPECIAL NOTES

The main attractions for me along the Coalition Loop Trail are the big trees and the access to Halibut Cove Lagoon, China Poot Bay, and China Poot Lake.

Wildflower treasures found along the forest path

43

Goat Rope Spur

Total distance: 3 miles one way from the Halibut Cove Lagoon dock, including a steep 1-mile ascent up the Goat Rope Trail itself from the junction with the Halibut Cove Lagoon Trail that leads up to it.

Hiking time: Three hours one way, which includes a one-hour straight-up effort on the Goat Rope Trail after first spending 1.5 to 2 hours to get there along the Halibut Cove Lagoon Trail

Elevation change: 3,200 feet to the Goat Rope Knob summit (includes Halibut Cove Lagoon Trail section from sea level to spur trail)

Rating: Very difficult

Best season: July and August

Maps: Kachemak Bay State Park by National Geographic Trails Illustrated, and Kachemak Bay State Park and State Wilderness Park Map (www.dnr.state.ak.us/parks/units/kbay/kbaymap.htm)

Special features: Heart-pounding, flower-strewn scramble to spectacular views of Kachemak Bay, Halibut Cove Lagoon, and surrounding peaks.

A quick scramble (once you reach the actual Goat Rope Trail) to a great view. The Goat Rope is a short trail, only about a mile long, but it gains more than 2,100 feet. It ascends straight up the fall line (steepest slope angle) along a ridge route to a spectacular overview knoll. There are terrific views and wonderful wildflowers all along the way, and snow glissading (sliding) is possible in late spring and early summer. If you like steep, challenging, thigh-burning hikes up to rewarding views, you'll love this one. The view from the top of the trail offers a unique perspective of Halibut Cove and Halibut Cove Lagoon.

GETTING THERE

Take a water taxi to the public dock at the head of Halibut Cove Lagoon and hike for about 2 miles northeast along the southern section of the Halibut Cove Lagoon Trail* to the trailhead for the Goat Rope Spur Trail. This southern section of the Halibut Cove Lagoon Trail is the most passable part of that trail, which is poorly maintained. Definitely check in with the State Park Service about the condition of Halibut Cove Lagoon Trail leading to the Goat Rope.

*Writer's Note: I have not included a description of the Halibut Cove Lagoon Trail in this book due to its long lack of maintenance and difficulty. At this point the trail is way overgrown and just plain nasty to traverse.

THE TRAIL

From the public dock at the head of Halibut Cove Lagoon, the Halibut Cove Lagoon Trail, which provides the best access to the Goat Rope Trail, winds a short way at sea level around the southeast edge of Halibut Cove Lagoon. It then passes over a small hill and begins a steep switchback ascent to heavily forested slopes. The trail is fairly well maintained here (though you'll want to check with the State Park Service before you start this hike to be sure), but you'll still encounter many roots and rocks and it's often wet and slippery as you climb steeply to about 700 feet in less than one-half mile. Following this initial steep section, the Halibut Cove Lagoon Trail extends about a mile along the slope in front of the Goat Rope summit. You then climb rapidly to about

1,100 feet over one-quarter mile to the intersection with the Goat Rope Trail itself . . . now the real fun begins!

For the Goat Rope Trail itself, there is not a lot to explain. It pretty much goes straight up the fall line from 1,100 feet to 3,200 feet. You're hiking directly up along the ridgeline to the Goat Rope summit, which is actually a false-summit knob along the ridgeline that continues up into even higher elevation. If it's early in the season or has been raining, the lower parts of this trail can be muddy and slippery. About two-thirds of the way up, the trail begins to level out, relatively speaking, so you are mostly hiking rather than scrambling from this point on. Anywhere along this upper third of the trail is a great place to stop and look back

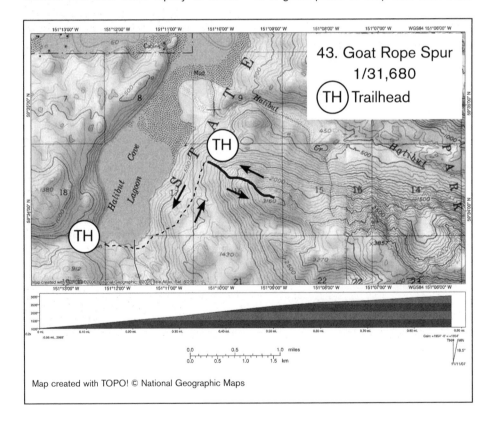

Map created with TOPO! © National Geographic Maps

50 Hikes in Alaska's Kenai Peninsula

across Kachemak Bay and the surrounding areas. The views are spectacular. And besides, it's a great excuse to help you catch your breath!

On the summit you have spectacular views of Halibut Cove to the west, the Moose Valley country to the east and south, and of the chocolate drop of Poot Peak from a seldom-seen perspective. You also have a unique view of the forest and peninsula that pinches the north end of Halibut Cove Lagoon and the Halibut Creek delta.

Early in the season the Goat Rope Trail is a relatively easy way to access snow slopes for glissading, which is a fancy word for sliding down the snow on your butt. For the best rides, put on your slick rain pants and be prepared to end up on tundra grass or alder bushes.

In spring and summer, if you are a berry picker you may well find success in some of the brushy areas surrounding the summit, but you'll likely have to share with the many birds that take up residence here in the warm months.

SPECIAL NOTES

This trail is a great workout and offers spectacular and unique views of the environments of Kachemak Bay. You can hike farther up the ridge, but be aware that many of the upper slopes are steep and unstable, so proceed cautiously.

Stunning highcountry view of the southern Kenai Mountain peaks

44

Alpine Ridge

Total distance: Roughly 2.5 miles to where the lower trail peters out at an outlook knoll; another 2 to 3 miles up and across the Alpine Ridge Plateau

Hiking time: 2.5 hours to where the lower trail peters out; 2 to 4 more hours, or more, cross-country to the upper elevations of Alpine Ridge Plateau

Elevation change: 2,200 feet to the end of the lower trail; 3,647 feet to the top of Alpine Ridge

Rating: Moderate to difficult on trail section, very difficult to ridgetop and easy across the top

Best season: July and August for lower trail section, August only for the higher portions

Maps: Kachemak Bay State Park by National Geographic Trails Illustrated, and Kachemak Bay State Park and State Wilderness Park Map (www.dnr.state.ak.us/parks/units/kbay/kbaymap.htm)

Special features: Spectacular views west and southwest across Kachemak Bay and down to the Grewingk Glacier and across the southern reaches of the Harding Ice Field. Special Note: Bring gear for stream crossing such as Crocs® and a spare pair of woolen hiking socks.

Along with Grace Ridge (Hike 36) and Red Mountain (Hike 34), Alpine Ridge is one of the three high-altitude alpine hikes in the Kachemak Bay State Park region. The lower section is on a well-defined trail, mostly through spruce and hemlock forest with steep switchback sections and lower-slope fields of wildflowers. The upper section runs cross-country above tree line and offers boggy, brushy tundra in the middle elevations and sweeping, lichen-encrusted rock outcrops in the upper elevations of the Alpine Ridge Plateau. These broad, shallow slopes allow easy exploration in many directions.

GETTING THERE

The most direct access to Alpine Ridge involves taking a water taxi from the Homer Spit to the base of the Saddle Trail (Hike 45) on the north end of Halibut Cove. From the trailhead beach, hike one-half mile and 400 feet to the saddle on the Saddle Trail. (A saddle is a curving dip in the topography between two higher points.) Continue hiking along a 0.3-mile section of the Halibut Cove Lagoon Trail to the trailhead start for the actual Alpine Ridge Trail.

THE TRAIL

The Alpine Ridge Trail ascends steeply uphill through spruce forest on switchbacks for about one-half mile. For the next three-quarters mile the trail then alternates between mild slope and somewhat steeper sections as you move out of the forest into subalpine alder thickets and meadows

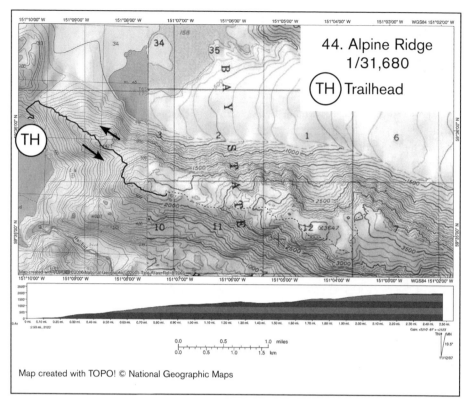

44. Alpine Ridge
1/31,680

(TH) Trailhead

Map created with TOPO! © National Geographic Maps

filled with wildflowers. You have several opportunities to stop and enjoy great views back across Kachemak Bay. The trail can be muddy in several places, particularly in spring when patches of reluctant snow linger.

There is a brief downhill section between humps in the ridge in the upper alder groves. At about 1.5 miles you leave the alders behind and the trail steepens again as you begin to traverse the alpine zone. This is characterized by rock outcrops covered by lichen, low scraggly windswept bushes, and small swatches of short grass.

About 0.2 mile from the top of the trail, the slope levels out once again, and you enjoy easy hiking across alpine tundra with expansive views in all directions. The end

of the trail, at 2,200 feet, is a wonderful place to have lunch, gawk at the scenery, and gaze down onto the Grewingk Glacier. On most days a nice breeze blows across this knoll, which helps keep the mosquitoes grounded, but it's always a good idea to have long pants and a long-sleeved shirt along too. If the breeze is not blowing, you will want to have plenty of repellent handy due to the great mosquito breeding habitat provided by the moist boggy areas along the trail.

For many hikers this will be the end of the Alpine Ridge Hike, and a fine stopping point it is. This is a great change-your-socks stop even if you plan to continue on. However, if you are adventurous and you started early enough, you might turn your attention to the upper slopes of Alpine

Alpine Ridge

Ridge and the many geological, botanical, and viewing treasures to be discovered there.

To continue on, you head first down into a boggy bowl containing wetlands and one small alpine lake with several inviting camping spots. Several trails start out across this bowl, but most disappear somewhere around the lake. You have to pick your own way across this area, trying to stick to high and dry ground. If the area is wet throughout you might consider wearing your stream-crossing gear, such as your Crocs®, to traverse this boggy section.

For some of the best views down to the Grewingk Glacier, head left (north) to the ridgeline that forms the top of the southern slope of the Grewingk Glacier valley. You can stand right above the glacier and see it and the huge landslide scar where a large section of the slope gave way and thundered down into Grewingk Glacier Lake. If you look carefully, you'll see other sections of the slope about to give way.

From the glacier overview, your best approach to the upper Alpine Plateau is back south and up the right (south) ridge that forms the upper slopes of Halibut Creek. As you move up and out of the basin, you might notice the weak bands of soil on some of the slopes. They look like rumpled rugs. These are rolls of soil caused by a process known as solifluction, where the upper layers of permafrost melt during the summer months and flow gently downhill in slow-moving waves on top of the still-frozen permafrost or solid rock below.

Above the low and boggy areas the hiking, while steep in some areas, is much easier as the brushy soft vegetation gives way to shorter grasses and lichen-covered rocks. Hiking along the southern shoulder of the ridge will provide you with dramatic views down into the wild upper drainage of Halibut Creek. As you hike up onto the top of the eastern shoulder of the Alpine Ridge Plateau, you are gifted with sweeping views of the upper plateau, as well as dramatic views back into the still-glaciated terrain of the upper Kenai Mountains and the Harding Ice Field. If you have time, follow the edge of the plateau counterclockwise around to the north side. Once again, you are peering down on top of the Grewingk Glacier. The views are grand. And of course you'll curse yourself if you forgot to bring your camera.

SPECIAL NOTES

From above, try to imagine the Grewingk Valley 12,000 to 15,000 years ago, completely filled with ice by a glacier three times as thick as it is today. The slopes on which you are standing, including the entire upper Alpine Ridge Plateau, were completely covered with ice. Picture too the vast expanse of the Harding Ice Field extending all the way over onto this ridgeline. The ice flowed over all but the very highest peaks, and the plateau itself was smoothed by a glacier. All the valleys you see to the west were also completely filled with glaciers merging together in what is now Kachemak Bay to form one massive valley glacier, which deposited thousands of tons of sediment across its melting front, or terminus, to form what we know as the Homer Spit.

Getting to, and exploring, the upper Alpine Ridge Plateau and then back down in one day can be quite a challenge. I've done it several times and enjoyed it, but I'm always a whipped puppy at the end—tired but smiling as I down huge quantities of spaghetti. Another approach is to hike up and camp near the end of the maintained trail on day one, then use day two to explore the upper reaches of the plateau. You might even consider camping on the high plateau, a grand experience if the weather is calm. If you have enjoyed a high camp on Grace Ridge (Hike 36) as well, you can decide which is your favorite. You might have to sample both again to make up your mind!

Alpine Ridge (right) towers above Grewingk Glacier at the edge of Kachemak Bay

45

Saddle Trail to Grewingk Glacier Lake

Total distance: 1.1 miles

Hiking time: 1 hour one way, but add another hour to enjoy the view

Elevation change: 400 feet

Rating: Moderate

Best season: Spring through fall

Maps: Kachemak Bay State Park by National Geographic Trails Illustrated, and Kachemak Bay State Park and State Wilderness Park Map (www.dnr.state.ak.us/parks/units/kbay/kbaymap.htm)

Special features: Rapid access to the lakefront of Grewingk Glacier and provides access to the Alpine Ridge Trail (Hike 44)

If you don't have a lot of time, or if you're not a super-ambitious hiker but would still like to get your heart pumping, see some beautiful scenery, and gaze across a lake at the front of a massive glacier, then this is the hike for you. The Saddle Trail is short, only 1.1 miles, and it's the fastest way to get to an upfront and personal view of the Grewingk Glacier after taking in some spruce forest hiking along the way. You can easily make the round trip in half a day and still have time to sun yourself on the Saddle Trail Beach while waiting for your water taxi. Or you can plan to explore the country around Grewingk Lake, or perhaps continue on to Glacier Spit and be picked up there (Hike 46).

GETTING THERE

Take a water taxi from Homer Spit to the beach at the Saddle Trail trailhead at the north end of Halibut Cove.

THE TRAIL

From Saddle Trail Beach you climb steep wooden stairs, and then immediately start up through a predominantly spruce forest along a series of switchbacks that rise to 400 feet over the first one-half mile and give the trail its moderate rating. At the top of the switchbacks, you reach the saddle, the high point of this trail nestled into a sunny spot in the spruce forest. You'll know when you get there because your heart will stop pounding so hard and your legs won't hurt so much. This is also the intersection of the north end of the Halibut Cove Lagoon Trail that you would take for 0.3 miles to access the Alpine Ridge Trail (Hike 44).

For the next one-quarter mile you gradually lose about 100 feet of elevation down through the spruce forest on the long, sloping side of the saddle. You then hike down a steeper section for 0.1 mile, quickly leveling out for most of the remaining descent toward Grewingk Valley. There is one final short, steep section just before the end of the trail.

At the bottom of the switchbacks, the trail flattens onto the gravelly outwash plain formed several thousand years ago by the floods of water and sediment deposited by the retreating Grewingk Glacier. Follow the well-worn trail until you come to a large rock cairn. Cairns are man-made stacks of rocks used to act as trail markers when there are no places to place signs, such as here on this rocky, glacial outwash plain. Cairns are also commonly used in high alpine treeless areas.

This cairn is technically the end of the Saddle Trail, but nobody stops here so neither should you. The most common destination is Grewingk Lake. Turn right at the cairn and hike one-half mile gently downslope across the outwash plain to the front of the lake. This is a terrific lunch spot, but also one of the most highly trafficked areas in the park. If you want some solitude, hike from the cairn off to the north (left) side of the lake. Hang around for a while and ogle the front of the glacier and the icebergs that have recently calved off. Cool winds off the glacier frequently blow the icebergs westward across the lake to

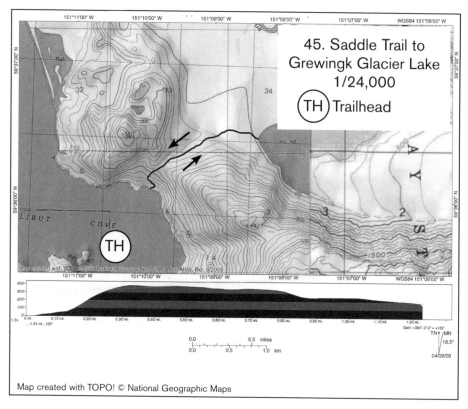

45. Saddle Trail to Grewingk Glacier Lake
1/24,000
(TH) Trailhead

Map created with TOPO! © National Geographic Maps

where you are standing. These constant winds occur because air over the glacier is cooled by the ice, becomes denser than the surrounding air, and then drops and flows down and away.

As you stand on the north end of the lake's cobble beach, be sure to look up onto the steep slope of the southern wall of the valley. You will see a sheer, vegetation-free scar where in 1969 a landslide broke away taking millions of tons of rocks down into Grewingk Lake. All this landslide material forms the small peninsula jutting out into the lake.

SPECIAL NOTES

If you are just in Homer and the Kache-mak Bay area for a day or two and only have time for a quick hike, this is a dandy. You'll see a variety of terrains and ecosystems, including the bay, a steep cobble beach, spruce forests, a glacial outwash plain, a glacial lake, a landslide scar and debris pile, and of course the glorious Grewingk Glacier itself, all in the space of about a mile and a half—not bad for a half-day hike.

Are you wondering about the blue green color of the ice? It is created by the selective absorption of the longer-wavelength red and yellow light by the hydrogen bonds in the ice. Once the reds and yellows have been absorbed, all that is left for you to see are the blues and greens.

Grewingk Glacier and Lake with icebergs for your viewing pleasure

46

Glacier Spit to Grewingk Glacier Lake

Total distance: About 3 miles from the Glacier Spit to the Grewingk Glacier Lake; another 1.5 miles on Saddle Trail to your pickup at Saddle Trail Beach

Hiking time: 1.5 to 2 hours to the lake; another hour to enjoy the scenery; and one more for the Saddle Trail

Elevation change: 250 feet to the lake and another 150 feet to the top of the Saddle Trail

Rating: Easy; moderate if you take the Saddle Trail

Best season: Spring through fall; often accessible during the winter, but snow likely on Saddle Trail then.

Maps: Kachemak Bay State Park by National Geographic Trails Illustrated, and Kachemak Bay State Park and State Wilderness Park Map (www.dnr.state.ak.us/ parks/units/kbay/kbaymap.htm)

Special features: Of course, there's the gorgeous Grewingk Glacier and the glittering lake, but the sweeping vistas and high-energy crashing waves on Glacier Spit are always a highlight of this trip for me.

If you want a relatively easy hike to Grewingk Glacier Lake but want to see more of the countryside than the Saddle Trail (Hike 45) affords, this is a wonderful hike to consider. You start out on a wild, high-energy, steep-sloped cobble beach and then trek through a sparsely forested glacial outwash plain to the glacier and lake. For your return trip, you can head back to the Glacier Spit or, as most hikers do, go up and over the heavily forested Saddle Trail to catch your water taxi to Homer.

GETTING THERE

Take a water taxi from Homer Spit to Glacier Spit, where access is good at most tidal levels. You may have to exit your water taxi quickly if the waves are high, so be prepared to get a bit wet.

Wearing your crocks for access to the beach may be a good choice. Don your dry boots and socks once you have secured higher and dryer ground.

THE TRAIL

The water taxi will drop you off somewhere along Glacier Spit that is conducive to a safe landing and exit from the boat. Where you exit will depend upon wind, waves, and tide levels and where it looks best for a beach landing. Usually, you'll have a one quarter- to one-half-mile hike north along the Glacier Spit beach. But this is a good thing. Take some time to explore the dunes and grassy supratidal areas. The dunes offer all sorts of treasures like driftwood, animal tracks, and birds.

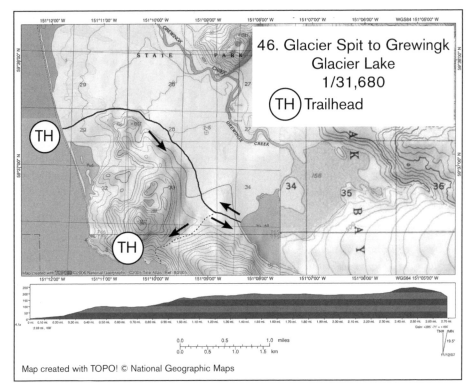

46. Glacier Spit to Grewingk
Glacier Lake
1/31,680

(TH) Trailhead

Map created with TOPO! © National Geographic Maps

The beach is usually pretty steep due to the high energy of the waves, which are driven by strong southwesterly winds from as far as Kamishak Bay, over 100 miles away. Hiking is often easier up near the dune line where the sediment is not so coarse and the beach levels out as you approach the supratidal zone. Plus, the orange trailhead marker is easier to spot.

At the trailhead marker, you turn east away from the beach and immediately enter a forest of spruce, cottonwood, and alder. There are some amazingly massive cottonwood trees growing here thanks to all that fresh water flowing from the glacier through the gravels on the outwash plain. After about one-half mile you come to a trail junction. Take a right if you want to hike into Rusty's Lagoon. There is a campsite back there, as well as lots of wildflowers along

the short trail through the back dune area behind the Glacier Spit beach. Otherwise, continue hiking for another mile through open-canopy forest that thins out here and there near recently active high-water stream flow channels.

At about 1.5 miles you reach a second intersection, this one on the left (north) side of the trail. This turnoff leads to many adventures, including the hand-pull tram over Grewingk Creek, the start of the Grewingk Glacier Trail, a back-trail entrance to the Humpy Creek area, and an access to the Emerald Lake Trail (Hikes 47, 48, and 50). Past this junction, the trail leads out of the forest and begins to traverse the flat, open gravels of the outwash plain. (An outwash plain is where a glacier used to be, now the flattened, gravelly, watery area in front of it as it retreats.) You continue across this area until you reach the intersection with the Grewingk Glacier Lake Trail and then the Saddle Trail. A large rock cairn marks the intersection. Turn left (east) at the cairn and hike for about one-half mile slightly downhill to the shores of Grewingk Glacier Lake. This is a nice spot for lunch or camping. Cool winds blow off the front of the glacier almost continually so pitch your tent behind a little cover if you're staying overnight.

Hang out at the lake and marvel at the glacier and the ever-present icebergs, newly calved off the front of the glacier. Also, look up on the south wall of the valley, about halfway across the lake toward the glacier, to see a huge scar formed by a 1969 landslide that occurred when an enormous section of the slope gave way and thundered down into the lake. A massive pile of debris has formed a small peninsula that juts out into the water. If you pay attention you may see and hear some of the small rock falls that frequently careen down this steep landside scar—a reminder that it could become active again at any time.

SPECIAL NOTES

The flat plain you hiked across from Glacier Spit was formed by the deposition of several hundred feet of sediment, known as ground moraine sediment, on this valley floor as the Grewingk Glacier retreated up its valley toward where it is today. Several thousand years ago Grewingk Glacier extended all the way down to Kachemak Bay where it joined an even larger Kachemak-Bay-valley glacier that flowed all the way out into Cook Inlet. As the climate has warmed over the past 10,000 years, the larger Kachemak Bay Glacier melted back and eventually retreated into disappear-

ance. For a while after the larger valley glacier retreated north, Grewingk Glacier was a tidewater glacier that calved off icebergs into Kachemak Bay.

You could return to where you came in at Glacier Spit, but it is shorter and faster to hike up and over the Saddle Trail to Saddle Trail Beach, which will also give you the chance to see new country. It's about one-half mile back to where the Saddle Trail begins, and from there, about an hour to an hour and a half of hiking to reach the beach (Hike 45 contains a description of the Saddle Trail). Hopefully you've arranged for a water taxi to pick you up on Saddle Trail Beach; if not, you might be able to bum a ride with another group.

While you can reverse the direction of this hike and trek from the Saddle Trail to Glacier Spit, the water taxi pick-up at the Saddle Trail is much easier and less exposed.

Glacier Spit's beach

47

Grewingk Glacier

*Total distance: 7 miles total (one way)
from Glacier Spit to the face of Grewingk
Glacier itself. Includes 1.5 miles along
the Glacier Spit to Grewingk Glacier Lake
Trail (Hike 46).*

Hiking time: 5 hours (one way)

Elevation change: 580 feet

Rating: Moderate

Best season: Spring through fall

*Maps: Kachemak Bay State Park by
National Geographic Trails Illustrated, and
Kachemak Bay State Park and State Wilderness Park Map (www.dnr.state.ak.us/
parks/units/kbay/kbaymap.htm)*

*Special features: The hand-operated tram
over Grewingk Creek, terrific views from
the high point on the Foehn Ridge Trail,
good bird viewing at Grewingk Glacier
Lake, a visit to the glacier and the opportunity not only to touch it but to drink
thousands-of-years-old glacier water drip-
ping off the front of the ice. Special Note:
Bring binoculars as well as your camera.
Also each hiker should bring a pair of
protective gloves for operating the tram.*

The Grewingk Glacier Trail has several
interesting challenges, including a hand-
operated tram you use to pull yourself over
the Grewingk Creek gorge. It is about 14
miles up and back over a variety of terrain
from your drop-off point at Glacier Spit. Be
sure to bring your camera and a drinking
cup.

GETTING THERE

Take a water taxi from Homer Spit to Glacier Spit, and then hike about 1.5 miles to
the intersection with the Grewingk Glacier
Trail. (Hike 46 contains more details on this
section.)

THE TRAIL

From the start of the Grewingk Glacier
Trail, you hike out of the forest for about 1
mile across the open outwash plain formed
by the retreating and melting glacier. This
trail segment terminates at the Grewingk
Creek gorge, and you must use the hand
tram to pull yourself across. For your safety,
please follow the instructions posted at the
tram (see Special Notes below for more
information). The pull across the gorge is
a lot of fun and a great upper-body workout. Take time to look up and downstream,
as you have a unique perspective down
to Grewingk Creek. Besides providing a
good opportunity to take pictures, stopping
mid-way across offers a good excuse for
resting.

On the other side of the gorge, your
path intersects with the trail from Humpy
Creek, which comes in from the left (west).

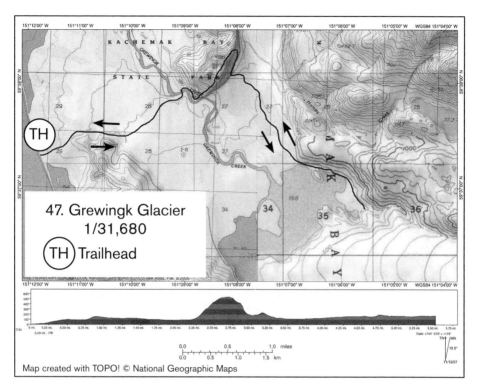

47. Grewingk Glacier
1/31,680

(TH) Trailhead

Map created with TOPO! © National Geographic Maps

Turn right (east) and continue toward the glacier. Immediately you begin to head up onto Foehn Ridge. It is a moderately steep climb to an elevation of 580 feet, challenging but well worth the multiple spectacular views of Grewingk Glacier. I call this section the Up & Over section. As you go, you are treated to some beautiful wildflower meadows, featuring the startling blues of columbine and lupine, as well as red elderberry bushes.

From your perch along the top of the Foehn Ridge line, you continue the hike first through a spruce forest and then descend on a slightly steeper grade via a series of three long switchbacks leading down to the current outwash plain in front of Grewingk Glacier.

Once you get down, you hike about 2.6 miles through an open-canopy, wildflower-strewn spruce, aspen, willow, alder, and cottonwood forest to the northern edge of the lake. The trail is rocky but well worn in most places and easy to follow, and it is marked intermittently with rock cairns and occasional orange trail markers tacked to trees. The Emerald Lake Trail enters from your left (see Hike 50) as you approach.

Grewingk Glacier Lake is a good place to relax with a snack, which you will likely be sharing with the squadrons of dive-bombing arctic terns. If you have remembered to bring your binoculars, turn them toward the island—which I call Bird Island—out in the middle of the north end of the lake. It is home to hundreds of birds going about their daily business of living . . . and they don't do this quietly! Also, look south across the lake to see a large dark scar on the sheer cliff face of the high southern

Grewingk Glacier and Lake, the glacial outwash plain, and Alpine Ridge

valley wall. This is from the massive landslide that broke loose in 1969, depositing a huge debris pile that now forms a small peninsula into the lake. At this point you're about 1.5 miles from the glacier.

To reach it, traverse around the north edge of the lake and hike up and over mounds of sediment recently deposited—in the past few hundred years—by the retreating front of the glacier. You pass to the left of a huge elongated mound of sediment the glacier deposited, which is called a lateral moraine. As you approach the glacier, you can see similar lateral moraines forming where sediment is piling up and being deposited along the edge.

You have now hiked about 7 miles from Glacier Spit and are standing at about 350 feet of elevation. Now is the time to drop your pack and fish out that cup you brought.

Go over to the side of the glacier and catch yourself a cup of water melting from glacial ice that's thousands of years old.

Don't be surprised if there is a constant breeze blowing off the end of the glacier. Air is cooled by the glacier, becomes denser, and then flows off its front most of the year. Have fun nosing around the edge and on the slopes next to the glacier, but beware of climbing on the ice itself—this is very dangerous.

You have several options for the return trip. You can simply hike back out to Glacier Spit the way you came in. Or, you can hike back out to the Glacier Lake Trail and then hang a left to exit via the Saddle Trail (Hike 45). Or, you can hike out to Humpy Creek (Hike 48). If you need to catch a water taxi, both the Glacier Spit and Saddle Trail Beach access points are bet-

50 Hikes in Alaska's Kenai Peninsula

ter bets, as they are far less dependent on tides for boat access.

SPECIAL NOTES

The sign at the tram says it is rated for two people at a time, with a 500-pound weight limit, but I don't recommend that two people cross together. Instead, I suggest that one hiker get in the tram while the other work the line from the outside. The hiker who then arrives at the other side of the gorge can return the favor from where she/he is standing.

TRAM INSTRUCTIONS AND TIPS

- Tuck all clothing in before getting on the tram.
- Secure all long hair, dogs, and other loose items.
- Secure all gear so that nothing can fall off the tram.
- Wear gloves when operating the tram.
- If the tram is at the opposite shore, pull the rope to move it closer to the opposite A-frame support to disengage the restraining hook, and then pull the tram across.
- Engage restraining hook before loading the tram by swinging the hook up into the eyebolt.
- Use the hooks on the outside of the tram to secure your gear.
- If only two hikers, one person crosses while the other works the line from the bank (unless of course you like the challenge of pulling two people across at once, which some of us just can't resist!).
- Enter the tram through the door and take a seat.
- Secure door chain.
- Remain seated at all times while the tram is in motion.
- Pace yourself; the second half of the pull is all uphill.
- When finished, return the tram to the center of the river-crossing to make the next hiker's access easier.
- This is not a toy, be cautious and pay attention at all times.

Katie and Zip prepare for their tram trip

48

Humpy Creek South to Glacier Spit

Total distance: 2.2 miles to the Grewingk tram, 4.7 miles to Glacier Spit

Hiking time: 1 hour to the tram, 2.5 hours to Glacier Spit (including the tram crossing)

Elevation change: 100 feet

Rating: Easy, although the tram is a fun challenge

Best season: Year-round, but spring through fall is best

Maps: Kachemak Bay State Park by National Geographic Trails Illustrated, and Kachemak Bay State Park and State Wilderness Park Map (www.dnr.state.ak.us/parks/units/kbay/kbaymap.htm)

Special features: A beautifully pleasant trail that crosses back and forth between the open stream channel flats of Grewingk Creek and the forested lower slopes of the uplands.

The main access for Humpy Creek is in the middle of a longer trail, which for this book I've broken into two separate hikes: one that goes north from that access point to Mallard Bay (see Hike 49), and this one heading south from that same entry point to Glacier Spit. Access to the main Humpy Creek trailhead depends upon the tides, and often results in wet feet, but once out of the water you are treated to the typically serene delta and stream channel of Humpy Creek. This trail also accesses some spectacular salmon fishing on the creek. From this path, you can also get to several other trails such as the Emerald Lake Trail (Hike 50), the Grewingk Glacier Trail (Hike 47), and the Grewingk Glacier Lake Trail (Hike 46), as well as the entire Mallard Bay area.

Special Note: Bring Crocs® or some other footwear besides your hiking shoes, to use when your feet have to get wet, such as when coming and going from the water taxi.

GETTING THERE

The main trailhead in the middle of the Humpy Creek Trail is obtainable by water taxi from the Homer Spit. Be sure to consult with your water taxi beforehand, however, to pick a time when the tidal level is conducive to accessing Humpy Creek. Higher tides are typically needed. If you are planning to reach the trailhead by kayak, though, you can gain access at just about any tide level.

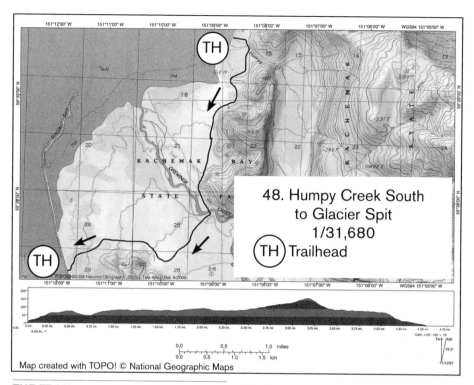

48. Humpy Creek South to Glacier Spit
1/31,680
(TH) Trailhead

Map created with TOPO! © National Geographic Maps

THE TRAIL

Count on getting your feet wet when you exit the water taxi. This is a time when having some "get-wet" footwear is a bonus. Crocs® are a good solution for entering and exiting water taxis. Once you're on dry land, swap your Crocs for hiking boots.

The first part of the hike to the trailhead is across the flat alluvial gravel area that is often cut by several small channels of Humpy Creek. This is an engaging environment worthy of a little hang time as you look for fish or enjoy some photography and dry off your toes.

There are several game trails leading back into the woods around Humpy Creek, so look for the trailhead kiosk with sign-in station. To locate the kiosk, look for the COMMERCIAL FISHING sign located in the open coastal grassland, and then walk directly back toward the forest. You will see the kiosk as you approach the trees. If you enter the forest without seeing the trailhead kiosk, you have gone too far, so back out and try to locate the kiosk again.

From the trailhead kiosk, you can hike north toward Mallard Bay (Hike 49) or south toward the Grewingk tram and Glacier Spit. The trail in both directions is marked with orange triangular markers.

Walk south back into the spruce-rich woods to begin your hike toward the Grewingk tram. The trail is generally flat and follows the edge of the open stream channel gravel at the base of the upland. In addition to the spruce you will encounter aspens, willows and some cottonwoods, along with the floral treats of lupine in July and fireweed in August. The route is fairly well defined, but if you stray from the path just look for the orange trail markers to help get back on track.

In several places you pass small ponds known as kettle lakes. These small water-filled gouges formed when the Grewingk Glacier scoured over and then retreated back across the ground moraine, filling the gouges in with melting water. Constantly high groundwater levels maintain them to this day. If you have time, wander off the trail to explore both the open outwash flat and the forest.

About three-quarters mile into the hike, the trail climbs up to around 100 feet in elevation and remains there. The second half of the path nestles up close to the steep slopes that form Foehn Ridge. At a little past 2 miles, you come to the Grewingk tram. (Hike 47 contains more information, and please read it, as this tram is a dangerous device that must be properly used.) The tram crosses Grewingk Creek where the icy creek cuts a gorge through the ground moraine and stream-channel sediments deposited by the retreating Grewingk Glacier. Take a look at the depth of this gorge—which tells you how much sediment the retreating glacier deposited. In many places the sediment can be hundreds of feet thick. Imagine too the height of the glacier that used to be on top of it. The Grewingk Glacier on top of where the tram is today was 1,000 feet high 10,000 years ago.

From the tram you could continue east up and over Foehn Ridge on the Grewingk Glacier Hike (Hike 47). But on this hike you ride the tram and hike for about 1 mile through flat, open gravel areas deposited by the retreating glacier, punctuated by sparse spruce, cottonwood, and aspen with a variety of wildflowers. After this 1-

Zip and Katie enjoying a sunny afternoon at the mouth of Humpy Creek

mile, near-level jaunt, you reach the Grewingk Glacier Lake Trail. If you were to turn left here you would hike a little under 2 miles to the lake. But on this hike you turn right and proceed 1.5 miles to the beach at Glacier Spit. (Hike 46 contains a more detailed description of this section, as well as information on the hike toward Grewingk Glacier Lake.)

As you cross the flats toward Glacier Spit, keep an eye open for moose and black bear that frequent this area. Visibility is generally good so the big beasts will be easy to avoid.

SPECIAL NOTES
Humpy Creek is a favorite local fishing spot for salmon and Dolly Varden trout. You're most likely to encounter anglers in late July and August when the salmon are running. This area is also replete with other wildlife, including black bears, which like to compete with fishermen for the salmon. Eagles and a variety of birds like plovers, sparrows, and woodpeckers are also common. The entire area around the creek is also well suited for just exploring. My favorite time of year here is late August through late September, when the air is cool and the trees are changing colors—a photographer's paradise. By fall the salmon have had their day and few people are about.

49

Humpy Creek North to Mallard Bay

Total distance: 3 total miles; 1.8 to the trailhead, 1.2 down to Mallard Bay

Hiking time: 2 hours

Elevation change: 875 feet

Rating: Moderate

Best season: Spring through fall

Maps: Kachemak Bay State Park by National Geographic Trails Illustrated and Kachemak Bay State Park and State Wilderness Park Map (www.dnr.state.ak.us/ parks/units/kbay/kbaymap.htm)

Special features: Mallard Bay is a terrific place to camp near the tidal zone, hike the varied coastline up to the mouth of the Portlock River and/or Neptune Bay, or just hang out or kayak. One of my favorite activities is hiking up and over into the wild and seldom-visited and fascinating drainage basin of the Portlock River and glacier, which boasts a trailless area packed with moose and bear surrounding a glacial stream valley draining nearby Portlock Glacier.

You will hike from Humpy Creek flats at sea level up and over a forested ridge before slanting down into Mallard Bay and the Portlock Drainage. You can start this hike from either end, but Mallard Bay is even more tidally challenged than Humpy Creek.

Prior to planning this trip, be sure the check with Kachemak Bay State Park (http://www.dnr.state.ak.us/parks/asp/ trailcondition.htm) about the condition of this trail. The last time I hiked it, the path had not been cleared in over two years and there was significant alder overgrowth and many multitree downfalls of thick trees and tangled branches blocking the trail– basically a journey that only a masochist could love. When cleared this is a well-designed and delightful trail for hiking and exploring. In its current condition, however, I do not recommend taking dogs, unless you plan to use them to help rescue you. Likewise, do not attempt this hike if you are not active enough, and survivalist enough, to endure some very harsh, very remote conditions. If you miss the water taxi ride home for any reason, you will be up a creek, so to speak, and one in remote wilderness Alaska.

GETTING THERE

The starting trailhead for this hike is located in the middle of the Humpy Creek Trail, which typically is accessed by water taxi from Homer Spit. Consult your water-taxi service in advance to pick a time when the tide is conducive to a drop-off at Humpy Creek. Exiting the boat here will require you

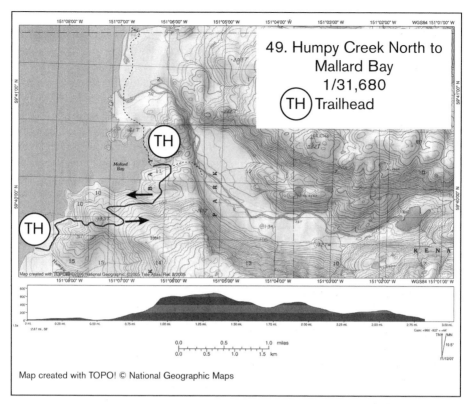

to get your feet wet, so bring your get-wet footgear. Crocs® are a good choice. You can don your dry socks and hiking boots after a short slog across the wetlands at the delta of Humpy Creek.

Option two for accessing this trial is in reverse, from the other side at Mallard Bay. Be aware that you'll face even more drastic tidal challenges if you decide to hike this trail from that direction. In fact, at tides below +2 feet Mallard Bay is dry. No matter where you begin, be sure to don some mosquito repellant.

THE TRAIL

The hike begins at the same Humpy Creek trailhead kiosk as the Humpy Creek Trail (Hike 48). Finding the initial kiosk and then the trailhead can be tricky because

there are many false trails, coastal embayments, and game trails leading back into the spruce forest. Look for the Humpy Creek trailhead kiosk directly inland from the COMMERICAL FISHING sign located on the open tidal grassland. From the kiosk, hike north on the Humpy Creek Trail, rather than south toward the tram.

As you hike north across the tidal flats stay at the edge of the spruce forest for about one-third mile. At the northern end of the tidal flat grasslands where it ends along the rock cliffs, look for the orange "T" trailhead marker showing the way up into low- to middle-elevation forested slopes. (Note this section of trail can be under water at tides higher than 17 feet.) The trail is not well marked but can be fairly well worn. If you end up straying into the forest, backtrack to the trail at the forest edge.

The northern portion of the Humpy Creek Trail is used far less than the southern half, so you're likely to have it to yourself even at lower elevations. Once you locate the orange "T" trail marker head up into a heavy forest of alder at first, and then more spruce as you climb the moderately steep slope with several short switchbacks. This steep section runs one-half mile before the trail levels out, then winds across a saddle area for another one-half mile. You may encounter a deadfall or two, depending upon how recently the trail crews have cleared this section.

One more steep section takes you to the trail's high point at about 875 feet before dropping down again to about 650 feet at the intersection of the trails for Humpy Creek, Mallard Bay, and Emerald Lake. From this high vantage spot, you will have some long views south across the Grewingk River valley as you climb the trail. So, take time to stop and look back across the Humpy Creek/Grewingk Glacier Creek area, over the delta areas of Grewingk and Humpy creeks, and then across the southern Kenai Mountains with its jewel of Sadie Ridge. Also be on the lookout for black bears, who leave much bear berry-filled sign (aka poop) along the trail.

On the hike up to the turnoff to Mallard Bay, you will hike through plenty of alder and devil's club, the latter of which serves up huge, wide, flat leaves that are tempting to use as toilet paper–but don't. Their name comes from the surprising spikes underneath. Also joining this dense undergrowth in this shady forest are lush fern, dwarf dogwood, lupine, elderberry, and wild rose.

The Mallard Bay tent platform is located on the shoreline above the tide's reach

50 Hikes in Alaska's Kenai Peninsula

Turn left (north) on the path to Mallard Bay, where the trail is flat at first, then descends on a moderate slope for about 0.5 mile through a couple of long switchbacks. After that, the path descends more steeply at first and then levels out on more gradual uphill and downhill slopes as you pass through lower hills in the middle of the Mallard Bay drainage. From the higher points, looking north toward Mallard Bay you are treated to good views of the northern half of Kachemak Bay, including Mallard Bay, Aurora Lagoon, and the Fox River delta in the distance. Picture what this looked like 10,000 years ago when all the mountain valleys were filled with glaciers. Kachemak Bay itself was in the process of being carved out by a huge valley glacier formed by the confluence of all the alpine glaciers flowing down the western flank of the Kenai Mountains.

You will encounter and hike along an unnamed stream channel as you near the lower sections of the trail. Near the end of the hike you come to another junction whose right-hand path leads up and over a saddle to the wild Portlock River drainage. The path to the left takes you down the stream channel to Mallard Bay. I suggest you plan for time to explore both sides, particularly the Portlock River drainage, which is secluded and seldom visited.

At the end of the trail where the stream channel meets the bay, look for and set up your tent on the wooden tent platform located just south of the trailhead marker on Mallard Bay. The platform is easy to miss because it is about 10 feet above the beach and hidden behind vegetation. Do not camp on the beach, as even moderate high tides flood this area completely.

SPECIAL NOTES

As I mentioned at the end of Hike 48, (Humpy Creek to Glacier Spit), the area around the trailhead is a paradise for anglers, photographers, and wildlife lovers. Mallard Bay at the other end of this hike offers its own set of charms. Camping here is a treat as Mallard is nestled back away from the main section of Kachemak Bay and often protected from its stiff winds. This is a great base camp for combined kayaking and hiking adventures. Spend some time kayaking around Mallard Bay and then hike over to explore the Portlock River and glacier drainage. It's neat to be so close to the water when high tide arrives but be sure to perch on the tent platform!

As the tides recede plan to hike north along the rocky edge of the tidal flats around the undulating coastline. Have fun exploring the high-tide islands located just offshore and if you have time, hike up to the mouth of Portlock Glacier (1 mile) and even to Neptune Bay (2 miles). You will likely see moose and at least signs of bears.

If you have packed a raft (see Information Resources pages 33–35), the Portlock River would be a good choice to hike up and raft down. Bring your get-wet footwear for making your way upstream.

You can easily devote a great day to exploring these two areas. Bring your hiking poles for crossing the channels of the Portlock River. This area is often filled with large flocks of shore birds that will entertain you with all their raucous behavior.

Taxi tip: If you need to be picked up at any time other than high tide, arrange to meet your water taxi just north of Mallard Bay near the southern end of Aurora Spit. That additional distance to hike is about 2 miles from the tent platform.

50

Emerald Lake

*Total distance: 15 miles (one way); 2
miles along the North Humpy Creek Trail,
6.5 miles on the Emerald Lake Trail, 5
miles along the Glacier Trail, and 1.5
miles along the Glacier Lake Hike*

*Hiking time: 2 days; you can do it in 1,
but don't if you can help it*

*Elevation change: 2,100 feet, with a lot of
up and down*

Rating: Moderate

Best season: Summer and early fall

*Maps: Kachemak Bay State Park by
National Geographic Trails Illustrated, and
Kachemak Bay State Park and State Wilderness Park Map (www.dnr.state.ak.us/
parks/units/kbay/kbaymap.htm)*

*Special features: Panoramic vistas of
Kachemak Bay and the high alpine peaks
from the trail's high points along the Portlock Plateau section; wide-open views
with easy hiking across the plateau itself,
the serene surroundings and great camping at Emerald Lake, and the buffet of
wildflowers and wildlife along the way*

Next to Grace Ridge (Hike 36), this is my
favorite hike in the Kachemak Bay area, for
it offers some of the most diverse scenery,
hiking, and natural environments near the
bay. You start on tidal flats near Humpy
Creek, continue along forested mountain
slopes, traverse the broad and beautiful alpine Portlock Plateau, visit gorgeous
alpine lakes, and enjoy astounding views of
mountains, glaciers, lakes, and bays.

GETTING THERE

From Homer Spit, take a water taxi to the
Humpy Creek landing site. Access to the
trailhead will force you to get your feet wet,
so bring your get-wet footgear . . . Crocs®
are a good choice here. You can change
into dry socks and hiking boots after a short
slog across the wetlands at the delta of
Humpy Creek. Be sure to coat yourself with
mosquito repellant.

You could also hike this trail from the
other direction, either heading south from
Humpy Creek toward the tram (Hike 48)
or starting at Glacier Spit to the Grewingk
Glacier Lake Trail (Hike 46) and then taking the Emerald Lake Trail north from near
the northern end of Grewingk Glacier Lake.
However, I recommend starting where indicated in the previous paragraph because
this clockwise route affords the best views
across the Portlock Plateau. Plus, hiking
out to Glacier Spit, rather than hiking in
from it, allows far more flexibility in terms
of spots to land the water taxi for your
departure. Also, hiking west-to-east across
the Portlock Plateau toward Emerald Lake

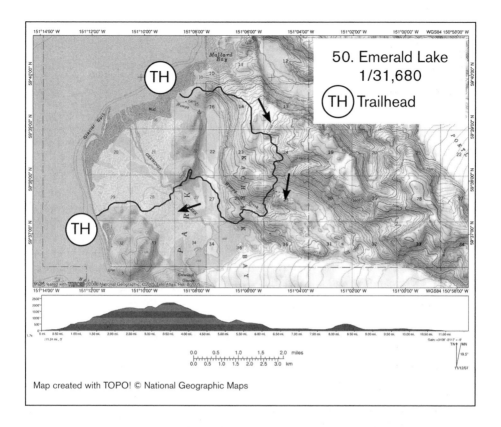

Map created with TOPO! © National Geographic Maps

as I've written this hike provides a continuously breathtaking panoramic vista.

THE TRAIL

Sometimes finding the trailhead at Humpy Creek can be tricky because there are numerous coastal embayments and game trails leading back into the spruce forest. Look for the trailhead kiosk directly inland from the COMMERCIAL FISHING sign located on the open tidal grassland. From the kiosk, hike north on the Humpy Creek Trail, rather than south toward the tram.

The first 2 miles from Humpy Creek take you north across rocky tidal flats and up into the forested lower mountain slopes toward Mallard Bay trailhead. (Hike 49 contains more details on this section of trail.)

From the turnoff to Mallard Bay, about 1.8 miles from the start of the hike at the north end of Humpy Creek flats, you hike up a moderately steep slope through mostly open alder thickets and a few spruce stands. You may encounter a few downfalls, but this section of trail is cleared regularly. As you gain elevation you begin to enjoy increasingly revealing views of the entire Kachemak Bay area. Your goal, Emerald Lake, is about 4.3 miles from the turnoff to Mallard Bay. As you hike up toward the alpine zone you enter fields of wildflowers—violet blue lupine and wild geranium in July and fuschia fireweed in August—that surround you on the trek into and through some wonderful *Sound of Music* scenery.

About 2 miles from the Mallard Bay trailhead, you begin my favorite part of the hike, a broad upland area known as the Portlock Plateau. You abruptly burst out into the alpine zone, which means there are no trees or bushes to hamper your view. Within another 100 meters, there are several terrific stop-rest-view-snack-&-snooze overlook points located close to the south side of the trail. Stop here to celebrate the end of your climb and take in the extraordinary sweep of sky, mountains, and icy world that is Alaska.

Once you resume your traverse across this alpine zone, my suggestion is to slow down and really absorb this mile-long section of the plateau. Hey, you just hiked up about 1,200 feet, so take some time to enjoy your reward. There are several lazy alpine stream channels to enjoy as well as the big scenery. Hiking is easy and the views wonderful! This upper alpine region offers many places to camp and enjoy the plateau environs. It would be a great place to camp on your first night of a three-day journey on the Emerald Lake Trail.

The trail then moves higher into the alpine region through willows and alders and becomes indistinct in areas. Well into June some slopes are covered with still-deep snow banks. Prevailing northern winds have deposited copious amounts of snow on the downwind (lee-side), mostly south-facing slopes (due to the predominantly northern winter winds) of many hillsides traversed by the trail. It's basically cross-country here.

Keep an eye out for rock cairns on the snow-free slopes and the orange trail markers where snow covers the trail. When you

Emerald Lake framed by high Kenai peaks and Grewingk Glacier

cross the steep, snowy slopes, be careful not to lose your footing. To help do that, keep your weight out from and perpendicular to the snow surface to minimize the slip potential.

The trail continues at high elevation for about one-half mile as it wraps around a ridge and back into the alder-filled drainage to a stream crossing. Then head upslope for about a mile to the high point on this trail at about 2,100 feet. From here the trail starts to wind its way down, zigzagging along a semi-ridgeline. Throughout this higher-elevation section you have to watch for trail markers. If you lose the trail, just head back to where you saw the last marker and begin looking for the next one.

As you move down the slope, again go slowly to take in some truly dramatic views of Grewingk Glacier, Grewingk Lake, the Alpine Ridge country (Hike 44), and of course lovely Emerald Lake itself–today's destination if you are doing this as a two- or three-day hike. You won't actually have a view of Emerald Lake until you are at the last ridge prior to the decent to the lake about 0.5 mile from the turnoff toward the lake itself.

The slope gradually moderates until you reach the bench that contains Emerald Lake. This high-elevation bench was scoured clean and the lake carved out by the Grewingk Glacier. Over 10,000 years ago, the glacier was at least twice its current thickness and covered the landscape from this ridge where you're standing all the way over to the alpine ridge on the other side of what is now Grewingk Valley. Solid ice over 1,000 feet thick carved and ground the glacial valley and ridges you see today.

A little over 4 miles from the Mallard Bay intersection, you encounter a short side trail of about 0.2 mile that leads off to the left (east) to Emerald Lake. In the spring and summer, you will have to cross a snow-field-fed stream just prior to reaching the lake, so keep your Crocs® or neoprene booties handy.

The lake sits at an elevation of 1,200 feet and is about 1.25 miles long. If you are spending the night here, and I hope you are, you will find at least one well-sited tent platform on the west end of the lake where you can pitch your temporary home. If the tent platform is occupied, there are several lakeside camping spots to be made on the pebble beach of the lake.

Keep in mind that the local bear and moose populations also think Emerald Lake is a cool place to hang out, so keep an eye out, and be sure to clean up well after dinner. And don't stash your food in your tent.

Enjoy a quiet and serene night by the lake and soak up all the landscape grandeur you can stand. Also be sure to visit the southwestern end of the water where Emerald Lake empties into the headwaters of Humpy Creek–the same one you stepped in when you exited the water taxi over 6 miles and several thousand feet ago!

After a lazy morning at Emerald Lake, you can continue on your way. Head back out the side trail on which you hiked in, and don't forget the stream channel crossing you have to make. I simply start in my Crocs®.

After you regain the main trail, for the first one-quarter mile or so the hike winds back and forth as it gently trends down through alders and grasses with plenty of wildflowers, including mauve wild roses. When you leave the subalpine zone and enter the spruce forest again, you are walking sharply downhill along the upper portion of the Humpy Creek drainage. You will recross the creek on a wooden post bridge, which is a good place to take a break and enjoy the sights, sounds, and smells of the creek's headwaters.

After a mile or so the trail flattens out on a bench and zigzags across wetlands with streams, small lakes, and plenty of wildflowers. Head down once again toward Grewingk Glacier Lake and the intersection with the Glacier Spit to Grewingk Glacier Lake Trail (Hike 46). The hike down offers continuously wonderful views of the lake, the glacier, and the entire valley. Early in the season, however, this section of the trail may have significant downfalls if the trail crews have not been through yet. The good news is this trail is a high priority one the State Park tries to keep open. If you encounter any trail crews please thank them for their heroic work, and better yet offer them a candy bar!

Following a flat wetlands section, the lower part of the trail then steepens again as it descends into the Grewingk Glacier Valley. Take some time to look past your gripping feet to the terrific views of Grewingk Glacier Lake and what I call "Bird Island" with all its raucous birds. Near the bottom of this lower steep section, the trail passes over some very interesting metamorphic rocks that have been cooked with lots of heat and pressure. This is a dandy place to stop for a lunch break before continuing on either to the glacier itself or beginning your trek back to your pickup point.

At the end of the Emerald Lake Trail at its intersection with the Grewingk Glacier Trail, you can turn left (east) and take a detour up to the glacier or turn right (west) to continue your hike. For the latter, follow the Grewingk Glacier Trail 2.6 miles to

A peaceful evening on Emerald Lake

the tram that takes you over the Grewingk Creek gorge, then go one more mile to the Grewingk Glacier Lake Trail, which you then follow out to your water-taxi pickup at Glacier Spit. (Hikes 46 and 47 contain more details on the Grewingk Glacier Lake and Grewingk Glacier Trails; Hike 47 also has instructions for using the Grewingk Creek tram.)

SPECIAL NOTES

If you are a photographer or wildlife enthusiast, the Emerald Lake Trail should be high on your list of hikes. Give yourself at least two days and preferably three so you can fully enjoy all its pleasures and not have to rush through areas like the Portlock Plateau and so you can linger appropriately at Emerald Lake for at least one evening.

Glossary

Alluvial: Area of deposition by stream channels. Can be coarser sediment deposited by stream channels, or finer sediment deposited on a flood plain.

Basalt: A high-temperature (hot enough to be molten/liquid) volcanic rock formed by volcanic action at the surface of the Earth. Basalts form the floors of ocean basins.

Chert or Radiolarian Chert: Sediment deposited on ocean floors that is rich in the shells of silica-rich single-cell marine organisms. Finding radiolarian cherts indicates these rocks were formed deep in the ocean.

Cirque or Cirque Bowl Basin: Rounded bowl carved out by alpine glaciers at their heads, where snow accumulates to form ice and then begins to flow.

Fluvial: Processes and features associated with the actions of stream channels. These can be erosional in nature, like a channel cut by a stream, or depositional like a flood plain.

Glacial Striations: Parallel scratches on rocks formed by the grinding of glaciers across them.

Glacier: A flowing mass of ice. There are two types: 1) Continental glaciers that form at high latitudes and flow as huge thick sheets over large areas (the current Antarctic Ice Sheet is a continental glacier); and 2) Alpine glaciers that form at high altitudes in mountain ranges, then flow more or less in channels guided by valleys (Alaska's glaciers fall into this category).

Ground Moraine: Glacial sediment deposited beneath a glacier, often forming thick sheets that fill in the underlying topography and create flat-floored valleys upon glacier retreats.

Kame Terrace: Flat terrace formed at the edge of a glacier by sediment falling down the sides of the surrounding valley walls. When the glacier retreats these flat terraces are left along the sides of the once-filled glacial valleys.

Lateral Moraine: Glacial-sediment-deposit feature formed along the sides of a glacier. These often leave elongated ridges parallel to the valleys' lengths when the glacier retreats.

Moraine: A feature formed by glacial deposition of sediment once caught up in the moving ice.

Recessional Moraine: Similar to a terminal moraine, but formed during glacial retreat (recession) when the terminus of a glacier remains in the same location for some time, thereby building up an elongated ridge of sediment deposited at the front of the melting glacier.

Scree Slope: A slope formed at the lower portions of steep slopes where falling and sliding sediments accumulate.

Tectonics: Large-scale movement of crustal plates, resulting in the formation of folded and faulted mountain ranges when the plates run into each other, or volcanoes where these plates slide under and over each other.

Terminal Moraine: Glacial-sediment-deposit feature formed at the end (terminus) of a glacier by the conveyor belt action of the flowing ice that melts at its terminus. Usually leaves an elongated ridge perpendicular to the flow of the glacier and the valley's length when the glacier retreats. The Homer Spit was initially formed on top of a terminal moraine.

Index

C

outdoor clubs, 35